# A PLAYER'S GUIDE TO
# *Chamber Music*

In memory of my father,
G.N. (Nelson) Jeffery,
who taught me to love music
and to play the violin.

*Also by Paul Jeffery*:
The Collegiate Churches of England and Wales
(Robert Hale, 2004)

England's Other Cathedrals (The History Press, 2012)

*Paul Jeffery (b. 1948) should not be confused with the author of the same name who lived from 1927 to 1997.*

# A PLAYER'S GUIDE TO
# *Chamber Music*

PAUL JEFFERY

ROBERT HALE

First published in 2017 by
Robert Hale, an imprint of
The Crowood Press Ltd,
Ramsbury, Marlborough
Wiltshire SN8 2HR

**www. crowood.com**

**British Library Cataloguing-in-Publication Data**
A catalogue record for this book is available from the
British Library.

ISBN 978 0 7198 1496 9

Typeset by Chapter One Book Production, Knebworth

Printed and bound in India by Parksons Graphics

# Contents

Preface 7

Introduction 9

Chapter 1.   The Chamber-Music Art-Form 11

Chapter 2.   Playing Chamber Music for Pleasure 28

Chapter 3.   Aspects of the Music 36

Chapter 4.   The Composers and Their Works

Arriaga 41

Bach 42

Barber 45

Bartók 46

Beethoven 49

Berg 68

Boccherini 69

Borodin 71

Brahms 73

Britten 81

Bruch 83

Bruckner 85

Chopin 86

Corelli 86

Danzi 88

Debussy 89

Dohnányi 90

Dvořák 92

Elgar 99

Fauré 100

Franck 102

Grieg 103

Handel 104

Haydn 109

Hummel 144

Janáček                                       148
Mendelssohn                                   149
Mozart                                        157
Poulenc                                       180
Prokofiev                                     182
Purcell                                       184
Rachmaninoff                                  185
Ravel                                         186
Reicha                                        187
Richter                                       190
Saint-Saëns                                   191
Schoenberg                                    194
Schubert                                      197
Schumann                                      208
Shostakovich                                  212
Sibelius                                      217
Smetana                                       218
Strauss                                       219
Stravinsky                                    221
Tchaikovsky                                   222
Vaughan Williams                              225
Verdi                                         226
Vivaldi                                       227
Weber                                         230
Webern                                        231
Appendix I. Further Composers                 235
Appendix II. Repertoire by Instrumental Combination   243
Glossary                                      248
Index                                         251

# Preface

Playing chamber music for pleasure has been an absorbing interest for most of my life. In my teenage years I began playing the violin and later the viola, and was soon able to enjoy informal music-making. Musical experiences multiplied at university. Not until I was in my early twenties, however, did I discover the string quartet: and chamber music became a passion. I played with many different groups, attended courses and classes, and bought sheet music and books on the subject. One thing I sought but could not find was a comprehensive source of information about the repertoire that might be played. So, having access to an excellent music library, I put one together for myself. I have used it ever since. It is the germ that now, greatly magnified, has become this book.

My years of playing chamber music have given me many good memories. These are often of musical enjoyment: first experiences of playing and studying some of the greatest works; inspiring coaching sessions sometimes with prominent figures. But chamber music is also a social pleasure: a special form of friendship, and fun. I think of the string quartet that never stopped playing until after midnight, when a bottle of wine was opened; the ensemble mainly distinguished by the volume of laughter coming from the room. Memories of those with whom I have shared musical friendships over the past half-century remain warm; and with some, I still play today.

Immersing myself in the subject in order to write this book has been fascinating, indeed often a pleasurable indulgence. Every work has been studied; some works that hitherto had eluded me have at last been played. Events, incidents and advice from players of greater knowledge or experience than mine over many years remain in my mind and have often informed my writing. Present friends, too, have helped. My principal thanks, however, are to my wife Margy, who has read the text in draft and has helped me very much by making both broad and detailed comments and suggestions.

# Introduction

Chamber music is a genre that is substantial in its character, yet executed by only small groups of players. Many of its composers wrote it at least partly for the enjoyment of its players, and though it is today widely enjoyed by listeners in concerts or recordings, it probably still gives the greatest pleasure to those who play it. Playing chamber music is a remarkable and delightful activity: a few instrumentalists of quite moderate proficiency can in their homes play some of the world's greatest music.

This book is intended for all who play chamber music for pleasure, or are interested in doing so. It sets no requirement in terms of technical expertise: players can range from some of very moderate ability up to others of high or professional standard. Players are mostly amateurs but they may be professional musicians, especially those whose usual musical activity is in other areas. Indeed, even members of that small and exclusive élite who have a career as performers of chamber music are not immune from sometimes playing it for pleasure.

The principal content of the book is a list of the important chamber compositions that exist, with information about each work from the point of view of the prospective player. Chamber music is considered broadly. Coverage extends from the baroque period which began in the seventeenth century up to music composed in the later twentieth century. All chamber-music combinations are addressed: those of strings alone, of strings with piano, of or including wind instruments, baroque groupings, and duet sonatas. The criterion for inclusion is musical: the basis is the corpus of great chamber music as it is generally recognized. Technical difficulty, or lack of it, is not a factor. This means that some works appear that few players will be able to approach; but the nature of chamber music is that most of the repertoire is accessible to reasonably capable amateurs.

Works are listed by composer, but other lists by instrument or instrumental combination are provided to assist readers in identifying the works available. Also included are chapters discussing the nature of chamber music and considerations in playing it. An appendix lists some further composers of chamber music beyond those addressed in detail.

Many sources have been consulted for information and opinions about the compositions discussed. However, all judgements expressed concerning both their musical value and aspects of playing them are ultimately those of the author. Players will no doubt in some cases disagree!

# Chapter 1

# The Chamber-Music Art-Form

Chamber music is a major branch of Western 'art music' or 'classical music'. Despite the small forces employed, the works are comparable in their character and importance to those written for a large symphony orchestra. Its repertoire includes some of the greatest musical works for any medium.

Perhaps surprisingly, there is no universally agreed definition of chamber music. Widely accepted, however, is the rather whimsical term 'the music of friends'. This indeed captures its essence, especially as it is addressed in this book: chamber music is intended primarily for the pleasure of its players. Though it may be performed in concert halls to an audience, its true home is the domestic environment, where the players sharing the enjoyment of it are most frequently amateurs, usually with no audience at all. At least in the earlier periods, composers wrote it with this environment in mind. This did not mean that they made it deliberately easy to play, but chamber-music writing normally avoided virtuoso display or technical difficulties that could be mastered only by highly trained professionals. This definition of chamber music remains valid today: there continues to be a substantial body of music lovers – friends – who play it for pleasure. The music they play is taken widely from the chamber-music repertoire: though concentrated in the classical and romantic ages it extends as far back as the seventeenth century and forward into the second half of the twentieth century.

This definition has, however, come to have problems. By the mid-nineteenth century, chamber music was widely performed in the concert hall; some lovers of chamber music were only listeners and did not play. Nevertheless, most of the music performed in these concerts was also played domestically for pleasure: when Brahms in 1873 published his op. 51 string quartets, he dedicated them to Dr Theodor Billroth, a surgeon and amateur violinist, viola player and pianist. Though sometimes technically demanding, works of the period were still accessible to reasonably capable amateurs. But since the turn of the twentieth century some new chamber works have been so difficult that they are hardly playable by any other than dedicated professionals. This does not exclude the possibility of such professionals sometimes playing them for pleasure, but their main life is in the concert hall. These works are not just a few on the margins: they embrace much of the mainstream of the chamber music of this era. The string quartets of Bartók, widely considered the summit of the string quartet in the twentieth century, fall into this category. Such works are undoubtedly chamber music; but they have largely excluded themselves from this definition of the art-form.

More explicitly, it is usually agreed that chamber music is for between two and nine performers, with a single player to a part. Music for only one instrument (including that for piano) is not chamber music. The instruments of chamber music are normally just the violin family of string instruments, the woodwind family, the horn and the piano. They do not include the voice. However, a few cases break some of these bounds.

Further limitations are that chamber works are substantial in both character and duration, usually having multiple movements. Short pieces or works of light entertainment character are not true chamber music. Moreover, chamber music should be democratic, with all parts on equal terms. Although that statement requires some qualification, music consisting entirely of a solo for one instrument with accompaniment by one or more others is not chamber music.

In two areas, the boundaries of chamber music are subject to disparate views. Some authorities consider that true chamber music requires a minimum of three players: by this, duet sonatas for a melody instrument and keyboard would be excluded. However, this is a minority view. Duet sonatas, and some other duets, are a distinct form of chamber music, and they are much enjoyed in the domestic environment. However, the large body of music for one instrument with a piano purely in an accompanying role is not chamber music. Also (perhaps perversely), music for two pianos, or for two players at one piano, is not considered chamber music.

The second disparity concerns baroque music. Many writers limit chamber music to that written since the start of the classical period around 1760–70, usually beginning with Haydn. However, music explicitly for small groups of players was composed in the baroque period, though it is very different from what came after. Most of the combinations that became established in the classical period did not exist in the baroque; moreover, baroque chamber music almost always includes a continuo part, which by its nature is not usually on an equal basis with the other part or parts. But this music meets the definition 'the music of friends': it was and still is enjoyed by players in their homes.

Another form of early music sometimes played domestically today is sixteenth- and seventeenth-century music for consorts of viols. However, being written for instruments that are obsolete, it is not generally regarded as chamber music, and it is not discussed here.

Two other forms of music may be mentioned that are not considered true chamber music. One is music arranged for chamber groups from other sources, chamber or otherwise. Some of this is popular and often played – for example, by string quartets at weddings. Normally only where the arrangement was made or approved by the composer can it be accepted as chamber music. Also not true is that chamber music is 'easy' music: original works and arrangements produced specifically for players of limited technical proficiency.

# HISTORICAL PERIODS OF CHAMBER MUSIC

Music, like other art-forms, has developed continuously since early times. Conventionally it is grouped into distinct periods for which dates are given; naturally these are approximate and there is much overlap. It is not the purpose of this book to discuss the character of the music of these periods; but something may be said about their chamber music.

## The Baroque Period

This long period is usually taken as roughly from 1600 to 1760. It saw many very important innovations, including the establishment of the system of major and minor tonality with key signatures as we know them, and the beginnings of sonata form. Many instruments became standardized and widely used that have continued to the present day, including the violin family. Although music written for orchestra may sometimes have been played with one player to a part, music was also composed that was specifically intended for just a few players – what we now call chamber music.

Of the chamber-music combinations of later periods, the only one to exist in the baroque period was the duet sonata; and that had significant differences from later practice. The other principal combination was the trio sonata. A few sonatas in four or more parts were also composed.

Baroque ensembles, orchestral as well as chamber, almost always included a continuo part (in full *basso continuo*, also called thoroughbass). In a duet or trio sonata, one of the parts is the continuo. This was normally written as a figured bass – a notation in which only the bass notes appear, together with numbers indicating the harmony. The specific instrumentation of the continuo was usually (though not always) unspecified; but the norm was for it to have two players. One played a chordal instrument such as the harpsichord (Italian *clavicembalo*, usually shortened to *cembalo*) or perhaps the organ or archlute. This player extemporized from the bass notes and the chordal information. The other player reinforced the bass on a cello, bass viol (often stated as a *violone*, a non-specific term) or bassoon. Both players often read from the same physical part. So a duet sonata usually required three players, and a trio sonata four.

Sonatas of the baroque period were sometimes specified as *sonata da camera* (chamber sonata) or *sonata da chiesa* (church sonata). The former were intended for entertainment, and usually included dance movements with titles such as *Sarabande, Allemande* and *Giga*. The *sonata da chiesa*, originally intended for use in church services, was more serious and abstract, without dances, typically having fast and slow movements alternating. Both types often had four movements, but could vary. The distinction between the two types largely vanished after about 1700.

Many of the most famous composers of the baroque period were Italian: for example, Corelli and Vivaldi. Others included Purcell in England. In the early eighteenth century, with Bach and Handel, German composers began their rise to dominance. The number of baroque composers who wrote chamber works is large; only the most prominent are addressed in this book.

## The Classical Period

This period lasted approximately from 1760 to 1830. The years following the deaths of Bach in 1750 and Handel in 1759 saw a fundamental change in the character of new music. Many of the conventions of the baroque period, such as the use of continuo, disappeared; so did the trio sonata. The symphony as a four-movement work for orchestra became established. The fortepiano, which had appeared early in the eighteenth century, continued to develop and grow in importance. The clarinet joined the other widely used members of the woodwind family. Over two or three decades at the beginning of the period, there appeared most of the chamber-music combinations that we now know, with the string quartet at their head.

Italy was no longer central to musical progress. The music of the classical period developed mainly in Germany and Austria, and particularly in Vienna. It was dominated by just four great composers: Haydn, Mozart, Beethoven and Schubert. Haydn was the earliest of these, and had a role in the beginnings of classical music and in establishing the forms in which it was composed. In the 1770s he was joined by Mozart in the composition of the first masterpieces of the classical chamber-music repertoire. From the mid-1790s, Beethoven came to prominence, and for almost three decades held a dominant position. He dramatically expanded the scope of music, including chamber music. In the last part of the period, Schubert lived his tragically short life and contributed further chamber-music masterpieces. Though in many ways a romantic, Schubert belongs to the classical period in his perfection, his clarity and his adherence to the forms established by Haydn and Mozart.

The music of these four composers still forms the basis and a major part of the chamber-music repertoire. All four composed extensively for string quartet and (to some extent excepting Haydn) for other combinations. However, although over-shadowed, other composers including Hummel and Weber also produced good chamber music in this period.

## The Romantic Period

The era of romanticism in music may be said to be approximately from 1830 to 1910. The deaths of Beethoven and Schubert in the late 1820s left the field clear for new composers. Most important to chamber music were Mendelssohn and Schumann, who both began promisingly with a series of fine works for string quartet and other combinations. However, both were cut short by their early deaths. After them came many other composers who wrote chamber music; but Brahms is the dominating figure. He is the only composer of the romantic age to have produced a body of chamber music that holds a position comparable to that of the great classical composers.

Mendelssohn, Schumann and Brahms were German, but other important composers came from elsewhere, including Russia, Scandinavia and what was to become Czechoslovakia. Most of the composers of these regions illustrate the rise of nationalism in music. In the late years of the period, too, England had in Elgar its first real master composer since Purcell.

Beethoven had begun in his late period to burst the bounds of classical chamber music: but in general no romantic composers followed him in this. Rather their models were the works of his early and middle periods, and those of the other classical masters. Composition seemed to become more difficult in the romantic period: most composers worked more slowly and produced a much smaller volume of music than had their classical predecessors. Many important figures, though interested in chamber music, contributed only two or three works. Some produced none. Other than Brahms, only Dvořák of the major later romantic composers composed chamber music freely. In compensation, however, the number of significant composers is large, so overall they have left a substantial body of chamber music. Important new works were written for string quartet, piano trio and duet sonata, combinations that had already been much cultivated in the classical period. Works were also composed for some groupings that the classical composers had neglected: larger ensembles offering richness and power, especially the piano quintet and the string sextet. As we have seen, the convention that chamber music was not of virtuoso character continued; though much of it is quite demanding, it is hardly more so than the later music of Beethoven and Schubert.

## The Twentieth Century

Although the term 'twentieth-century music' is often used, it covers a wide range and diversity of styles. Great changes took place through the century; and even at any one time, different composers were producing music of very different character.

There are terms used for particular schools of composition, such as twelve-tone and neo-classical, but their nature will not be examined here.

Meanwhile, many romantic composers continued to compose through much of the first half of the century. Such composers as Dohnányi, Elgar, Rachmaninoff and Strauss belong unambiguously to the late romantic period.

Composers continued to write chamber music in the twentieth century. The string quartet retained its especially important position, and works for it were produced by many of the major figures, although little was composed for some of the other established combinations. On the other hand, some works appeared for new and surprising groupings, sometimes including instruments that had not previously been used in chamber music such as the trombone, saxophone or bass clarinet. Moreover, some composers wrote works employing a miniature orchestral ensemble resembling a chamber group. Though not to be considered as true chamber music, these are sometimes mentioned in this book as of possible interest to players.

Some of the trends that became significant in twentieth-century music began before the turn of the century. An obvious example is the impressionism of Debussy, well represented in his string quartet of 1893. Despite the wide range of compositional styles in the twentieth century, there are common factors to many: the rejection of romanticism, the abandonment of some previously accepted conventions of harmony. One aspect must be recognized: a gulf or disconnection appeared in the twentieth century between many members of the musical public, including players, and much of the music being produced. This gulf has not closed: there continue to be many good musicians who do not understand or enjoy the music of some important twentieth-century composers. This applies perhaps most obviously to the atonal and twelve-tone compositions of Schoenberg and his school, despite the long period that has passed since such works first appeared. The music of some other composers of the period is more widely appreciated, but still not by all.

This gulf is one problem inhibiting the playing for pleasure of much twentieth-century chamber music. Another is technical difficulty, which renders most of the chamber works of composers such as Bartók, Berg, Schoenberg and Webern largely inaccessible to amateurs. On the other hand, other twentieth-century composers such as Barber, Prokofiev, Shostakovich, Sibelius and Vaughan Williams wrote chamber works as playable as many of the romantic period.

In the composition of chamber music in the earlier twentieth century, a factor in Britain was the work of W.W. Cobbett (1847–1937). He was a wealthy amateur violinist and passionate lover of chamber music. Among his varied activities in support of the art-form, he was responsible for the composition of many new works both by commissioning and by an annual competition. A requirement was usually the use of a form that he called 'phantasy': inspired by the English 'fancy' or 'fantasy' for viols of the sixteenth and seventeenth centuries, this was to be a work in a single movement containing sections in different speeds and rhythms. Composers often interpreted this as a condensation of a normal three- or four-movement work. The first competition was held in 1905, and Cobbett continued to be active for most of the rest of his life. The result is the existence of phantasy quartets, quintets, trios and duos by many British composers, notably Bax, Bridge, Britten, Howells, Ireland and Vaughan Williams. Few of these works, however, have established themselves in the repertoire. The requirement for the phantasy form, which has not otherwise been taken up, is perhaps to be regretted. Nevertheless, at least one masterpiece came out of this in the phantasy string quintet by Vaughan Williams.

Cobbett having been considered, justice demands mention also of Elizabeth Sprague Coolidge (1864–1953), who was a comparable patron in America. Unlike Cobbett, her interest was international, and she promoted no special form. Among her commissions were string quartets by Bartók, Britten, Prokofiev, Schoenberg and Webern.

### Contemporary Music

This book addresses chamber music only of composers active at latest until about the 1970s. What has happened since may (at present) be considered contemporary music. Composition of chamber music has continued, but it is too early to know which composers are important and enduring. This music is interesting to some, but it is confusing for many ordinary lovers of chamber music. Works have continued to be produced that are intended mainly for professional performance, and moreover their challenges may apply not only to the difficulties of instrumental execution. Instruments may have to be 'prepared', and there are sometimes further requirements. An extreme case is Stockhausen's *Helicopter* string quartet, of 1993. In addition to the players and their instruments, this calls for four helicopters, complete with pilots and other staff, together with extensive electronic equipment. One wonders whether any amateurs have attempted it!

## INSTRUMENTAL COMBINATIONS

Chamber music has been written for many instrumental combinations, which may be considered in groups. Of post-baroque ensembles there are strings alone, strings with piano, and groupings of or including wind instruments. Baroque ensembles form a fourth group. Duet sonatas are a fifth.

Many chamber groupings are commonly referred to by a shorthand terminology. Thus a clarinet quintet is not for five clarinets but for clarinet and string quartet; a piano trio is piano, violin and cello. A duet sonata for a melody instrument and piano is often referred to as, for example, a violin sonata. (This may vex pianists: but as with the other short names, it implies no inferiority of the unmentioned instrument or instruments!) These names are not always unambiguous: for example a piano quintet, for piano and four strings, has two alternative string groupings.

## Ensembles of Strings Alone

In these, the instruments involved are almost always violin, viola and cello, with a few appearances by the double bass. Of all chamber ensembles, those for strings alone perhaps come closest to the ideal of all parts being on equal terms. However, the violin or first violin is almost always 'first among equals', having a greater share both of musical prominence and of technical difficulties.

From early in the classical period, the string quartet, like the symphony, became established as normally having four movements. The string quintet and sextet have followed this convention, which largely continued through the romantic period but was often abandoned in the twentieth century. The string trio sometimes follows the four-movement plan but has been more variable, probably under the influence of Mozart's wonderful six-movement divertimento, K. 563.

### The string duo

Only a few significant works exist for this medium. Mozart's two for violin and viola stand out. The few duos by major romantic or twentieth-century composers are technically difficult. There are, however, many relatively minor works such as those by Haydn, Boccherini and various secondary composers of the classical period, also arrangements. These remain valuable for domestic use, especially in homes having two string players. Some were explicitly written for players of limited ability. Others are intended for teaching, one part being taken by the pupil, the other by the teacher. There are also some virtuoso display works mainly from the romantic period. Some music also exists for string duo with piano accompaniment.

### The string trio

A small repertoire of major works exists for three string instruments. The normal grouping is violin, viola and cello, but there are also some works for two violins and viola, two violins and cello and even other combinations. Haydn, Mozart, Beethoven and Schubert all composed for string trio. Few romantic composers contributed, the serenade by Dohnányi being probably the most significant work, but the medium made something of a comeback in the twentieth century. With only three players, all parts have plenty to do and playing them may seem quite hard work. The greatest string trios are Mozart's divertimento and the three trios of Beethoven's op. 9: these are all major works on a large scale. As well as the other trios by the major classical composers there are many works by lesser figures of the classical and early romantic periods, also arrangements. Some of them make enjoyable playing.

## The string quartet

The string quartet, almost always of two violins, viola and cello, is the supreme combination in chamber music, with a particular prestige and a repertoire larger than that of any other grouping. Its position in chamber music is similar to that of the symphony in orchestral music: the classic medium, the most important form in which a composer might write. This prestige was rapidly established by the quantity and superlative quality of the contributions of the four great classical composers.

### Origins of the String Quartet

The origins of the string quartet have been much discussed. It seems likely that, with the instruments of the violin family all existing from the later sixteenth century, groups of two violins, viola and cello sometimes played together. However, since continuo was almost universally used if available, and with the limited distinction between the use of single or multiple strings, such groups were probably seen as only a temporary makeshift until better forces were available. Claims for 'the first string quartet' have been made for a work by Gregorio Allegri (1582–1652), and for some four-part sonatas by Alessandro Scarlatti (1660–1725), but these works have remained in obscurity. Compositions for the string quartet combination appeared quite suddenly about the late 1750s. Haydn's two sets of divertimenti opp. 1 and 2 date from this time, as do works by other composers, notably Richter. These preceded the establishment of the string quartet in the form it subsequently took: the works by Haydn mostly have five movements; Richter's have three. The four-movement layout that became the standard was introduced by Haydn in his op. 9 of 1769–70. He rapidly followed with his opp. 17 and 20. As well as the layout, these works established the string quartet as being substantial in length and weighty in musical character; and by these developments Haydn has a legitimate claim as its inventor. Other composers quickly followed.

Haydn, after playing his role in the creation of the medium, went on to compose what is still today easily the largest number of quartets in the repertoire by any one composer. Mozart composed his splendid albeit shorter series. Mostly in the first decades of the following century Beethoven and Schubert followed. The works of these four classical masters still dominate the repertoire of the string quartet.

Many important string quartets were added to the repertoire in the romantic era, including substantial series from both Mendelssohn and Dvořák, and small numbers, often only one or two, from many other composers. Composition continued in the twentieth century; probably most notable are the series of fifteen by Shostakovich and that of six by Bartók. It is sometimes said that, of all composers of string quartets, three stand out. These three produced string quartets through-out their compositional lives, their string quartets are an essential part of their art and are representative of it at its finest. The composers are Haydn, Beethoven and Bartók.

---

### Beethoven's Late String Quartets

For many, Beethoven's string quartets, and in particular his late string quartets, are the pinnacle of the string quartet repertoire, the greatest works to listen to or play. The six late quartets (counting the *Grosse Fuge* as one) are of unique character, and their exceptional greatness is universally agreed. Nevertheless, at least for amateur players, this view should be put in perspective. There are some whose perceptions of the string quartet (or even of chamber music as a whole) have been unfavourably coloured by a superficial impression of Beethoven's late string quartets. It is no disparagement of them to say that not everything in them is obviously attractive. They are difficult musically; and they are difficult to play. They are not the music to choose when introducing either players or listeners to string quartets. Rather, they are a goal to be approached after experience has been gained in other areas of the repertoire.

---

A form that has nothing to do with true chamber music but had a place for a period in the early nineteenth century is the *quatuor brillant*. In this, the musical interest is concentrated in a concerto-like first violin part, with accompaniment by the remaining players. The most prominent composer of these was Louis Spohr. It is an extreme form of a tendency sometimes seen in normal string quartets.

### The string quintet

There are three string quintet combinations. What is effectively the standard combination is the 'two-viola quintet' – two violins, two violas and cello. Its repertoire is quite small, but it is remarkably fine. Its most important composers are probably Beethoven, Brahms, Bruch, Bruckner, Dvořák, Mendelssohn, Mozart and Vaughan Williams, most of whom appear at their best in these works. A distinctive feature of this repertoire is that it is spread remarkably evenly through the classical and romantic eras – there are no large numbers from the classical period, but surprisingly many from romantic composers.

This medium offers a greater scale and weight of utterance than the string quartet. The presence of two violas gives a distinctive, viola-rich sound to the ensemble. These works are usually gratifying to viola players, and the first viola may be given a prominence similar to that of the first violin.

One particular string quintet, Mozart's in G minor, K. 516, seems to hold a position with players as universal favourite. If an opportunity arises to add a viola player to a string quartet, this is often the work chosen. It is excellent, but so are others by Mozart – and by other composers!

The principal alternative string quintet combination is the 'two-cello quintet' – two violins, viola and two cellos. For this there is one dominating masterpiece by Schubert, in C, D. 956, considered by many the greatest chamber work ever written. One of its memorable qualities is the melodic freedom given to the cellos, sometimes together, which naturally gives it a special place in the affection of cellists. It stands almost alone, however: no other major work exists. Boccherini wrote many quintets for this combination, and there are others by lesser composers.

A third combination is two violins, viola, cello and double bass. Its most important work is by Dvořák.

### The string sextet

This combination is almost always two violins, two violas and two cellos. It offers power and richness of sound, which is doubtless why it was mainly romantic composers who wrote for the combination. There are just five major works. Dominating the repertoire are the two great sextets of Brahms; the others are by Dvořák, Schoenberg and Tchaikovsky. The exploitation of the two cellos naturally gives a character to the music that is enjoyed by cellists; and these works are also enjoyable for viola players. The two Brahms sextets are his most playable string chamber works and are much loved; amateur string quartets often grasp an opportunity to add a viola and cello in order to play them.

### The string octet

This largest medium of string chamber music contains one outstanding masterpiece, by Mendelssohn. This is for the standard combination of four violins, two violas and two cellos (and so may be played by two established string quartets coming together). It has a vigour, freshness and brilliance hardly excelled anywhere in chamber music. Few other composers have written for string octet. Finest after Mendelssohn's is that by Bruch, which is for four violins, two violas, cello and double bass. Lesser composers who wrote octets include Gade, Raff and Svendsen. Shostakovich contributed two pieces. Spohr wrote several works for double string quartet in which the two are treated antiphonally, and these are occasionally played.

## Ensembles of Strings with Piano

Chamber music for strings with piano, like that for strings alone, has a small number of standard groupings, the largest repertoire being that of the piano trio. The character of the piano chamber music of the early classical period, as of duet sonatas and sonatas for solo piano, was affected by the social aspect of music involving the piano in those years. It was intended for domestic performance by amateur pianists, often ladies, and so was seen as an intimate medium, moderate in its musical scope and not unduly heavy or serious. The works had only three or even two movements; typically there is no minuet or scherzo. Four movements, and a more weighty character, became normal from the turn of the nineteenth century. More will be said about this in the discussions of the piano trio and the duet sonata.

In ensembles with piano, the chamber-music principle of democracy still applies. However, the nature of the piano, with its power and its abilities to play chords and more than one contrapuntal line, so differs from that of string instruments that there cannot really be either musical or technical equality between each string instrument and the piano. The writing sometimes gives approximately equal roles to the piano and to the whole string group. Together with the violinist or first violinist, the pianist leads the ensemble. Especially in large-scale romantic music, a piano played with enthusiasm can drown the strings, a risk to which the pianist should be sensitive.

Playing a string instrument in an ensemble with piano can be very different from playing in a group of strings alone. The presence of the piano gives the composer (especially the romantic composer) opportunities for music of a power and scope not available with strings only; the individual can feel carried along as part of a great machine pounding forward with tremendous force and momentum.

The technical difficulties for the pianist are of very different character from those of the string players. For many amateur pianists, sight-reading of chamber music, at least later than Haydn and Mozart, is hardly practicable. Because of this, piano chamber music in a sense belongs to the pianist. It should be the pianist who in advance decides, or at least agrees, what will be played. It is not a good idea for string players to try to persuade a reluctant pianist to undertake a work that may have a formidable piano part! Before a chamber-music meeting, the pianist may have spent weeks or months preparing. By contrast the string players, even if conscientious, may have practised only for a few days. There is also a point here of courtesy: the string players, even if they are technically strong and their parts apparently straightforward, should not sight-read. It is exasperating to a pianist who has spent many weeks in preparation to find that other players repeatedly trip over minor timing or technical difficulties that would have been resolved by just having read through their parts in advance!

### The piano trio

This is normally piano, violin and cello. It has a large repertoire. As with the string quartet, an extensive basis was provided by all four composers of the classical period. The combination continued to be a favoured medium for composers through the romantic era, with notable contributions including multiple works from Brahms, Dvořák, Mendelssohn and Schumann. The medium was less cultivated in the twentieth century, though Ravel and Shostakovich composed important works.

## The Early Classical Piano Trio

A particular characteristic affects early classical piano trios. We have already seen that, for social reasons, chamber works with piano in this period were of limited musical scope and normally had only two or three movements. Such works were usually regarded as accompanied piano sonatas (and were so entitled in their published editions). In a piano trio, as in a sonata for violin and piano, the freedom allowed to the violin was limited. As for the cello, the memory persisted of its role in the baroque continuo, and in the early piano trio it continued to be restricted largely to supporting the bass being played by the pianist's left hand. It is worth remembering that the fortepiano sustained its tone for only a short time and had limited power in the bass, so its reinforcement by string instruments was a real improvement. This is the character of Haydn's long series of piano trios – which are nevertheless fine works. To a lesser degree it also affects those of Mozart and even the first two of Beethoven's initial set, op. 1. But once the nineteenth century had arrived, piano trios were fully democratic. However, these early classical piano trios are fully in the professional repertoire, and they are well worth playing. The violin parts, even though somewhat restricted, are enjoyable. The cello parts may not be to every player's liking, but for those who understand and appreciate the role (comparable to that in a baroque continuo), they can be satisfying. These trios also have the advantage of being technically available to many pianists and string players for whom later piano trios may be problematical.

It is amusing to remember that this combination was once very popular as background entertainment in cafés and hotels. It is unlikely, however, that the music considered in this book was often played by these ensembles. Their large repertoire, much of it arranged from other sources, was not what we would consider true chamber music. However, playing some of it from old sets of parts can provide variety and amusement.

### The piano quartet

This always means piano, violin, viola and cello. Its repertoire, though much smaller than that for piano trio, is substantial. Its basis is two beautiful works by Mozart; but there is otherwise not much from the classical period. Many romantic composers have contributed, and their works are often large and weighty. This was perhaps the heyday of the medium, its summit being the three magnificent and large-scale works by Brahms. Little was composed for piano quartet in the twentieth century.

### The piano quintet

The grouping of piano and four strings again has alternative combinations. What is effectively the standard grouping is piano, two violins, viola and cello – piano and string quartet. Its repertoire is substantial and important. This medium was not addressed by any of the great classical composers. Perhaps it was this absence of classical precedent, together with the potential for power and richness, that particularly attracted the romantics. The combination became a favoured medium for them: although they usually composed only one or at most two works, many of these are particularly splendid. Perhaps the most outstanding are those of Brahms, Dvořák, Elgar, Franck and Schumann, but there are many further worthy compositions by others. Shostakovich made a notable contribution in the twentieth century.

The second combination is piano, violin, viola, cello and double bass. This grouping had its heyday in the early years of the nineteenth century. By far its most popular work is the 'Trout' quintet by Schubert. Hummel also contributed, and there are many further works by lesser composers.

## Ensembles of or including Wind Instruments

There are some magnificent chamber works for ensembles that include wind instruments; but the numbers are relatively small, and the combinations are varied. As a result, wind players have only limited opportunities to form long-term groups meeting regularly. The instruments normally involved are flute, oboe, clarinet, bassoon and horn, and the combinations may be divided into those for wind and string instruments, wind instruments with piano, and wind instruments alone.

Nevertheless, there is one established standard grouping: the wind quintet, one each of flute, oboe, clarinet, horn and bassoon. This has sufficient repertoire for professional quintets to exist. Unfortunately, before the twentieth century no front-rank composer wrote for it, but an enjoyable basis to its repertoire was provided by Reicha and Danzi, both contemporaries of Beethoven, who between them left thirty-three large-scale quintets. Other secondary composers produced a few more through the nineteenth century. In the twentieth century, many further works were added, some by important figures such as Barber, Hindemith, Nielsen and Schoenberg. There are also just a few sextets for wind quintet with piano, notably that by Poulenc.

Otherwise, however, there are no standard combinations, and some groupings may have only one significant work. Mozart and Haydn both wrote a series of divertimenti for two oboes, two horns and two bassoons: but these are short and lightweight works. More substantial are Mozart's two serenades, K. 375 and K. 388, both for this combination plus two clarinets, a grouping for which there is also the octet, op. 103, by the young Beethoven.

There are, however, some excellent opportunities for wind players to play chamber music. Particularly popular with players and also audiences are Beethoven's septet and Schubert's octet, both for clarinet, horn, bassoon and strings. Fine quintets for piano, oboe, clarinet, horn and bassoon were composed by Mozart and Beethoven. Of groupings of one wind instrument with strings, best established is that of clarinet and string quartet. It has major works by Brahms, Mozart and Weber, the first two being among the best-loved works in chamber music. The combination also has many works by lesser composers. Hummel composed a quartet for clarinet and strings. Mozart left a quartet with strings for oboe and several for flute, also a quintet for horn. Other significant combinations are trios of piano with one wind and one string instrument. Clarinet trios – for clarinet, cello and piano – were written by Beethoven and Brahms; Mozart composed an exquisite work using viola instead of cello. In the Brahms horn trio, the string instrument is a violin. Bartók's *Contrasts* is for piano, clarinet and violin.

Many other works have not been mentioned. Several important twentieth-century composers, such as Janáček and Stravinsky, wrote works involving multiple wind instruments.

## Baroque Ensembles

Baroque chamber groupings were few: there were only duet sonatas, trio sonatas and a small number of sonatas in four or more parts. Baroque duet sonatas are included in the section on duet sonatas, below.

Orchestral ensembles in the baroque era were often small. Baroque orchestral works may be of interest to chamber players: groups of perhaps a dozen can gain much enjoyment from playing such works as *concerti grossi* for strings or strings and wind.

### The trio sonata

The trio sonata or *sonata a tre* was the characteristic chamber medium of the baroque period, and existed only in that era. The instrumentation is two melody instruments, usually but not always both treble, with basso continuo. It has a large repertoire. The most famous composers for the medium include Corelli, Handel, Purcell and Vivaldi, but there were many others. Trio sonatas were usually published in sets, sometimes of twelve.

The melody instruments are most frequently violins, but many other instruments may be specified, particularly flute but also oboe, recorder, bassoon and viola da gamba. There was often flexibility in the baroque period as to the instruments that were employed: it would be quite normal to play, for example, a flute part on an oboe or violin. It can be useful to apply this flexibility today. (But problems should be expected if playing a violin part on an oboe or flute because the bottom note of the violin is lower than those of the wind instruments, double-stopping could appear, and there may be violinistic figuration that is unidiomatic and difficult on a woodwind instrument.)

An attraction of much of this music is that it is technically straightforward, both in the string or wind lines and in the keyboard part (as realized from the continuo). The two melody parts are often equal, but sometimes the first is given extra prominence or even solo movements.

### The four-part sonata

Though much less numerous than trio sonatas, four-part sonatas – *sonate a quattro* – were sometimes composed. Their instrumentation varies, but almost always includes continuo. Sonatas for more than four parts are even rarer.

## Duet Sonatas

Substantial chamber works for a melody instrument with piano (or harpsichord or continuo) are usually entitled sonata, though other names such as sonatina or duo also appear. Having existed in the baroque period, this medium has a longer history than has any other combination, and its repertoire is large. More duet sonatas have been written for violin than for any other instrument; probably the next largest number is for cello. Duet sonatas for viola are scarce. There is a scattering of duet sonatas for wind instruments, with significant numbers from the baroque era for both oboe and flute. Especially in the romantic period, composers sometimes made or authorized arrangements of their sonatas for alternative instruments.

As with all forms of chamber music, the principle applies that the musical responsibility is shared between the players: the pianist is an equal partner, not an accompanist! (However, in some sonatas from the seventeenth and eighteenth centuries this equality is qualified.)

There also exists much other music for one instrument and piano. Some composers produced sets of variations: these normally share the interest between the players and are fully of chamber-music character. The many short pieces for one instrument with piano accompaniment, some of which are well known, do not usually warrant mention in this book. However, some more substantial sets of pieces, such as those by Schumann, may be regarded as chamber music and are addressed here. Certainly not chamber music are the many virtuoso display works for solo instrument with piano accompaniment, mostly composed by nineteenth-century performers.

Because of the widespread use of terms such as 'violin sonata' or 'oboe sonata' to refer to a duet sonata, a work for a non-keyboard instrument alone is usually identified as a solo sonata. However, confusingly, as some baroque duet sonatas employing continuo give much of the main musical interest to the melody instrument, they too are sometimes referred to as solo sonatas.

Through most of the baroque era, duet sonatas almost universally employed continuo. However, in the early eighteenth century the first fortepianos appeared, beginning the development that led eventually to the pianoforte as we now know it. The sonata for solo keyboard began its rise to prominence. At the same time, the keyboard parts of duet sonatas were sometimes given increased importance. This trend is illustrated by Bach, who composed some of his duet sonatas with, instead of continuo, a fully written out and musically important keyboard part.

This went further from the middle of the century when the previously mentioned vogue for the accompanied keyboard sonata affected duet sonatas as it did piano trios. (This was a reversal of those earlier baroque duet sonatas with continuo in which the melody instrument had most of the musical interest.) A typical publication title might be 'Sonata for harpsichord or forte-piano, with the accompaniment of a violin'. A frequent accomplishment of ladies in polite society being to play the harpsichord or fortepiano, the accompanied duet sonata, with a gentleman playing (most often) a violin, offered an acceptable and enjoyable way in which the sexes might mix. Sometimes the part for the violin or other instrument was actually optional. Usually it was required ('obbligato'), but might do little more than duplicate the melody in the keyboard right hand, provide ornamentation or fill out the harmony. The violin sonatas composed by Mozart in his childhood are of this type. Its effects continued to be felt to a limited degree in some of his mature sonatas, and vestiges of it are seen in Weber's sonatas, but generally it had vanished by the beginning of the nineteenth century.

Beethoven composed what remains the most impressive series of duet sonatas in the repertoire, totalling sixteen: ten for violin, five for cello and one for horn. Significant numbers were also composed by Mozart and Schubert. Numbers in the romantic era were generally smaller, but many composers produced at least one. Brahms published seven. Composition of duet sonatas continued in the twentieth century, including important contributions by Bartók, Debussy, Poulenc, Prokofiev and Shostakovich.

In the baroque era, duet sonatas typically had four movements, though other numbers also occurred. In the early classical period, duet sonatas, as with other chamber works involving the piano, usually had only two or three movements. Four movements subsequently again became more usual though some continued to be written in three.

Duet sonatas from the baroque and classical periods can make enjoyable material for music-making by amateurs of fairly moderate technical accomplishment. Most sonatas from subsequent periods, however, are more technically demanding.

# Chapter 2

# Playing Chamber Music for Pleasure

## Ensemble Meetings and Activities

There is much variation in what chamber groups do when playing for pleasure. Some only ever sight-read; others study a work in detail through multiple meetings and with much private practice of parts. Many fall somewhere between.

All players, however good, make errors, particularly when sight-reading. These may be the cause of much laughter. In an ensemble that works well in musical and human terms – with players who are truly chamber-music friends – errors made by one player can be pointed out by another with no sense of awkwardness. A chamber ensemble is not a place for feelings of personal pride!

An attractive option for a regular group can be on occasion to add a further player. A string quartet can add a piano, clarinet, viola or cello and immediately be presented with splendid new opportunities. A piano trio by adding a viola player has a large new repertoire. For wind groups, adding or omitting one or two players may be a way of life!

Playing different parts in a work on different occasions (perhaps with different groups of players) is an excellent way of gaining a deeper knowledge of the work. Violinists who also play viola can know three parts of a string quartet!

An additional pleasure of playing in a chamber ensemble can be that its members, though sharing a love of chamber music, otherwise vary widely in their characters, backgrounds and stations in life.

Attending a chamber-music course can be enjoyable musically and socially, and a good way of learning. Being coached by professional musicians can be inspiring and give memorable insights. One-week courses are offered at summer schools of music, and shorter courses or classes are available. Either individuals or complete ensembles may be accepted.

Some people advocate that established amateur chamber groups should sometimes perform to an audience. Indeed, doing so can be rewarding: it can give a deeper understanding of the works performed, and improve technique and musicianship. But it is demanding. It requires a great deal of time and commitment; it can also raise problems such as performance nerves. It is not the same as playing for pleasure!

Amateurs (as well as professionals) may sometimes play in a string quartet or other small ensemble for social events such as weddings. Financial gain is usually a motivation. It is not really to be considered as public performance: much of the audience will be inattentive so the music is mainly only a background. Moreover, most of what is played will not really be chamber music.

---

## Useful Aids

Players usually understand most Italian performance directions; but some works have directions in other languages. Those in German (used by such chamber-music composers as Bruckner, later Schumann and some twentieth-century Germans) are problematical for many. A suitable dictionary such as the *Oxford Dictionary of Musical Terms* can be useful.

Having parts is a necessity, but owning the score is a luxury. Nevertheless, the well-equipped chamber player possesses scores at least of music that is likely often to be played. A score may clarify what is happening in a passage that is causing difficulty. It can be consulted when there is discussion about surprising harmony or potential intonation problems. When a player questions a possible error in a part, the matter can often be decided by the score (which is frequently in a different edition from the parts). It is also valuable for privately studying a work or for following while listening to a recording. The fact that many scores are today available online can be useful.

A metronome may be valuable in holding tempo steady both for the ensemble and in private practice. A further use is for hearing the composer's metronome markings.

---

## Playing Baroque Music

Baroque chamber music offers a large repertoire, much of which is accessible to players of limited technical proficiency. It raises, however, questions concerning attitude to authenticity – though players should not let these discourage them from playing it!

Many professional performances today aim at being authentic – to reproduce a performance as it would have been in the composer's day. The instruments (and, with string instruments, their bows) are of baroque form, usually in modern reproductions. The continuo part is played on an appropriate instrument or instruments. A baroque pitch is used (usually about a semitone lower than modern pitch).

An authentic performance style (as it is understood today) is employed, different in many respects from modern style. Ornamentation is extensively used.

Some of those who play for pleasure, too, have similar objectives, at least in part. There are players who are sufficiently interested in baroque music to possess an instrument (or perhaps in the case of string players, just a bow) of period type.

Others, however, have only modern instruments. For any other than purists, there is nothing wrong in using these to play baroque music. For players who understand baroque performance style, it is possible to go at any rate half-way towards it using modern instruments. It is not unmusical, however, to play baroque music on modern instruments in modern style. Indeed, many players do this: it can be very enjoyable, and it should not be deprecated! Besides, many of those who play at least partly authentically probably started by playing in modern style.

Whatever the style, there is flexibility as to how the continuo part is realized, which will be determined by convenience and individual preference. Since it was in the baroque period typically played by whatever was conveniently available, unless authenticity is intended the use of a piano is legitimate. The pianist can, if preferred, play in a manner sympathetic to baroque style. Since a piano has a stronger and more sustained bass tone than has a harpsichord, it is unnecessary, and arguably inappropriate, also to have a supporting instrument such as a cello. Another option is to use an electronic keyboard set to either an organ or a harpsichord sound. With the latter, or a real harpsichord tuned to modern pitch, employing a supporting bass instrument could add further authenticity. The large proportion of keyboard players who are unable to play from a figured bass will be dependent on an editorial realization of the figured bass part. Playing from a clumsy, over-thick nineteenth-century piano realization is unsatisfactory if any degree of authenticity is intended – and may also be unnecessarily difficult!

When the continuo part is realized by a keyboard along with another instrument such as a cello or bassoon, the role of the latter in reinforcing the bass is a limited one and may have little participation in the musical dialogue. Nevertheless, for those who understand and enjoy baroque music it can be rewarding to play.

The instruments and performing practices of the classical period, and even to some extent those of the romantic age, also had differences from those of today. Specialist ensembles exist that perform works of these periods authentically. However, the great majority of professional ensembles play classical and romantic music in modern style on instruments of modern form, and those playing for pleasure will normally do likewise.

## Identification of Works

Some system for identifying works is normally necessary, at least with composers who produced a large output. There are, for example, eleven string quartets in E♭ by Haydn! The most frequent identification is by opus numbers (abbreviation op., plural opp.), which were usually allocated by the composer or with the composer's approval. Each number applies to a single work or sometimes to a set of works. Ideally the numbers are in chronological order of composition, and no significant work is omitted. Only too often, however, reality does not match this ideal. Since an opus number was often allocated only when a work was published, delays in publication could affect the number. A work that remained unpublished until after the composer's death might have no number. Moreover, publishers (and sometimes multiple publishers) might allocate numbers without the composer's approval, perhaps posthumously but also during the composer's lifetime. All this led to erratic numbering, and sometimes even duplications.

It is often desirable to know the period of composition of a work for consideration in the light of knowledge of the composer's dates and compositional life. Works from a composer's very early years will not be of the quality of later compositions; and many composers developed greatly through their compositional careers, affecting both the character and the playability of their works. Players may infer the approximate period of a work from its opus number, but unless done knowing the state of the composer's numbering this can be unwise. For example, Mendelssohn's sextet op. 110, which might be thought to be a late work, is actually from his immature years, published posthumously.

Some composers, mostly in the twentieth century, chose not to use opus numbers. Others, for example Bach, lack opus numbers because few works were published in their lifetimes. For such composers, or for those who have opus numbers that are confused, a scholarly catalogue of works has often been produced, the numbers from which have become the normal means of identification. These catalogues generally list all of the composer's works in chronological order (and can indeed be used as an indicator of composition dates). A few, however, usually for prolific earlier composers such as Handel, rather than being chronological list the compositions in groups by genre: their main purpose is to provide comprehensive and unambiguous identification.

With many other composers the opus numbers continue to be used, despite imperfections. For some of these, compositions that lack an opus number have been allocated WoO numbers (*Werk ohne Opuszahl* – work without opus number). Beethoven, Corelli and Hummel are examples.

Even with a series of works usually referred to by opus number or catalogue number, simple sequential numbering may also be encountered. For example, Beethoven's string quartet op. 132 is sometimes referred to as 'string quartet no. 15'. Such numbering may be confusing, however, as a result of factors such as irregularities in the opus numbers or changes to the canon of works resulting from modern scholarship. This particular quartet is actually the thirteenth that Beethoven wrote.

Some chamber works, usually popular ones, have a name or nickname. Most of these did not originate with their composers, though some did.

## Sheet Music

Even in this era of electronic data, parts printed on paper are normally necessary for playing music.

Most people frequently play from old editions. However, these editions, typically originating in the later nineteenth or earlier twentieth century, normally suffer from the style of editing favoured in their day. Phrasing indications are heavily altered as a matter of course, usually in string parts to be the editor's favoured bowings. Dynamic indications and hairpins are changed and additional ones introduced. Expression indications are added. Markings by the composer such as grace notes or different types of staccato are unlikely to be reproduced reliably. Few or no indications are given of what changes have been made. Fingerings are often added, and (for string instruments) instructions introduced to use harmonics or play high on a low string. All these markings are informed by ideas of both musical taste and playing technique that are often completely outdated. We would anyway now say that such matters should be the choice of the performer, based on a knowledge of what the composer wrote.

These alterations are usually worst in music from the baroque period. The editing of all parts is typically very heavy, and (as remarked earlier) the continuo is realized for piano, generally in a way that we would now consider inappropriate. In music of the classical period, too, the editing is often bad, though it can usually be lived with. Even music of the romantic era often has significant alterations.

Old editions may also have other problems. A difficulty for many cellists is the use of treble clef octave below for high-lying passages, unlike the modern usage of tenor clef or treble clef at correct pitch. (This also occasionally occurs in publications still available today or until recently, such as Simrock editions of works by Dvořák.) A different annoyance can affect pianists: fingerings may use the numbering (from thumb to little finger) x1234, instead of the modern 12345. A further shortcoming is that these editions generally do not have bar numbers. Most have rehearsal letters or numbers: but these may be sparse and some have none at all.

Another inconvenience is that old copies often lack the identifications of the works normally used today. Some that are for a series of works use their own numbering unrelated to anything else. Many compositions by Schubert are designated as 'Opus Posthumous' (not a very helpful identification!) but do not show the Deutsch number by which they are now generally known. When opportunity arises, it is worth writing such numbers in. Three long series of works where old publications without modern identifications remain widely used are the Haydn piano trios, the Mozart sonatas for violin and piano and the Schubert string quartets. To assist, musical incipits are shown in the entries for these works in Chapter 4.

It is possible to do something about bad editing in old editions, given access to a good modern edition or a score. (It is worth noticing that scores even when old are often without editorial alterations, although probably not up to modern standards of scholarship.) Marking-up in pencil will do, but using correction fluid to remove unwanted markings will give better results.

Acquiring sets of parts usually means purchasing them from a retailer (music shop or online). These are normally printed copies, but there are also online retailers that provide them in electronic form for the purchaser to download and print. There are even CDs available with electronic parts of multiple works. Though this method is cheap, parts printed at home will not be as readable and usable as professionally printed parts. They are also often old editions.

A difficulty in purchasing sheet music is the absence of any single source of information, online or otherwise, about who publishes particular music or how to obtain it. It is not always easy to locate publications of little-known works, or to identify all available editions of major works to allow an informed choice. A good music shop or bookshop music department will help. Searching online can find the answer, but may require investigating multiple retailers and publishers. Many publishers have online catalogues, sometimes including a specific catalogue for chamber music.

The best editions are normally modern and from reputable publishers. Since about the mid-twentieth century, the climate of opinion concerning editing has completely changed. Good editions are now urtext (original text), which are intended to show as accurately as possible what the composer intended. Another advantage of modern editions is that they usually have bar numbers. Most of the major classical chamber works have by now been made available in at least one urtext edition. However, these editions can have drawbacks. The most obvious is price. Also they are not always as well printed or laid out as an old edition of the same music. Moreover, it is possible to be irritated by careful annotations such as brackets put round markings to show that they are editorial introductions. Players who prefer parts that have performance suggestions such as bowings and fingerings may not like modern editions that lack them. It should also be appreciated that editions vary: not all those claiming to be urtext are up to modern standards.

Purchasing a new set of parts does not necessarily mean acquiring a modern edition. For many important chamber works and series of works, old editions continue to be printed. The editing is frequently late nineteenth century and has not been changed (though modern identification numbers may have been added). They can have other shortcomings: for example, the Peters edition of the Schubert string quartets in two volumes (still sometimes described as 'string quartets, complete') is by no means complete. Nevertheless, these editions are usually the cheapest, and the difference particularly when acquiring a series of works can be large. Buying these editions may be the right decision, but it is best to understand the alternatives.

## Free Online Sources of Sheet Music

A quite different resource is music available online free of charge, most prominently from the International Music Score Library Project (IMSLP, also called the Petrucci Music Library). This only contains music that is out of copyright, mostly in old editions. Provided they are out of copyright in the user's country, printed copies can be made and played from. Coverage and quality depend on what owners of printed music have scanned and downloaded to the library, and are variable. Some works do not appear at all, and others are available in score but not in parts. On the other hand, there are some works available in parts in multiple editions, sometimes including modern versions that are not subject to copyright restrictions. As already remarked, parts printed from a computer are not as good as publishers' printed copies; but this method of acquiring parts is very cheap. As such it can be useful, for example, as a way of trying out works by little-known composers that may never be played again.

The restrictions of copyright law apply when downloading and printing from the Internet (and also when photocopying paper music). Details for the UK are on Fact Sheet P-01, available online from the UK Copyright Service. Copyright duration in the UK is seventy years from the end of the year in which the composer died. For editions containing a new typographical arrangement, the duration is twenty-five years from the end of the year of publication. Note that IMSLP is hosted in Canada and operates under Canadian law, which has different durations.

Also sometimes available online are reproductions of the composer's manuscript, which can be fascinating.

One last problem often encountered in both old and modern sheet music is inadequate time for page turns. Adding at the top or bottom of a page a few bars or lines of music from the other side (photocopied or written out by hand) can be useful. A horizontal cut between lines of music in the middle of a page occasionally works. Photocopying pages to assist is always acceptable in copyright terms. It is possible to use a wooden frame that, when put on a music stand, is wide enough to support three or even four pages.

Publishers are numerous. Peters Edition is one of the best-known, offering at reasonable prices many popular chamber works in editions originating many years ago. Particularly known for their scholarly urtext editions are Bärenreiter and Henle: for many works these are the best available. Other publishers too (including Peters) offer urtext editions. Many smaller or specialist music publishers also exist. Two that provide a wide selection of out-of-copyright chamber works by less-known composers are, in Britain, Ourtext (formerly Merton Music) and, in America, Edition Silvertrust. Publisher information is occasionally mentioned in this book; it is, of course, liable to change with time.

Exploring music outside the normal repertoire can occasionally mean seeking sheet music that is a century or more out of print. Copies may exist only in the libraries of universities or music colleges, perhaps in other countries; they may be found by electronic catalogue searches. Such institutions are sometimes very helpful, and may scan and send them electronically for a small charge or none. With music that has never been published, it may be possible in a similar way to obtain copies of manuscripts. However, these will often be scores, so parts would have to be prepared before they could be played.

# Chapter 3

# Aspects of the Music

The core of this book is Chapter 4, the list of chamber works grouped by composer. This is essentially the repertoire as it is generally accepted today and is professionally performed in concerts and recordings. Just a few composers are included who may be thought surprising, but they are considered justified by the quality of their chamber music and the enjoyment it can give to players.

All the significant chamber compositions of each composer are discussed. Often not mentioned, however, are minor, unfinished or very early works. Devotees of particular composers who are anxious to know and play everything they have written should consult other sources.

Some further composers not included in Chapter 4 are listed in Appendix I, with a brief summary of their chamber output. Appendix II contains lists by instrument or instrumental combination of all works discussed or mentioned in this book.

## Duration

For every work discussed, a measure is shown of the time it takes to play. Knowing this can be valuable when considering playing it. The fifty-one minute duration of Schubert's G major string quartet is part of what makes that work formidable. Equally, it is worth appreciating that Haydn's C major divertimento for winds (Hob.II:14), despite having five movements, occupies only five and a half minutes.

The durations shown are averaged from a number of representative professional recordings. (Technical limitations may of course mean that amateur performances take longer!) The recordings have been selected for their choices concerning repeats. In sonata-form first movements, repeats of the first section (exposition) where marked are taken (even if the movement is long), but marked repeats of the second half are not. Other short repeats are taken, including in sets of variations both halves of each variation where so marked.

## Technical Difficulty

Technical difficulty is a fact of life. For amateurs, it can make the difference between being able to play and enjoy a work and being unable to do so. (Considering that some now-famous concertos were originally pronounced unplayable by their intended performers, we are reminded that finding music impossible to play is – or at least was – not limited to amateurs!) Even for those able to play a composition, greater technical difficulty usually means harder work, both together as an ensemble and often in individual study and practice.

Every work discussed in this book is given a rating of technical difficulty, described below. However, a warning is necessary. No system of ratings can reliably indicate whether a particular ensemble or player will be able to play a work, how well they might play it or how much practice will be necessary in order to do so. All players – or, at least, all amateurs – have frailties in their technique, which are different for every individual. There are many types of technical difficulty, even on one instrument. Different instruments have different inherent difficulties. A further problem can be complicated timing. Even if all players can play their notes and manage the timing difficulties, maintaining ensemble may not be easy. The ratings try to take all these factors into account, but they are inevitably approximate.

A rating of difficulty is given for each work as a whole, not normally for each of its parts. It is a basic tenet of chamber music that all parts share in the musical burden: in consequence they usually share comparable technical difficulties. However, in chamber music involving strings, the violin or first violin part is (as has already been discussed) normally more technically demanding than the others; this is to be understood within the overall rating. Certain works may place particular demands on other parts. Difficulties for all instruments depend on how well the composer understood their characteristics and so wrote for them. A further consideration is the piano, so completely unlike all other chamber-music instruments and possessing difficulties unique to itself. Difficulty ratings for works involving piano should be considered by pianists with caution.

One factor not included in the ratings, however, is musical difficulty – the problems of understanding what the music is saying, which parts are important at each moment, and so of performing the work as the composer envisaged. Beethoven's late string quartets are generally considered particularly challenging in this respect. It is also well known that the music of Mozart, even when technically straightforward, can be even to professionals particularly difficult to play musically. A low difficulty rating does not necessarily mean that a work is undemanding.

Ratings given are on a five-point scale (similar to those employed by some music publishers): D1 = easy; D2 = fairly easy; D3 = average difficulty; D4 = fairly difficult; D5 = very difficult.

These may be illustrated by some string quartet examples: D1 – Charles Wesley; D2 – most early Mozart; D3 – mature Haydn; D4 – Brahms; D5 – Bartók.

In the chamber-music repertoire, D1 hardly occurs, and D2 rarely after the classical era. For most amateurs D3 is playable, though for many it can be problematical in places. D4 is generally playable by experienced amateurs, though it may require a lot of work. For the great majority of amateurs, D5 is impossible.

Although greater precision than this five-point scale is not reasonable, the ratings are often modified by the addition of a plus or minus. This usually expresses a comparative distinction. For example, almost all mature Haydn string quartets have a family likeness in their technical characteristics, and are rated D3. Nevertheless, some stand out as particularly difficult, while for a few the opposite is the case. These are designated respectively as D3+ and D3–. No modifiers are used, however, with the D5 rating.

A further distinction is occasionally made. Although the ratings apply to the whole ensemble, in cases where a particular part deviates noticeably from the difficulty of the others, this is indicated: for example 'D3 (cello easier)' or 'D2 (piano harder)'.

Other aspects for particular works may be amplified in the text.

## Beyond the Bounds

Players may occasionally enjoy opportunities to play music outside the normal bounds of chamber music, of which the following are a few examples.

String players may like to play Bach arrangements, including those for string quartet of music from the *Art of Fugue*. Another field of interest is sixteenth- and seventeenth-century English music for viol consort. Many of the works (which do not employ continuo) are entitled *Fantasia*; they culminate in a notable series by Purcell. There are domestic groups who play them using reproductions of original instruments, but they can also be played on modern instruments (for which editions may be available).

Wind players have a significant repertoire of works for ensembles larger than nine players. Notable examples are Mozart's Serenade ('Gran Partita'), K. 361/370a, for thirteen instruments, Dvořák's Serenade, op. 44, for eleven instruments, and several works by Strauss for either thirteen or sixteen instruments.

A quite different opportunity is to play with a singer. Well-known examples are Vaughan Williams's song-cycle *On Wenlock Edge* for tenor, piano and string quartet, and Barber's *Dover Beach* for baritone and string quartet. There is also a small repertoire of songs with piano and another instrument. Notable examples are Schubert's *Auf dem Strom*, for tenor, horn and piano, his *Der Hirt auf dem Felsen* (*The Shepherd on the Rock*), for soprano, clarinet and piano, and Brahms's two songs, op. 91, for contralto, viola and piano.

## Suggested Works for Inexperienced Players

For players new to chamber music, especially those of limited technical skill, suggestions are given below of reasonably straightforward works that might be tried. They are offered for three combinations, each having a large repertoire that includes many works from the classical period (among which are usually to be found those that are least technically demanding). Only employed in these are string instruments and piano. Other combinations, including those involving wind instruments, have a smaller repertoire: so there is little choice.

In addition, for violinists, flautists, oboists and keyboard players, there are from the baroque period many playable duet sonatas and trio sonatas, and these too may make a useful introduction to playing chamber music. This applies also to cellists and bassoonists playing in the continuo of baroque sonatas.

Also potentially useful are the many publications of duets and trios for various combinations of instruments, both original works and arrangements, usually deriving from smaller works by classical composers such as Boccherini, Haydn and Mozart or lesser composers of the late eighteenth and early nineteenth centuries.

*String quartets*

Easiest are the six quartets of Charles Wesley (*see* Appendix I).

The following are a step more difficult, but still straightforward:

Mozart: most of the early quartets, particularly K. 157, K. 158, K. 159, K. 160 and K. 173. The great quartets of Mozart's maturity are all more demanding than these early works; the most playable is probably K. 458 ('The Hunt')

Haydn: any of the early quartets of opp. 1 and 2, especially op. 1 nos 3, 4 and 6 and op. 2 nos 1, 3 and 6. Also, from op. 3 (probably not actually by Haydn) nos 2, 3 and 5. Haydn's mature quartets are almost all significantly more difficult than these. Probably the most straightforward are op. 33 no. 3 ('The Bird'), op. 42 and op. 64 no. 6

Schubert: D. 32 and D. 87 (op. 125 no. 1)

Mendelssohn: in E♭ (of 1823)

*Piano trios*

Haydn: any of his many piano trios (though their cello parts have little freedom). The famous 'Gypsy Rondo' trio (Hob.XV:25 in G) is as suitable as any

Mozart: K. 254, K. 542, K. 548 and K. 564. Of these, K. 254 and K. 564 are easiest

Beethoven: though not a full-scale work, his Allegretto in B♭, WoO 39 of 1812, makes a delightful and undemanding introduction to playing piano trios. Of his full-scale trios, op. 1 nos 1 and 2 are the best to begin with

Hummel: any of opp. 12, 22, 35, 65 and 96

*Sonatas for violin and piano (or continuo)*

Handel (including some of doubtful authenticity): 'no. 3' (op. 1 no. 12, HWV 370), 'no. 4' (op. 1 no. 13, HWV 371) and 'no. 6' (op. 1 no. 15, HWV 373)

Mozart: K. 301, K. 302, K. 303 and K. 304

Schubert: D. 384 and D. 385 (sonatinas, op. 137 nos 1 and 2)

Beethoven: op. 23

Hummel: op. 5 nos 1 and 2

# Chapter 4

# The Composers and Their Works

25m   duration in minutes
D3    difficulty (D1 = easy; D2 = fairly easy; D3 = average difficulty; D4 = fairly
      difficult; D5 = very difficult)

## ARRIAGA
### 1806–1826; Spain

Juan Crisóstomo de Arriaga was a composer of remarkable promise, but died
shortly before his twentieth birthday. He is sometimes referred to as 'the Spanish
Mozart'. Born in Bilbao (in the Basque country), he went to Paris to study at the
Conservatoire, where he died. His three string quartets are probably his most significant works, and have a real musical interest. They are classical in character, with
touches of early romanticism and of Spanish flavour. Though only occasionally
performed professionally, they are popular with amateurs as playable and distinctive alternatives to the great classics. Arriaga also left two sets of variations for
string quartet, which some may wish to investigate.

### String Quartets
Published in 1824 and probably composed about 1823, these quartets are interesting to play, with their material well distributed between all the parts. Their
difficulties are not formidable but they are not trivial either.

#### No. 1 in D minor                                                    25m; D3
This is perhaps the most impressive of the three quartets. In particular the *Adagio
con espressione* second movement has surprising power and feeling.

#### No. 2 in A                                                          25m; D3
Cheerful, fresh and interesting throughout. Most memorable is the set of variations

that forms the *Andante* second movement. A soulful *Lento* variation is given to the viola, whereas the second violin's variation is fast.

No. 3 in E♭                                                                                    25m; D3

In character this differs from the others, but again is interesting. The bucolic *Pastorale* second movement contains a surprisingly dramatic middle section. Perhaps finest is the *Presto agitato* last movement.

# BACH
## 1685–1750; Germany

Johann Sebastian Bach, the supreme member of his large musical family, is considered by some the greatest of all composers. He lived a relatively unspectacular life, occupying a succession of musical positions in different towns in Germany. From 1717 to 1723 he was Kapellmeister at Cöthen, and from 1723 until his death he was Cantor at St Thomas's Church, Leipzig. His greatest fame in his lifetime was as an organist; his compositions gradually became widely known only from the early nineteenth century. He composed in many forms, but never opera; much of his output is religious choral music. There is only a relatively small amount of chamber music (though some more may have been lost). Most consists of duet sonatas, of which some, in accordance with the convention of the time, are for solo instrument with basso continuo. In others, however, he was innovative in providing a fully-composed harpsichord part.

Few of Bach's works were published in his lifetime; hardly any have an opus number. They are normally referred to by their number in the *Bach-Werke-Verzeichnis* (BWV – list of Bach's works), compiled by W. Schmieder and first published in 1950. (S is occasionally used instead of BWV.) Numbers are not chronological; they are grouped by medium. Accurate dates are rarely known for Bach's works, and for many even the period is uncertain. No dates are shown here, but most of his chamber music is thought to date from his mature years at either Cöthen or Leipzig. Some further works not listed here (including some that have a BWV number) are now considered spurious.

In addition to the chamber works discussed below, other works may well be played. The six Brandenburg concertos are usually considered orchestral music, but two of them are normally played with single players per part. No. 3 in G (BWV 1048) is for three violins, three violas, three cellos, double bass and harpsichord. No. 6 in B♭ (BWV 1051) is for two violas, two violas da gamba, cello, double bass and harpsichord. In both works the last two instruments form a basso continuo, so can be played by any convenient instrumentation. In no. 6, in the absence of violas da gamba, their parts can be played (given sheet music in the appropriate clef) by either violas or cellos (if the former, the work becomes very much a viola party!).

Other Bach works may be played in arrangements. Foremost is the *Art of Fugue*, BWV 1080. This unfinished work from Bach's last years was written in open score (each voice written on a separate stave) with no indication of the intended instrumentation (indeed, it is not even certain that performance was envisaged). Consequently it is valid to use any instrument or group of instruments able to play the notes, and many different published editions exist. Performances by keyboard instruments (including organ) are probably most frequent, but string quartet is also prominent. The complete work consists of up to twenty-one pieces, mostly fugues but also including canons and a chorale. When played by a string quartet most pieces use all four instruments, but some require only two or three.

## Trio Sonatas

Of five trio sonatas individually allocated BWV numbers (1036–1040), only two are full-scale works and considered probably authentic. (Six other works entitled trio sonata, BWV 525–30, are indeed trios but are to be executed by one player at an organ: left hand, right hand and pedals.)

Trio sonata in G (BWV 1038) (flute, violin, continuo)         8m; D2
Short, straightforward and attractive. Its authenticity has been questioned.

Trio sonata in G (BWV 1039) (2 flutes, continuo)         13m; D3–
This attractive work is more substantial in both length and content than its predecessor. It may be an arrangement of an earlier version for two violins and continuo.

Trio sonata in C minor from *The Musical Offering* (BWV 1079) (flute, violin, continuo)         20m; D3
In May 1747 Bach visited Frederick the Great of Prussia, where he improvised on a long theme given to him by the king. He then returned to Leipzig and composed a series of contrapuntal pieces, all based on the king's theme, which he dedicated to the king. These are known as *The Musical Offering*. One piece is this trio sonata, a four-movement work. It is a tour de force – probably the most powerful of all Bach's chamber works. Its themes all derive from the king's theme, though not always obviously.

## Duet Sonatas with Full Harpsichord Parts

These sonatas with a fully composed harpsichord part have a true partnership between the instruments, rather than being for a solo instrument with continuo accompaniment. They resemble trios in that they have two melody lines with the keyboard left hand playing a continuo-like bass. Interest is shared democratically between the instruments, though overall the keyboard carries more of the musical responsibility.

## Violin

Six sonatas are for violin and harpsichord; Bach stated that optionally a viola da gamba could be added. Many today will use a piano. All except the last are in four movements, slow-fast-slow-fast. The technical difficulties are moderate; the violin parts have nothing of the virtuosic demands of the works for solo violin.

Sonata in B minor (BWV 1014)                                    14m; D3

Sonata in A (BWV 1015)                                         13m; D3
It is usual to arpeggiate the three-note violin chords in the second movement.

Sonata in E (BWV 1016)                                        16m; D3

Sonata in C minor (BWV 1017)                                  17m; D3

Sonata in F minor (BWV 1018)                                  17m; D3

Sonata in G (BWV 1019)                                        16m; D3
This sonata has five movements, starting with an *Allegro*. The third movement is a harpsichord solo.

## Viola da gamba

The three sonatas for viola da gamba and harpsichord are often played using a cello, though the rather high tessitura adds to the difficulty of the cello part. Alternatively, the viola may be used, but editions for this have to make alterations, usually raising some low passages by an octave.

Sonata in G (BWV 1027)                                        13m; D3
This is a probably later arrangement of the trio sonata BWV 1039.

Sonata in D (BWV 1028)                                        14m; D3+
The last movement is technically quite demanding.

Sonata in G minor (BWV 1029)                                 14m; D3+
In only three movements, but substantial. The main material of the first movement is reminiscent of the third Brandenburg Concerto.

## Flute

There are three sonatas for flute and harpsichord. All are in three movements, but they are not a uniform set. The first is excellent, but the second is of uncertain authenticity and the third has suffered the misfortune that a part of it has been lost.

Sonata in B minor (BWV 1030)                                 18m; D3
A very beautiful work, the largest and arguably finest of all the flute sonatas.

Sonata in E♭ (BWV 1031)                                     10m; D3–

Attractive, enjoyable and straightforward to play, but modest in scale and musical character. It may be by C.P.E. Bach.

Sonata in A (BWV 1032)                            12m (complete); D3

Good; but the only source is the manuscript, from which most of the second half of the first movement is missing. Various reconstructions have been made, but some editions omit this movement.

## Duet Sonatas with Continuo

Unlike the sonatas with harpsichord, these are largely solos with accompaniment. In consequence, their violin and flute parts are more concertante and brilliant. Musically, though fairly lightweight and arguably less fine than those with harpsichord, they are perhaps more immediately attractive.

*Violin*

Sonata in G (BWV 1021)                                       8m; D3

Discovered only in 1928.

Sonata in E minor (BWV 1023)                        11m; D5 (violin)

This is variously considered as in three or in four movements, because the first two are linked. It is a display piece for the violin, some of it of virtuoso difficulty; the continuo is entirely subservient. The first movement has figuration reminiscent of the prelude of the E major partita for solo violin.

*Flute*

Sonata in C (BWV 1033)                                       9m; D3+

The authenticity of this sonata has been questioned. The first two of its four movements are made difficult mainly by their speed.

Sonata in E minor (BWV 1034)                                14m; D3

Sonata in E (BWV 1035)                                      12m; D3

# BARBER
## 1910–1981; America

Samuel Barber began as a pianist, singer and composer. In the early 1930s he rapidly achieved success in the last role, becoming one of the most frequently performed and highly regarded of American composers both in his own country and elsewhere. Unlike many others of his time, he rejected most of the trends of modernism, and wrote music of lyrical character based on conventional tonality. He also made little use of specifically American elements. Nevertheless his music is recognizably his own, and is not completely without influences of his time. There are only a few chamber works, but his string quartet includes a movement that has become one of his most famous works. Also, though not chamber music, players may be interested in the well-known early song *Dover Beach* for baritone and string quartet.

## String Quartets

Serenade for string quartet, op. 1 (1928)                                         11m; D3
In three short movements; pleasant but immature. It is mainly known in the version of 1944 for string orchestra.

String quartet, op. 11 (1936)                                                     18m; D4
This quartet is often described as being in B minor. It is known mainly for its central movement, *Molto adagio*, which is famous in the version Barber shortly afterwards made for string orchestra as *Adagio for strings*. (He also much later produced a choral version, *Agnus Dei*.) This is a lyrical and emotional movement, rising to a powerful climax; it distributes its interest fully between the players. The first movement is equally substantial; much of it is vigorous and has distinctive rhythms. Barber had problems with the finale, rewriting it twice after the first performance in December 1936. It is short, continues without a break from the slow movement, and recapitulates material from the first movement.

## Wind Quintet (flute, oboe, clarinet, horn, bassoon)

*Summer Music*, op. 31 (1955)                                                    12m; D4+
In a single continuous movement, though there are many time changes. It is challenging to play: the notes are sometimes difficult for all players, and brilliant flourishes are called for especially from the flute and clarinet. Timing complexities also mean that it is not easy to fit together.

## Duet Sonata

Sonata, op. 6 (1932) (cello, piano)                                              19m; D4
In three movements, with richly romantic writing for both instruments.


# BARTÓK
### 1881–1945; Hungary

Béla Bartók is widely considered one of the greatest composers of the twentieth century. An important part of his output is chamber music, dominated by the series of six string quartets composed at intervals throughout his career. These are often considered the finest of all twentieth-century quartets. It has been suggested that in them Bartók continued from where Beethoven in his late quartets left off.

Bartók's outstanding position in chamber music is reflected in frequent professional performances. However, matters are different when it comes to playing for pleasure. Bartók wrote for the concert hall, and his chamber music is almost all formidably difficult. For most amateurs these works are out of reach, and even by professionals or others who have the necessary technical ability they are hardly to be played casually.

Bartók collected Magyar (Hungarian) peasant folk music, and also that of other eastern European countries such as Slovakia, Romania and Bulgaria. The spirit of this folk music is fundamental to his mature compositions. His style is very personal to him. Particularly in the middle years of his career, it is very dissonant and can be harsh and even violent. It may be sardonic and employ parody and satire. His music is not enjoyed or understood by all.

Bartók used opus numbers only until 1921. Compositions are now sometimes referred to by numbers from two alternative catalogues compiled since his death; but there is no reason for confusion among the chamber works.

Although not true chamber music, the forty-four duos for two violins, of 1931, are of interest to amateurs. These are teaching pieces, typically about one minute long, and are of progressive difficulty. The early ones may be categorized as D1; later ones go up to D4, but their greatest difficulties are their rhythmic and harmonic complexity rather than their notes. They can be fun to play and are helpful for growing the ability to handle twentieth-century music. Also perhaps of interest to some is the piano quintet, an early work of 1903–4. It is massive and heavily romantic, with little sign of the later Bartók.

## String Quartets

The technical difficulty of these quartets, always severe, if anything increases through the first four, then moderates a little in the remaining two. From the third quartet onwards, Bartók employed a range of extended instrumental techniques – col legno, sul ponticello, long portamento, pizzicato portamento, and forceful playing of repeated multi-note chords. He also asks for pizzicato played so as to strike the fingerboard with a snapping sound, which has become known as Bartók pizzicato.

String quartet no. 1 in A minor, op. 7 (1908–9)                      30m; D4+

This quartet is considered immature, though still a fine work. Aspects of the later Bartók are evident, but the character of the music is still related to late romanticism. There are three movements. The first, contrapuntal and very slow, has been compared with the opening of Beethoven's op. 131. Bartók referred to it as a funeral dirge. The other movements are progressively faster and less sombre. This quartet is very difficult, but experienced and well-motivated amateurs may with practice make something of it.

## String quartet no. 2, op. 17 (1915–17) 27m; D5

This is perhaps the most immediately attractive and comprehensible of the quartets. It has frequent grinding dissonances, but in their context they give meaning and point to the music. There are three movements. The opening *Moderato* is lyrical, almost melodious. Very striking is the *Allegro molto capriccioso* second movement – a wild sequence of folk-inspired dances. The *Lento* finale makes a subdued ending. Musically this would perhaps be the best quartet to approach first: but unfortunately even experienced amateurs will probably find it technically too difficult.

## String quartet no. 3 (1927) 15m; D5

In the ten years since the previous quartet, Bartók developed his style to what might be called the most 'advanced' he reached – harsh and not easy to comprehend. Technically it is very demanding. Of the instrumental effects, sul ponticello and long portamento in particular are extensively indulged. This is Bartók's shortest quartet. It is played without a break, being effectively in one movement though divided into four sections.

## String quartet no. 4 (1928) 23m; D5

Dating from only a year after no. 3, this uses a similar harmonic language and similar instrumental effects. However, its structure is quite different: it is in five movements, in so-called arch form. Movements one and five have aspects in common, as have two and four. Movement three stands alone: it is calm, *Non troppo lento*. Movement four is entirely pizzicato, including much 'Bartók pizzicato'. This quartet is perhaps more easily understood than no. 3. It is uncompromising and consistent in its aims, much of it with an elemental force and power. Its technical difficulties are immense and there is little in it that could be contemplated other than by virtuosi.

## String quartet no. 5 (1934) 31m; D5

Like its predecessor, this quartet is in arch form. Here, the central movement is a scherzo with trio, and the second and fourth movements are slow. The harmonic language and instrumental effects are comparable to those of no. 4, but this quartet is less strident and dissonant. The level of difficulty is again very great. However, the *Adagio molto* second movement is technically relatively straightforward, and might be tried by capable amateurs wanting to attempt some mature Bartók.

## String quartet no. 6 (1939) 29m; D5

Bartók here returns to a four-movement form. Moreover, all movements are united by what might be called a motto theme. The atmosphere is tragic: the motto theme, which is slow and marked *Mesto* (sad), forms an introduction to each of the first three movements; in the last movement it continues throughout. The quartet is less dissonant than its predecessor, and sometimes more obviously melodious. Some passages in artificial harmonics are given to the first violin. The slow final movement is technically not unduly demanding, and is another possibility for experienced amateurs to try.

## Ensemble Work including a Wind Instrument

Contrasts (1938) (clarinet, violin, piano)                    17m; D5
This three-movement work was written for the violinist Joseph Szigeti and the jazz clarinettist Benny Goodman. The contrasts are between the timbres of the instruments. For listeners, this is an attractive and fascinating work, in Bartók's later, less severely discordant style. However, whilst the piano part is relatively subordinate, the violin and clarinet parts are of virtuoso character. Clarinets in both B♭ and A are required. Unusually, the violinist too needs two instruments, one tuned normally, the other (for just the opening section of the last movement) tuned to G♯-D-A-E♭.

## Duet Sonatas

Both sonatas require virtuoso players.

Sonata no. 1 (1921) (violin, piano)                    36m; D5
In three remarkably expansive movements. It is often meditative or gentle in mood.

Sonata no. 2 (1922) (violin, piano)                    21m; D5
In two movements.


# BEETHOVEN
## 1770–1827; Germany, Austria

Ludwig van Beethoven is universally regarded as one of the greatest composers of all time. Only perhaps Bach and Mozart might be considered of comparable stature. Coming as a young man into the Viennese classical world of Haydn and Mozart, he first showed that he could compose music that stood beside the works of those masters. He then went on and developed in a way that expanded the whole scope, scale and expressive power of music, moving its emotional content towards the romantic era. One reason why he was able to achieve so much is that he lived to the age of fifty-six – a relative maturity that was denied to Mozart and Schubert; and he composed with energy and commitment throughout most of his life. Moreover, chamber music was always a major and essential part of his output, so that his position in chamber music (as in other areas) is based on the quantity as well as the quality of his contribution.

Beethoven is almost unique among the great composers in that his musical development continued at an undiminished rate throughout his life. His output is often divided for convenience into three periods: early, middle and late. There was, of course, no abrupt alteration in his style between the periods; but so great is the change in the character of his music through his life that this simplistic distinction is almost essential to an understanding of his output and what will be involved in playing it. Moreover, most of the chamber works fall neatly in both date of composition and musical character into one or other of the periods. Of string quartets, he wrote an almost equal number in each period. A quartet from the early period and one from the late seem almost unrecognizably different in character.

Unlike Mozart, Beethoven was not a youthful prodigy as a composer; his very early works are weak (though they may have charm), and it was not until probably 1794 or 1795 that he began to produce music of real quality. His first or early period may be considered to run from that time until about 1802. During these years, he largely conformed to the conventions of the classical period, and in their size and musical scope the works are comparable to those of Haydn and Mozart. In his second or middle period from 1803 onwards, however, he burst the bounds of those conventions, both in the scale of the music and in the power of its expression. The most dramatic example came in the third symphony, the 'Eroica', composed in 1803; but the change was soon seen to an equal degree in the chamber music. This period is usually considered to continue to about 1812, with the third or late period beginning in 1813. For some years from this time, Beethoven had major problems in his life, and his compositional output slowed. Indeed, even after this crisis, the rate at which he composed was slower than it had been earlier – though conversely the intensity of the works was greater. In chamber music this period is only fully expressed in the series of string quartets composed from 1824 to 1826 – for many, among the supreme achievements in music.

Beethoven is a consistent composer: after the very early years, there are really no weak works. His writing is always democratic, giving good opportunities to all. In terms of technical difficulty, his works are demanding but manageable. Those of his early period are comparable in their difficulty to other music of the classical period; but as he developed, they become more difficult, in their musical as well as technical aspects, culminating in the late string quartets.

Beethoven's greatest importance in chamber music is for his dominating contribution to the repertoires of the string quartet, the piano trio and the duet sonata both for violin and for cello with piano. His output is a great and essential part of the repertoire of these combinations. However, there is also much more, and players of most instruments and most combinations have reason to be grateful to him. His contribution to the repertoire of ensemble chamber music involving wind instruments is quite large, though these works are all from his early period. He wrote more significant string trios than did any other composer, though these again are early works. He also provided enjoyable additions to the repertoire of the string quintet with two violas.

In addition to the compositions fully addressed below, there exists a substantial miscellany of further works. Some are very early, from the earlier 1790s or before, and have been published since the composer's death. Others are arrangements, usually made or approved by him. There are also a few short, small-scale works and some unfinished fragments. Simply because they are by Beethoven, they are of interest; and publications of many of them are available. Most (though not all) are mentioned in the relevant sections below.

Beethoven's opus numbers broadly reflect the order of composition, but they do not always do so accurately. Moreover, there are a few numbers that are badly out of chronological order: usually early works, or arrangements of them, that have misleadingly high numbers. Opus numbers above 137 may be encountered, but were not allocated in Beethoven's lifetime and are not normally used today. Most very early or miscellaneous works are now referred to by a WoO number; Hess numbers are also sometimes used.

## String Duo

Duet *With two obbligato eyeglasses,* WoO 32 (c.1796) (viola, cello)          13m; D3+
Unfinished: there are just a first movement and a minuet; a slow movement is incomplete. Four movements must have been intended. Moreover, Beethoven never finalized what we have by adding dynamics or articulation indications. Editions therefore have editorial markings – or players can use the Henle edition and make their own choices. It is lightweight but good entertainment, and (especially for the cello) not technically trivial. The 'title' was written on the autograph by Beethoven.

## String Trios
The first two of Beethoven's trios are relatively lightweight works; the second in particular offers a type of entertainment music rare in his chamber music.

Op. 3 in E♭ (1794 or earlier)                                                   42m; D2
In six movements, structurally modelled on Mozart's divertimento for string trio, K. 563. This first work of Beethoven's string chamber music is immediately democratic. Its musical intent is serious and it is attractive, well written for the instruments and good fun to play. It can, however, sometimes seem immature and insipid. Being technically quite easy, it is probably the best trio for players to begin with.

Serenade in D, op. 8 (1796–7)                                                   29m; D2+
This is a much more mature work than op.3, and only a little more difficult. It is

very lightweight musically, and is great fun to play. It opens and ends with a march and among its other movements are a minuet, a scherzo and an *Allegretto alla Polacca*. Many of the tunes are largely presented by the violin, but opportunities also come to the others; and the scoring is so resourceful that accompanying parts are never boring.

———•——•——•———

The three trios of op. 9 that follow are dramatically different from the previous two works. They are all in four movements: large-scale, serious and powerful. They were perhaps part of Beethoven's preparation for the creation of the op. 18 string quartets that were soon to follow. Musical responsibility is very democratically shared between the instruments. Technically they are much more demanding than their predecessors. Moreover, this powerful music from just three string players adds an element of strain that makes them in some ways more difficult to play than the op. 18 string quartets.

### Op. 9 no. 1 in G (1797–8)          26m; D3+
Large-scale and fine. Generally the mood is serene throughout. Much of the *Presto* last movement has the nature of a *moto perpetuo*.

### Op. 9 no. 2 in D (1797–8)          23m; D3
This is the most gentle and intimate of the trios in this set; it is also technically the easiest. It starts *pianissimo*, which illustrates the relaxed but musically delightful atmosphere that is maintained throughout. Critics often consider this the least important of the set of three, but for pleasure of playing some may find it the best.

### Op. 9 no. 3 in C minor (1797–8)          24m; D3+
Often considered Beethoven's finest string trio, this is a powerful and impressive work, with the intensity characteristic of Beethoven's music in C minor. Only the second movement *Adagio con espressione* brings a contrasting relaxation. Remarkably, the work also contains at least one foretaste of his much later music: the opening four-note motif is almost repeated in the string quartet in C♯ minor, op. 131 (finale, violin I, bar 21 – *see* below).

## String Quartets
The six early quartets, op. 18, written from 1798 to 1800 and published in two sets in June and October 1801, are of comparable scale and character to those of Haydn and Mozart. However, they immediately represent a new voice, and already show signs of a new ambition for what can be said in the medium. They are very varied, and not one could be mistaken as being by any of Beethoven's predecessors. The

musical interest is excellently spread across their parts. Though not much more difficult to play than the mature Haydn and Mozart quartets, they sometimes assume rather greater virtuosity from the first violin. They are a staple of the repertoire for many amateur quartets. Their numbering differs from their probable order of composition.

Op. 18 no. 1 in F                                                                                        30m; D3

A fine, large-scale work. Particularly impressive is the long and deeply felt *Adagio affettuoso ed appassionato*, which was probably inspired by the tomb scene in *Romeo and Juliet*. It may perhaps be questioned whether the three brilliant fast movements, good as they are, are quite adequate as companions for this slow movement.

Op. 18 no. 2 in G                                                                                        24m; D3

Sometimes called 'The Compliment', a nickname that refers to the formal opening gesture of the work; and indeed of these quartets this is the closest in character to the eighteenth century. It has nothing of the power and ambition of the first quartet, but is filled with exuberance and good humour. Even the song of the *Adagio cantabile* is surprisingly interrupted by an *Allegro* episode. The whole requires sparkling and often agile playing.

Op. 18 no. 3 in D                                                                                        25m; D3

Perhaps the first-written quartet of the set, this is one of the most delightful. The first three movements are consistent in their beautifully quiet and thoughtful character, while the 6/8 *Presto* finale is a brilliant and amusing expression of high spirits. None of the movements is especially difficult, though some will need advance notice before tackling the finale.

Op. 18 no. 4 in C minor                                                                                  24m; D3

Although C minor is the key of some of Beethoven's most powerful and iconic works, critics have been divided on the merits of this quartet. Some have suggested on stylistic grounds that it originated early, perhaps even before his move to Vienna in 1792; but others disagree. Whatever the facts, this quartet is popular with both players and audiences. The first movement especially has much forceful C minor writing. Surprisingly, the quartet has both a scherzo and a minuet, though the former with its marking of *Andante scherzoso quasi allegretto* stands substitute for a slow movement. This movement has a gentle, contrapuntal texture, is easy to play and most charming.

Op. 18 no. 5 in A                                                                                        28m; D3

Beethoven had a particular admiration for Mozart's string quartet in A, K. 464, and in structure as well as key this quartet, the quietest and gentlest of the set, seems to be modelled on it. Like the Mozart, it has a set of variations for its slow, third movement. These variations are especially delightful; second violin, viola and cello will enjoy their hilarious domination of Variation 5. For some, this is the favourite quartet of op. 18.

### Op. 18 no. 6 in B♭                                                 25m; D3

Much of this quartet is fresh and enjoyable. Particularly original is the bluff humour of the scherzo, in which the continual syncopations are tricky to play. Nevertheless the quartet is perhaps not entirely convincing as a whole, and some of it is arguably experimental. This applies particularly to the long *Adagio* introduction to the last movement, entitled *La Malinconia* ('melancholy' or 'depression'). It progresses with surprising modulations and sharp alternations of *piano* and *forte*, and is hard to play well. It is followed by what can seem in contrast a rather facile *Allegretto quasi Allegro*. The *Adagio* twice returns briefly before the *Prestissimo* dash to the end. This movement has parallels with some movements in the late quartets.

---

Six years then passed before Beethoven in 1806 completed his next string quartets, during which he had developed to an extraordinary degree as he entered his middle period. The quartets of 1806 are a set of three, op. 59. Two further separate quartets followed – op. 74 in 1809 and op. 95 in 1810. All these quartets occupy a vastly different world from those of op. 18. With the exception of op. 95, they are much longer. But more important is their content: tremendously greater are their scope and boldness, their breadth and the range of experience that they express. Along with this, they are technically more difficult than the early quartets; and with their length they can be gruelling. Those of op. 59, having been commissioned by Count Andreas Rasumovsky, the Russian ambassador to Vienna, are known as the 'Rasumovsky Quartets'. As is well known, Beethoven included a *thème russe* in the first two, probably in response to a request by his patron.

### Op. 59 no. 1 in F (1806)                                            40m; D4

This first quartet of the set is the largest – it is on a massive scale. Cellists will appreciate the solo with which they open the first movement. This movement achieves its length of nearly eleven minutes without an exposition repeat, although where this would be expected it seems to happen – but then after four bars veers off in a different direction. However, the longest movement is the third, *Adagio molto e mesto*. Mesto means sad, and this is indeed a sorrowful movement. It is also difficult. At its end the mood is broken by a quite difficult cadenza mainly for the first violin leading without a break into the finale, which opens (again on the cello) with the Russian folk-tune. This is technically the most difficult movement of the work. As well as its notes, the passages where the quartet divides rhythmically into two opposing halves can cause problems.

<u>Op. 59 no. 2 in E minor (1806)</u>        37m; D4

The outer movements of this quartet are vigorous. However, it is especially memorable for its long, rapt, contemplative and beautiful second movement *Molto adagio*. There is a story that the idea for it came to Beethoven when he was contemplating a starry night sky: this seems plausible and appropriate to the character of the music. Beethoven himself wrote on the score 'This piece must be played with great feeling'. The third movement *Allegretto* has a trio built on the *thème russe*. Unusually, Beethoven instructs that after the normal *Da Capo*, the trio should be played again, followed by a second *Da Capo*.

<u>Op. 59 no. 3 in C (1806)</u>        32m; D4

This is probably the best of the op. 59 quartets to try first: it is the shortest and in some ways the most straightforward. It opens with a mysterious, slow introduction, in which the long, scarcely moving *pianissimos* make a difficult beginning for a performance to an audience. The slow movement (*Andante con moto quasi Allegretto*) is a memorable highlight, strange but compellingly beautiful, notable for its haunting use of cello pizzicato. Probably the most popular movement is the brilliant, quasi-fugal finale, which maintains an almost perpetual motion. Particularly exhilarating are the passages given to each instrument in turn, *sul una corda*, inviting them to show off their technical prowess.

<u>Op. 74 in E♭ ('The Harp') (1809)</u>        32m; D4

The nickname comes from the pizzicato figurations that are prominent in the first movement. This quartet is on the same large scale as those of op. 59, but its musical character is perhaps more direct and charming. Some past observers have suggested that it is a lesser work, but that view is outdated and it is now generally accepted as an equally great masterpiece, albeit different in character. It is Beethoven's most Schubertian quartet. A slow introduction leads to an *Allegro*, which develops a remarkable power and spaciousness. At its climax the first violin is given a brilliant and spectacular semiquaver figuration, which is not actually as difficult as it sounds. The slow movement is lyrical, an exquisite song throughout. In great contrast is the *Presto* third movement, effectively a scherzo. Its trio is even faster and is exceptionally forceful. Though it continues the 3/4 time of the scherzo, Beethoven writes (in Italian) 'Think of it as being in 6/8'. The trio is played twice and the scherzo three times before a coda quietens the mood and leads without a break into the finale. This is a set of variations and is calmer and more conventional. It gives gratification to all the players, especially the viola in the second variation.

<u>Op. 95 in F minor (Quartetto Serioso) (1810)</u>        21m; D4–

The name is due to Beethoven himself (and the word *serioso* also appears in the tempo direction for the third movement). This is a wonderful and remarkably original quartet. It is big Beethoven, yet it is much shorter than its predecessors

– indeed, this is Beethoven's shortest quartet. It is of tremendous scope – a work of concentrated passion and power. Technically it is the least demanding of the middle period quartets, and there is so much that is enjoyable to play. The slow second movement has a beautiful central fugal section. This movement leads without a break into the third, which is forceful, almost violent. Yet this movement too has a calm and beautiful section, effectively a trio, which appears twice. In this section, below the busy movement of the first violin, the tune is with the other parts, led by the second violin. The finale eventually turns to F major and a fast and seemingly lightweight dash to the end. This ending has troubled many critics, but from the players' point of view it makes a satisfying and exhilarating conclusion.

Fourteen years passed before Beethoven again composed for the string quartet medium, and the change in style represented by these late quartets is enormous. Their composition followed the completion of the ninth symphony, and was initially in response to a commission from Prince Galitzin for three quartets. They were composed successively, and after completing the three, Beethoven carried on and wrote two more. They are sometimes seen as having a sense of finality as the ultimate summit of Beethoven's achievement. However, this sense is only a consequence of his death in March 1827, which occurred shortly after their completion: he had been full of ideas for new works. Before being overtaken by his final illness he was working on a string quintet, and he was considering a tenth symphony.

Something has already been said about these quartets. They have a reputation almost unique in music. For some they inspire reverence; they are surrounded by an almost religious aura of respect. Accounts talk of them 'revealing the secrets of the universe', of giving 'visions of another world', of 'heaven glimpsed', or that playing them is 'a veritable devotional act'. Certainly they have a spiritual quality, a sense of profound meaning. Even sober musicologists regard them as a pinnacle of greatness. But although they are undeniably exceptional, they are in some ways strange: they go to extremes, and many movements lack outward attractiveness. Their attributes do not necessarily make for enjoyable listening, let alone enjoyable playing. In the nineteenth century they were widely considered to be incomprehensible, which was often attributed to the fact that Beethoven was almost completely deaf when he composed them. Whilst enjoyment of music does not usually require it to be intellectually understood, in these quartets it can seem to be desirable. Familiarity is necessary before their beauties can be fully appreciated. They are unlikely to give much satisfaction on a first attempt to sight-read. But for some, playing these quartets is the highest pleasure in music. Most string players should play them at some time.

These quartets are technically difficult, not in a showy way but simply because Beethoven's ideas are difficult to execute. They are also, of course, difficult to play in a musical sense. One of the problems is to understand what part or parts need to be brought out at any moment. When first trying these quartets, probably the best because of both its moderate dimensions and its less severe technical demands is op. 135. Also more approachable is op. 127. The toughest challenges are opp. 132, 130 and 131. In a class of its own is the *Grosse Fuge*, which will probably have to remain out of reach for many.

With the exception of the last quartet, op. 135, and the *Grosse Fuge*, all these quartets are long. The first, op. 127, is the shortest of the first four, and is outwardly normal in having four separate movements. The following three quartets throw aside this convention, being successively in five, six and seven movements. Moreover the last of these, op. 131, is played without a break. Then in his final complete quartet, op. 135, Beethoven returns to four movements and a modest size. The three quartets opp. 132, 130 and 131 have often been considered as forming a trilogy. It has been argued that Beethoven's work on them overlapped, and that there are thematic relations between them. However, it was Beethoven's normal practice to work on more than one composition at a time, and it is debatable whether the supposed thematic connections are significant. Certainly Beethoven gave no indication that he considered them to have any special relationship to each other. What they do have in common is that they are all on a particularly massive scale, they reject many conventions of classical precedent, and they break new ground in their character and expressive content.

The opus numbers of these quartets are not entirely in the order of composition, the principal defect being that op. 132 should follow op. 127 and precede op. 130.

## Op. 127 in E♭ (1824–5)                                              37m; D4+

Of the late quartets, this is the most normal and in some ways the most accessible. Normality applies to the layout: it is in four movements of which the second is slow and the third is a scherzo. It also applies to the music: as with all the late quartets it seems strange at first, but it is among the easier to grasp. The general mood is lyrical, pastoral and happy, without any great intensity. In the opening movement, the main theme of the *Allegro* is marked *teneramente* – which means tenderly. The slow movement is a set of variations on a theme of similar character to that of the Benedictus in the recently completed *Missa Solemnis*, and the whole movement has a calm, rapt and spiritual quality. In some ways this is the most difficult movement to play.

## Op. 132 in A minor (1825)                                             45m; D4+

This quartet is in five movements, of which the fourth and fifth are played without a break. In character, it encompasses a very wide range. It was written after Beethoven had been ill – sufficiently so that for a month he was unable to compose. Its centrepiece is the great *Holy song of thanksgiving to God on recovery from an illness, in the Lydian mode.* Beethoven here gives expression to his long-standing interest in the techniques of early music. The movement is marked *Molto adagio*, but contains two long *Andante* sections, in which the Lydian mode is replaced by D major; the first of these is marked *Feeling new strength*. The movement typically lasts about seventeen minutes, and that alone makes it formidable – especially for players who suffer from aching arms in slow music. The prayerful mood of this movement is broken by a short and deliberately worldly march, which leads into a substantial recitative for the first violin. The following finale eventually brings the quartet to an A major conclusion in a joyful mood.

### Op. 130 in B♭ (1825; finale 1826)         41m; D4+

As published, this quartet ends with a replacement movement provided by Beethoven, the last completed music that he wrote (*see Grosse Fuge*, below). The quartet is in six separate movements, which might suggest that it resembles a divertimento: but that is not its character. This is a formidable and demanding quartet, perhaps more so than any other of these late quartets. The lengths of the movements are very varied; the first is longest, while the second and fourth are short. The latter is marked *Alla danza tedesca* ('A German dance') and is musically and technically relatively straightforward. Best known and most memorable is the fifth movement *Cavatina*, of intensely emotional expression. Beethoven himself said that nothing else he had composed had so moved him; even the thought of it brought tears to his eyes. What it expresses must be left to the response of the individual, but its beauty indeed seems to have profound depths. It contains a remarkable section marked in the first violin part *Beklemmt* ('oppressed' or 'heavy of heart'). This movement too is technically not unduly difficult, and its expression is direct enough that it can be played and enjoyed by those for whom the complete quartet is not practicable.

Note that the finale has a repeat of bars 20 to 33, which is contained within a longer repeat of bars 3 to 98 and so is played altogether four times. (To avoid confusion, some editions write out the short repeat.) This finale is sometimes criticized as being trivial and inadequate: but others disagree. Though of course smaller than the *Grosse Fuge*, which it replaced, it is substantial and (especially for the first violin) not easy. For most, it seems an appropriate conclusion to this huge quartet. Nevertheless, some professional performances instead forge on into the fugal finale that Beethoven first thought of.

### *Grosse Fuge*, op. 133 (1825)         16m; D5

Beethoven originally composed this 'Great Fugue' as the final movement of the quartet in B♭, which was first performed in that form. Controversy resulted, and for publication Beethoven agreed that it be issued as a separate work; he subsequently composed a new finale for the quartet. Preferences are divided today. Some consider that op. 130 should conclude not with the published finale but with the *Grosse Fuge*, on the grounds that it was Beethoven's original intention. Others, however, argue that Beethoven genuinely came to see that op. 130 is better with a more moderate finale. Whatever one thinks about this, from the players' point of view the published finale of op.130 is much the more manageable.

On the title page, Beethoven described the *Grosse Fuge* as *tantôt libre, tantôt recherchée* ('sometimes free, sometimes studied'). It is a gigantic and exceptionally complex work. It has a series of sections, and is not entirely fugal. The whole has tremendous power, and is uncompromising in its force and character. Its great difficulty means that for those who love Beethoven's late quartets it represents, technically, the ultimate pinnacle to be scaled.

Op. 131 in C♯ minor (1825–6)                                                                                       39m; D4+

Of the late quartets, this is widely regarded as the greatest of all, the most perfect and most profound of the series. It is unique in its structure: there are seven movements and they are marked to be played without a break. Whilst on the one hand it encompasses a very wide range of moods, the changes between movements are managed so that they seem natural. The movements are of widely varying lengths. The shortest is the third, which lasts less than a minute and is mainly a link between the adjacent movements. It is sometimes not counted as a movement: but that cannot be right, since Beethoven himself numbered the movements in the manuscript. The first movement immediately takes us to what seems a new world: it is a fugue, but a slow fugue: the tempo is *Adagio ma non troppo*. Its atmosphere seems to be of profound thought. The emotional heart of the quartet is the fourth movement, which is a set of variations. (Variation 3 is marked *Andante moderato e lusinghiero*: the last word means 'coaxing'.) The slow, thoughtful music of Variation 6 may be felt to be the highest point. Yet shortly after this comes the *Presto* fifth movement, a scherzo of uninhibited and straightforward high spirits. The finale is a galloping *Allegro*, still in the minor key.

Op. 135 in F (1826)                                                                                                      24m; D4

Following the extraordinary outpouring of the three preceding quartets, Beethoven here surprises us by this much shorter work in the normal four-movement layout. It is nevertheless still late Beethoven, and in parts is profound, though also sometimes puzzling. The first movement is open and enjoyable, and feels like a thoughtful conversation between the four players. Strangest is the scherzo that follows: fast and rough, with what might be considered sardonic humour. It contains a most extraordinary long passage in the (effective) trio section: three players pound out an unchanging *fortissimo* ostinato, above which the first violin executes a wild (and difficult) dance. There follows, in great contrast, an intense slow movement in the form of variations, meditative and perhaps sorrowful but both moving and very beautiful. Most enigmatic is the finale, which is headed *The difficult decision*. Over the opening *Grave* are the words 'Must it be?'; the answer follows, *Allegro*: 'It must be'. Beethoven's meaning in this has been much discussed: it could be trivial or profoundly serious, but no-one can say. Whatever the meaning, however, the result is a relatively straightforward and enjoyable movement, with tunes that stay in the memory. Technically most of this quartet is relatively easy to play; but the second movement is difficult. Nevertheless, for amateurs this is technically the most approachable of the late quartets. Its range of moods is typical of what is to be found in the other late quartets, and the depth and beauty of the slow movement is a memorable high point.

In addition, in 1802 Beethoven transcribed his three-movement piano sonata in E, op. 14 no. 1 of 1798, for string quartet. This involved changing the key to F and drastically rewriting the music to be idiomatic for strings. Playing it makes a pleasant, relatively undemanding change from the other quartets.

### String Quintets (2 violins, 2 violas, cello)

Beethoven wrote only one original string quintet: op. 29. The other two works listed here strictly are arrangements, but both (for different reasons) warrant inclusion. All three works belong to Beethoven's first period. They form an enjoyable contribution to the string quintet repertoire.

Op. 4 in E♭ (1792–3; 1795–6)                                                          32m; D3–

This, Beethoven's first published string quintet, was only discovered after his death to have been originally an octet for wind instruments composed a few years earlier (which was then published as op. 103). For the string quintet version, Beethoven made many changes and also added new material including a second trio to the minuet. It has charm and is entertaining for all players, but it remains lightweight and musically relatively weak. After Mozart's K. 174 it is technically probably the easiest work in the repertoire for this combination.

Op. 29 in C (1801)                                                                    35m; D3

A delightful and expansive work, with some charming lyrical writing. It is warm and mellow but its character is mainly entertaining: for some it is a favourite for the sheer pleasure given by playing it. Once the sometimes fast-moving notes are mastered, it has no significant problems of ensemble. It is sometimes called 'The Storm', from the rushing figures above measured tremolo accompaniment in the whirlwind *Presto* finale. This movement contains two surprising episodes marked *Andante con moto e scherzoso*, which have a first violin solo of *opera buffa* character above a light accompaniment: further entertainment value.

Op. 104 in C minor (1793–5; 1817)                                                     32m; D3

This is an arrangement of the piano trio in the same key, op. 1 no. 3, one of Beethoven's finest early works. In 1817, an amateur composer submitted to Beethoven his arrangement of the trio as a two-viola quintet. Beethoven was interested but regarded the arrangement as inadequate (jokingly describing it as a 'three-voiced quintet'!); he made major alterations, with wholesale rewriting of the parts in many passages. It was published in 1819 as op. 104. The result is arranged so well for the string ensemble that one feels the music could have been written for it. It is sombre but beautiful: a really fine work, which all two-viola quintet groups should play. It has been relatively little-known, but some attention came from its prominent role in Vikram Seth's 1999 novel *An Equal Music*. The slow movement is a set of variations. An appropriate tempo for the finale is not as fast as might be suggested by its *Prestissimo* indication.

## Piano Trios

Beethoven contributed a fine set of piano trios to the repertoire. Unlike those of Haydn and Mozart, almost all are in four movements. The three of op. 1 are the works with which Beethoven chose to introduce himself to Vienna. Though still early, they are arguably his first real masterpieces – especially no. 3. The remaining trios are ripe works of his middle period. There are no trios from his late period. In addition to the works listed here, the clarinet trio, op. 11, is often played with violin instead of clarinet. Players looking for the first time at Beethoven's piano trios are recommended to start with the first or second of op. 1.

Op. 1 no. 1 in E♭ (1793–5)  30m; D2 (piano harder)

Light-hearted and attractive: good entertainment. Much of the musical responsibility is with the piano, and in this early work there is still something of the restricted freedom allowed to the cello in eighteenth-century piano trios. However, it is enjoyable playing for all.

Op. 1 no. 2 in G (1793–5)  32m; D2+ (piano harder)

As compared to its predecessor, this is a more solid and serious work. It is also a little more difficult, although it shares with no. 1 the relatively unenterprising use of the cello.

Op. 1 no. 3 in C minor (1793–5)  29m; D3

This trio is in many ways a substantial step up from its two predecessors. It is Beethoven's first masterpiece in C minor, and it is full of the power, seriousness and poetry he could draw from the key. Along with this, the use of the medium seems richer and more mature, and the cello is now fully emancipated. Technically this trio is more difficult than its two predecessors.

Ten variations on *Ich bin der Schneider Kakadu* ('I am the tailor Kakadu'), op. 121a (1803, rev. 1816)  17m; D4–

This is not the late work that its opus number would suggest (it was not published until 1824). The theme comes from a *singspiel* by Wenzel Müller (1764–1835), and is unsophisticated. Beethoven's variations open with a long introduction in the minor key, *Adagio assai*. The theme is *Allegretto*, and the following variations are ingenious and entertaining. They include one for piano solo, one each for violin and for cello with piano accompaniment, and one for strings without piano.

### Op. 70 no. 1 in D ('The Ghost') (1808)                                    27m; D4

In three movements only – but this is not a work of small scope: its music is powerful and expansive. It is vigorous in the outer movements, but it is the central *Largo assai ed espressivo* that is the core of the work. This is exceptionally slow in tempo, and its character is intense but often strange and mysterious. There is extensive use of low piano tremolo. These characteristics make the nickname appropriate; moreover there is some reason to believe that Beethoven had ghostly ideas in mind when he composed it. The notes of this trio are not especially difficult, but it is difficult to play so slowly in the central movement. The writing for the instruments throughout is wonderful; that for the cello is predominantly melodic, and it participates in every-thing as fully as does the violin. When they play together, the cello may be higher!

### Op. 70 no. 2 in E♭ (1808)                                                30m; D4

This trio returns to Beethoven's usual four-movement layout. However, in contrast to the power, drama and mystery of no. 1, this seems quiet and at times almost withdrawn. This no doubt is why it is not well known and is relatively rarely played. However, it has much of beauty and interest, and its calm and generally happy music is playable and rewarding.

### Op. 97 in B♭ ('Archduke') (1811)                                         43m; D4

The nickname comes from its dedication to Beethoven's patron and pupil Archduke Rudolf. For this work, only superlatives apply. It is Beethoven's greatest piano trio, indeed one of the greatest works in chamber music. It is exceptionally spacious, and this reflects the character of the music, which is noble, dignified and mag-isterial. This character is immediately apparent from the broad and magnificent opening theme. The second movement is a scherzo, which nevertheless maintains the overall mood. The *Andante* third movement is a set of variations on an exqui-site twenty-eight-bar theme. The fourth variation, *Poco più adagio*, is especially moving. It is followed by a long coda that leads *attacca* into the finale. This is a rondo, *Allegro moderato*, finally moving to *Presto* and at the end *Più presto*, without ever breaking the majestic dignity of the whole.

The enterprising writing for the cello is again noticeable, frequently being used melodically and often lying high in its range. This trio is demanding to play but there are no excessive problems. Its length is itself a challenge. Players who can manage Beethoven's earlier trios may look to this as the ultimate objective. When achieved, they will find it one of the most rewarding of experiences.

In addition to the works discussed above, Beethoven left a number of further com-positions for the medium. Another piano trio, WoO 38 in E♭, probably dates from

1791. Op. 42 is a set of variations on an original theme, from 1792. An allegretto in B♭, WoO 39, was composed in 1812 for 'my little friend' Maximiliane Brentano (then not quite ten years old) 'to encourage her in her piano playing'. It is a six-minute movement, beautiful, enjoyable for everyone yet not difficult.

## Piano Quartets

Op. 16 in E♭ (1796)                                                                                  26m; D3

This is Beethoven's arrangement of the quintet for piano and winds: but both versions were published simultaneously in 1801 as op. 16, so playing this version is fully legitimate. The piano part is identical in both versions, but the string parts contain surprisingly extensive changes and additions as compared with those for wind instruments. There are three movements; it is classical in style, warm and attractive but musically undemanding.

-----

As well as the above work, in 1785 the very young Beethoven composed a set of three piano quartets, WoO 36. They are occasionally played.

## Ensemble Works including Wind Instruments

Beethoven wrote a substantial body of chamber music for combinations that include wind instruments, though wind players may regret that it all comes only from his early period. These works – eight are considered here – fall into two groups. The quintet for piano and winds, the clarinet trio, the serenade for flute, violin and viola, and the septet, all composed between 1796 and 1799, are typical and excellent examples of Beethoven's music from his early period. The septet is one of his most celebrated works. As their relatively low opus numbers suggest, they were all published within a few years of their composition. The other four are earlier, all dating from between 1792 and 1796 (but perhaps in some cases begun earlier), and they are more mixed. They were not published until many years later (and so have misleadingly high opus numbers). Nevertheless they have plenty of charm and interest, and are valuable as contributions to the limited repertoire of wind chamber music; but not all can be considered as first-rate works.

Octet in E♭, op. 103 (1792–3) (2 oboes, 2 clarinets, 2 bassoons, 2 horns)      22m; D3

This was not published in Beethoven's lifetime (though in 1795–6 he arranged and rewrote it as a string quintet which was published as op. 4, discussed above). It is enjoyable, lightweight entertainment music, though weak by Beethoven's standards. The first oboe most often has the leading role. The clarinets are in B♭.

Sextet in E♭, op. 81b (1795) (2 horns, string quartet)   17m; D2 (horns much harder)

This is an attractive but musically unadventurous work in only three movements. It almost resembles a miniature concerto for the horns, giving them difficult parts with plenty of opportunities for enjoyment. Though the string parts are undemanding, they too are given some interest. Publication was in 1810.

Trio in C, op. 87 (1795) (2 oboes, cor anglais)                                    22m; D3
An excellent trio, probably the best of the four earliest works involving wind instruments. It is remarkable that Beethoven should have written this full-scale four-movement work for so specialist a combination. Presumably because of its limited sound-world, it rarely appears in the concert hall: but for players it is a splendid possession! Beethoven also approved a transcription for two violins and viola – itself a rare combination – which is valued by players of those instruments.

Sextet in E♭, op. 71 (1796) (2 clarinets, 2 bassoons, 2 horns)             20m; D3
This is an attractive work in four movements, of undemanding classical cast. Much enjoyment is offered to the clarinets and bassoons, for which the writing is energetic and varied. The horns, however, are rarely given anything more than accompanying harmony. The clarinets are in B♭.

Quintet in E♭, op. 16 (1796) (piano, oboe, clarinet, horn, bassoon)        26m; D3
This forms a companion piece to Mozart's quintet in the same key and for the same instruments, K. 452; moreover it is clearly modelled on that work. It is in three movements, classical in manner, and has no strongly individual or forward-looking features. However, this is a fine and very attractive work, if arguably not quite the equal of its prototype. Good opportunities are given to all the wind instruments, with the clarinet most favoured. The clarinet is in B♭.

Serenade in D, op. 25 (1797?) (flute, violin, viola)                              25m; D3
In six short movements. This is music of a very light character – entertainment music. But in terms of compositional technique it is excellent, and the interest is almost equally distributed across the three parts: it is highly enjoyable to play. Four of the movements have multiple repeated sections and end with a *Da Capo*. Another is a theme and three variations, one of which is allocated to each instrument. (This work can also usefully be played, without arrangement, by two violins and viola.)

Trio in B♭, op. 11 (1798) (clarinet, cello, piano)                              22m; D3
This clarinet trio is in only three movements; it is a simpler and more direct work than the op. 1 piano trios that preceded it. It is entirely democratic in its distribution of the interest between the instruments. The relaxed and lovely *Adagio* second movement can seem almost an indulgence to play. The finale is a set of variations on a song by Joseph Weigl which was popular at the time. Its perky triviality may irritate some, but Beethoven's treatment in his variations should reconcile them! The clarinet is in B♭.

Beethoven provided an optional alternative part for violin instead of clarinet.

Some publications include this trio with his other piano trios, though not necessarily with a part for clarinet.

Septet in E♭, op. 20 (1799) (clarinet, horn, bassoon, violin, viola, cello, double bass)

40m; D3 (violin harder)

Ever since its first appearance this has been one of Beethoven's most popular works. The popularity applies to players as much as to audiences – this is a delightful opportunity for a mixed group of wind and strings to play together. There are six movements, providing enjoyable, entertaining playing. With the exception of the double bass, every instrument is given opportunities to shine. Of the wind instruments, the parts for clarinet and bassoon are particularly gratifying. The cellist should look in advance at least at the high-lying solo in the trio of the scherzo. The most prominent part throughout, however, is for violin, which also includes near the end a virtuoso cadenza – a strong violinist is necessary when assembling a group to play this septet. The clarinet is in B♭.

In addition to the works discussed above there exist various others; most are early, arrangements or fragments. The trio in E♭, op. 38, for piano, clarinet/violin and cello, is an arrangement of the septet, op. 20. The trio in G, WoO 37, for piano, flute and bassoon is of about 1787. Three duos for clarinet and bassoon, WoO 27, are perhaps of about 1790–2 though their authenticity is uncertain; they are enjoyable and useful (and are also available for violin and cello). A set of variations on Mozart's *La ci darem la mano*, WoO 28, for two oboes and cor anglais, dates probably from 1797. The rondino in E♭, WoO 25, is for the same instrumentation as the octet, op. 103.

## Duet Sonatas and other Duets

Beethoven's contribution to the duet sonata both for violin and piano and for cello and piano has a dominating position in the repertoire. There are ten for violin. The first eight of these, coming from his early period, are called in their original publications sonatas for the piano 'with a violin' or 'with the accompaniment of a violin'. But from the first the musical responsibility is shared equally between the instruments. The series ends with two very different and important works. For the cello, Beethoven was the first composer to write true duet sonatas, previous sonatas having had only a continuo accompaniment. The five sonatas are splendid; unlike those for violin, they are distributed almost equally across Beethoven's three periods. Also valuable and enjoyable for cellists are the three excellent sets of variations. Violinists have one lesser set of variations. Beethoven also gave a sonata to horn players. Although he composed nothing for viola and piano, he endorsed an arrangement, which considering the shortage of works for the viola is included here.

## Violin

Op. 12 no. 1 in D (1797)                                    21m; D3

Like both others in this set, this sonata has three movements. The second is a set of variations.

Op. 12 no. 2 in A (1797)                                    17m; D3

A particularly lyrical and elegiac sonata.

Op. 12 no. 3 in E♭ (1797)                                   20m; D3+

This is the most ambitious of the op. 12 sonatas, and is correspondingly demanding of the players.

Op. 23 in A minor (1800–01)                                 18m; D3–

Some musicologists have been critical of this sonata. From the point of view of players, however, it is particularly valuable, being in both parts technically the easiest of the sonatas for violin and piano. It is enjoyable and interesting throughout but never very complex.

Op. 24 in F ('Spring') (1800–01)                            25m; D3

Fresh, lyrical and happy, this is with both players and audiences one of the most popular of all duet sonatas. It is the first of Beethoven's duet sonatas to have four movements (though the quicksilver scherzo that is added to the three-movement form lasts scarcely more than a minute!).

Op. 30 no. 1 in A (1802)                                    24m; D3

Beethoven here returns to three movements. The central *Adagio molto espressivo* is particularly memorable: one of the composer's great slow movements.

Op. 30 no. 2 in C minor (1802)                              26m; D3

A powerful yet very playable example of Beethoven's C minor mood. Alone of this set, it is in four movements.

Op. 30 no. 3 in G (1802)                                    18m; D3

Light, delightful and straightforward to play.

Op. 47 in A ('Kreutzer') (1802–3)                           39m; D5

Beethoven said: 'written in a highly concertante style, almost like a concerto'. This is a monumental and wonderful work, in three movements, and its bravura style is thrilling. In popularity with audiences it stands alongside the 'Spring' sonata: but virtuoso players are needed to handle its technical demands.

Op. 96 in G (1812)                                          28m; D3+

Almost the antithesis to its predecessor: thoughtful, unassuming and without any sense of display. However, written on the verge of Beethoven's late period, it is utterly unlike any of his earlier sonatas and is musically profound.

Twelve variations on Mozart's *Se vuol ballare*, WoO 40 (1792–3)     12m; D2

Unadventurous and weak: but it may be valuable for amateurs who are not ready to tackle the sonatas. The theme is an aria from 'The Marriage of Figaro'.

## Viola

Notturno in D, op. 42     29m; D3

This is an arrangement by F.X. Kleinheinz (corrected by Beethoven) of the serenade for string trio, op. 8, of 1796–7. (Some may find the title surprising, but it reflects contemporary usage of the word.)

## Cello

Op. 5 no. 1 in F (1796)     24m; D3

The op. 5 sonatas are in three movements, but in both cases start with a slow movement that can alternatively be regarded as an extended introduction to the following *Allegro*.

Op. 5 no. 2 in G minor (1796)     25m; D3

Original and powerful: perhaps an even more striking work than its companion.

Op. 69 in A (1807–8)     27m; D4

This is the most popular of Beethoven's cello sonatas: a glorious work, a wonderful exposition of melody and lyricism. The writing for the cello often lies high.

Op. 102 no. 1 in C (1815)     16m; D4

A work of Beethoven's late period, more elusive and less immediately enjoyable than the earlier sonatas.

Op. 102 no. 2 in D (1815)     20m; D4

Both vigorous and expansively lyrical, this sonata is more obviously attractive than its companion. Its profundity is especially evident in the *Adagio* second movement – the only full-scale slow movement in the cello sonatas. The final movement is a fugue.

Twelve variations on Handel's *See the Conquering Hero Comes*, WoO 45 (1796)

13m; D3

Excellent music and enjoyable playing. The theme comes from the oratorio 'Judas Maccabaeus'.

Twelve variations on Mozart's *Ein Mädchen oder Weibchen*, op. 66 (1796)  11m; D3

Again interesting and delightful. (Its possession of an opus number, not allocated at its first publication in 1798, carries no implication of superiority over the other two sets of variations.) The theme is an aria from 'The Magic Flute'.

Seven variations on Mozart's *Bei Männern welche Liebe fühlen,* WoO 46 (1801)

10m; D3

Also very good. This theme, too, is an aria from 'The Magic Flute'.

## Horn

Op. 17 in F (1800)                                                                                15m; D3

Modest in its scope and limited in its demands on the horn: but it is delightful music. Beethoven made or approved an alternative version for cello.

---

In addition to the works discussed above, there are some other compositions for one instrument with piano. A sonata in B♭ for flute and piano may date from about 1790–92, but its authenticity is uncertain. Op. 41 is an arrangement for flute/violin and piano of the serenade, op. 25. A set of German dances for violin and piano, WoO 42, dates from 1796. There are also from 1818–19 (in his late period) two sets of *National Airs with Variations*, opp. 105 and 107, for flute/violin and piano; many of the airs are Scottish.

# BERG
## 1885–1935; Austria

Alban Berg was born and died in Vienna. With Schoenberg and Webern he is a member of what is known as the Second Viennese School. He was a pupil of Schoenberg from 1904 to 1911, and remained in close contact with him after that period. He followed his master in adopting atonality, and later the twelve-tone system. However, he differs from Schoenberg and also Webern in that they were not employed to the complete exclusion of tonality, and he continued to give his music emotional and romantic qualities. This has made him the most widely accepted of the composers of the school. His output was small, and includes just two substantial chamber works. There is also a chamber concerto for piano, violin and thirteen wind instruments. He gave opus numbers from 1 to 7 to works completed from about 1910 to 1923, and then ceased the practice.

## String Quartets

String quartet, op. 3 (1910)                                                             21m; D5

This was the last work that Berg composed while still a pupil of Schoenberg. There are only two movements; it is freely atonal but not without harmonic references. Technically it makes severe demands. Extended playing techniques such as sul ponticello and long portamento are employed, and rhythms are complicated. Playing it is not a viable proposition for most amateurs.

_Lyric Suite_ for string quartet (1925–6)                                    29m; D5

One of the most remarkable works of the twentieth century, this is the earliest composition for string quartet to employ, at least partially, the twelve-tone technique. Yet it is also extraordinarily passionate and emotional. In fact it is programme music. The markings in the score suggest this, but many years after Berg's death his programme was discovered: the whole work, to a remarkably detailed degree, concerns his love for a married woman. There are six movements. It starts fairly moderately, with an _Allegretto gioviale_. Successive movements become more extreme, the fifth and sixth being _Presto delirando_ and _Largo desolato_. The technical difficulties make playing impossible by any other than virtuoso professionals.

### Duet with Piano

Four pieces, op. 5 (1910) (clarinet, piano)                                   8m; D4+

The clarinet is in B♭. Unlike the works for string quartet, these short pieces are possible for experienced amateurs.

# BOCCHERINI
## 1743–1805; Italy, Spain

Although usually classified as an Italian composer, Luigi Boccherini went to Spain in 1768 and spent probably the rest of his life there. Spanish influence is often apparent in his music. He was very prolific, and a large proportion of his output was chamber music. He belongs to the classical period and was a contemporary of Joseph Haydn. A number of his compositions are popular; he is a significant figure and his style is distinctive and recognizable. However, the vast bulk of his music, though pleasant and playable, is lightweight and scarcely memorable. Nevertheless, such works as the string duos and trios are valuable for home music-making. The string quartets are not difficult and they distribute the interest to all the players: sight-reading them can be enjoyable, but most of them hardly warrant further attention. Boccherini wrote more string quintets with two cellos than anything else. He was a virtuoso cellist, and consequently his cello parts, especially in these quintets, are often demanding.

Most of Boccherini's works were given opus numbers, often in sets of six. However, these numbers are sometimes confused and they cannot always be relied on. Modern references use G numbers, from the catalogue published in 1969 by Yves Gérard.

### String Duos

2 violins: at least twelve.
2 cellos: two.

## String Trios

2 violins, cello: twenty-four.

Violin, viola, cello: twenty.

## String Quartets

About ninety-one, mostly in sets of six. Some were identified by Boccherini as *quartetti*, others as *quartettini* (little quartets). A published selection of nine quartets is readily available.

## String Quintets

2 violins, 2 violas, cello: twelve.

2 violins, viola, cello, double bass: three.

2 violins, viola, 2 cellos: approximately 110. Many of these have technically ambitious parts for both first and second cello. As with the quartets, some are identified as *quintetti*, others as *quintettini*. A few particular works for this combination stand out and are discussed individually:

String quintet in E, G. 275 (op. 11 no. 5) (1771)          20m; D3 (cellos harder)

This four-movement quintet contains the famous 'Boccherini's Minuet' – well known in numerous arrangements. This is frequently played alone: a four-minute movement. It is much easier than the quintet as a whole, and requires no particular cello virtuosity. In the other movements the cello parts are sometimes difficult.

String quintet in D, G. 276 (op. 11 no. 6: *l'Uccelliera – Bird Sanctuary*) (1771)
                                                            18m; D3 (cellos harder)

There are five sections, usually grouped as two movements. The second movement is entitled *Li Pastori e Li Cacciatori* (*Shepherds and Hunters*). This is amiable and pleasant music throughout, with plenty of birdsong effects. Both cello parts have some technically demanding passages.

String quintet in C, G. 324 (op. 30 no. 6: *La Musica Notturna delle Strade di Madrid*)
(c.1780)                                                              12m; D3

This is an evocation of the sounds of the streets of night-time Madrid – an amusingly original piece of picture-painting in music. The textures are sometimes surprising. Among other instructions, there are requests for players to imitate the sound of bells, and for the cellists to strum their instruments like guitars.

String quintet in C                              16m; D2 (first cello harder)

This quintet, published by Peters, is well known at least among amateur players; but it is not what it seems. It was put together by Johann Lauterbach (1832–1918) from movements of different string quintets by Boccherini. Although they are not much altered, this goes against all normal principles of authenticity. Nevertheless, it is a good selection: this is attractive music, straightforward and enjoyable to play. Significant virtuosity is confined to the first cello part.

## String Sextets
Six.

## Piano Quintets (piano, string quartet)
Twelve.

## Guitar Quintets (guitar, string quartet)
There are eight of these, although all are arrangements by Boccherini of music originally written for other combinations. The guitar plays mostly a supporting role, but its presence contributes strongly to the distinctive texture. Two warrant individual attention:

Guitar quintet no. 4 in D, G. 448 ('Fandango') (1798)        18m; D3 (cello harder)
The fourth movement is the famous Fandango, for which Boccherini asks also for a castanet player. Virtuoso technique is sometimes expected of the cello.

The original setting of the Fandango is the string quintet in D major, G. 341, with two cellos – which players of that combination may be interested in looking at.

Guitar quintet no. 8 (or 9) in C, G. 453 (*La Ritirata di Madrid*) (1799)        31m; D3+
This is a remarkably large-scale and impressive work. The name ('Retreat from Madrid') comes from the last movement, a set of variations expanded from the last movement of the string quintet G. 324 (discussed above).

## Ensemble Works including Wind Instruments
Quintets for flute, string quartet: six.
Quintets for flute/oboe, string quartet: twelve.
Sextet divertimenti for flute, 2 violins, viola, 2 cellos, double bass ad lib: six.
Sextet for horn, 2 violins, viola, 2 cellos.
Divertimento notturno for oboe/flute, bassoon, horn, violin, viola, double bass.
Divertimento notturno for oboe/flute, bassoon, horn, 2 violins, viola, cello.

## Duet Sonatas
Violin, keyboard: six.
Cello, continuo: at least nineteen (G. 18 in C minor is for either cello or viola).

# BORODIN
### 1833–1887; Russia

Aleksandr Borodin's second string quartet is considered by some the finest Russian chamber work of the nineteenth century. Yet remarkably, though of outstanding musical talent, Borodin was an amateur composer. His main career, after initial training as a doctor, was as an academic chemist. He was distinguished both for his discoveries in chemistry and for his work in encouraging education in Russia. In 1862 he met Balakirev and became a member of Balakirev's circle, known as 'The Five', whose objective was the pursuit of music of a distinctively Russian character. The other members were Cui, Musorgsky and Rimsky-Korsakov. Borodin was a cellist who enjoyed playing chamber music, and chamber music is a significant part of his small output. From his mature years there are essentially only two chamber works, both string quartets. Naturally, they give enjoyable parts to the cello. Two other mature movements for string quartet also exist: *see* 'Russian collaborative chamber music' in Appendix I. Borodin also left a number of early chamber works, none published until the mid-twentieth century. Most are incomplete, but the last, a piano quintet, was finished and is considered here.

## String Quartets

No. 1 in A (1875–9)                                                    39m; D3
Although it stands in the shadow of its popular successor, those who like the strongly Russian idiom of the latter will enjoy this quartet too. Its character and quality are consistent throughout its four movements, and it distributes the musical interest excellently. With Borodin's good understanding of string instruments, its demands whilst significant are never awkward. Arguably, however, it is too long. The title page of the score says 'Inspired by a theme of Beethoven' – the opening theme of the first *Allegro* has a resemblance (presumably accidental, and not very obvious) to a theme in the finale of Beethoven's op. 130.

No. 2 in D (1881)                                        29m; D3 (cello harder)
This is one of the best-known and most popular of string quartets: and it deserves its celebrity. The first three movements are of entrancing lyricism. Many cellists will enjoy Borodin's enterprising writing for their instrument. The third movement *Nocturne* is very widely known in arrangements, but the original is an excellent piece of writing for string quartet, giving gratification to every player. Moreover, obviously attractive though it is, most players find that it keeps its freshness even with repeated playing. The last movement differs very much from the others: vigour and counterpoint have here replaced lyricism. Nevertheless, many feel it makes a fine conclusion to this unique quartet.

## Piano Quintet (piano, string quartet)

Piano quintet in C minor (1862)                                        23m; D3
Although this is an early work, it is well written and shows some Russian character. There is much that is good to play in all parts, and it has the advantage of being one of the most technically straightforward of all piano quintets.

# BRAHMS
## 1833–1897; Germany, Austria

Johannes Brahms was born in Hamburg, but from the early 1860s he lived in Vienna. He is generally recognized as the greatest figure in chamber music of the romantic era. Chamber music is an important part of his output, and in it he is the only composer who has a stature comparable with that of the great classical composers. The twenty-four chamber works are without exception masterpieces, firmly established in the professional and amateur repertoires. Although a romantic, Brahms was a strong advocate of classical ideals, of following in the traditions established by Bach, Haydn, Mozart and Beethoven. He opposed the developments in his time particularly associated with Liszt and Wagner of programme music and music drama; the importance he gave to chamber music is one aspect of this. Brahms had established himself by the early 1860s, and for the following three decades and more he was the dominant figure in instrumental music.

Brahms's style, combining romanticism with a firm commitment to the classical framework, remained largely consistent throughout his compositional life. It is perhaps not obvious to us now how original it is. A well-known feature is his fondness for themes in a gypsy or Hungarian style. He was methodical and cautious in his approach, had high ideals and was self-critical. Music for publication must be worthy of his standards. This sometimes meant lengthy consideration and revision: we know that some works existed in earlier forms many years before their publication. It is because of this that his output is exceptionally consistent. Unlike most other composers (even Beethoven), there are no immature or weak works. This is especially true of the chamber music, where his only published early work, the piano trio in B major of 1854, was late in his life subjected to drastic revision. Moreover, his opus numbers are in good order: there is no confusion, there are no works unworthy of the mature composer masquerading under a late number, and no significant music is without an opus number. Dates of works given here are those of publication.

His chamber music output is distinctive for being spread over a wide range of instrumental combinations, including some, such as the string sextet, that had been little addressed previously. There is no emphasis on the string quartet. Did he have a long-term plan, in which three works was the maximum he would publish for any chamber combination? This is the number of his string quartets, piano trios, piano quartets and sonatas for violin and piano. For other combinations he published two or one. With his two string sextets he is without rival the greatest contributor to the medium. The three great piano quartets, too, have a dominant position, challenged perhaps only by Mozart's two. His last four chamber works, written under the inspiration of the great clarinettist Richard Mühlfeld whom he first met in 1891, all include the clarinet, making him an outstanding contributor to the repertoire of that instrument.

However, arguably there were also costs to his methods. His synthesis of musical romanticism with classical form and procedures is basic to his achievement. Nevertheless, there can sometimes seem to be an excess of technical devices to the detriment of spontaneity: the ingenious deployment of canon, imitation, inversion, augmentation, diminution and the rest may be felt to replace inspiration. This is mainly noticeable where he was perhaps less at ease with the medium in which he was composing, as in the two string quartets of op. 51.

Brahms was more prolific than we appreciate, because he destroyed a good deal of what he had written. We know that the list of destroyed works includes multiple sonatas for violin and piano, piano trios and string quartets. The works initially proposed in October 1853 for his first publications included a sonata for violin and piano in A minor and string quartets in F♯ minor and B♭, all now vanished. When twenty years later he finally released two string quartets for publication, he said that he had already composed twenty others. Even in his maturity he tended to compose works in pairs, and then to destroy whichever he subsequently deemed the weaker. Sometimes works were shown to those in his confidence, seeking their opinions, but then destroyed. We must respect his decisions that these works should not survive, and we can be sure that he gave us his greatest works. Nevertheless, amateur players especially may regret the losses: even Brahms at less than his best would be greater than most of his contemporaries. The possibilities are illustrated by one work he was unable to suppress – the scherzo in C minor of 1853 for violin and piano given (with other movements by Schumann and Dietrich – the 'FAE sonata') as a present to Joachim. Since publication in 1906 it has established itself in the repertoire and is often played in recitals and by amateurs. (There is also a piano trio in A major, published in 1938: but this is of doubtful authenticity.)

Brahms's chamber music is technically quite difficult. He was not a string player, and despite the advice he was given by Joachim and others his string writing is not always idiomatic. The middle string parts of an ensemble often involve much double-stopping and can be awkward and unrewarding. They also tempt players with insufficient experience or sensitivity to play too loudly, drowning the melodic lines and producing a thick, muddy texture. Concerning the piano, Brahms was a virtuoso who gave the first performances of many of his works that include the instrument, and the piano writing in his chamber music is rich and demanding. A prominent aspect of Brahms's writing concerns rhythm: he relished rhythmic complexities. Many players can cope with them; but for some with a less secure rhythmic ability, they can be severe problems.

In the five works that include wind instruments, Brahms provided or authorized alternative parts for viola and sometimes also for cello or violin. For amateurs, these can be useful additions to the repertoire. In the case of the two sonatas for clarinet and piano, the viola alternatives have become the principal sonatas in the viola repertoire and appear in recitals and recordings perhaps as much as the clarinet originals.

## String Quartets

Brahms's three string quartets have an important place in the repertoire, much loved and valued by both players and listeners. Nevertheless, they are arguably not the finest of his chamber music. In part this is probably because his rich romanticism was more at ease with larger forces. But it is also clear that he was affected by the comparison he had to face with the great quartets of the classics, especially Beethoven. The two quartets of op. 51 probably originated in the 1850s; certainly we know that they existed in 1866. They had to wait for many years of revision and polishing before Brahms reluctantly allowed their publication. Technically Brahms's string quartets are rather harder to play than are his works for larger ensembles of strings or strings with piano. None of the three is obviously easier than the others.

Op. 51 no. 1 in C minor (1873)                                    33m; D4

This is a powerful and tough quartet, presenting Brahms's very personal version of Beethoven's C minor mood. The outer movements are intense and strong, with little of lyricism; the last movement shows relationships in material and mood with the first. Both inner movements are much more relaxed. The *Poco adagio*, entitled *Romance*, is one of the composer's most heart-easing and lovely utterances – but to enjoy it the rhythmic subtleties that begin in the central section must be mastered. The third movement, effectively an intermezzo, also has timing difficulties that demand maximum concentration.

Op. 51 no. 2 in A minor (1873)                                    34m; D4

Overall this is a much more melodic and less intense work than its companion. However, it is especially full of ingenious counterpoint, and it has plenty of rhythmic complications. Though not dedicated to Brahms's friend Joachim, such a dedication had probably originally been intended, for the opening theme uses the notes FAE, a motto *Frei aber einsam* ('free but lonely') that the young Joachim had taken. Later Brahms contrapuntally combines it with FAF, for *Frei aber froh* ('free but happy'), which he had used himself. The central movements, though slower, have complications that make them no easier. Perhaps the most straightforward movement is the vigorous Hungarian-inspired finale, which makes a satisfying conclusion.

Op. 67 in B♭ (1876)                                               36m; D4

This quartet presents Brahms in a light and spirited character unusual for him. Though more relaxed than its predecessors it is still full of ingenuity. The first movement, basically in 6/8, introduces a theme in 2/4 and builds up to a fraught passage in which the two metres are combined. Especially beloved of viola players is the third movement in which that instrument takes the lead, the others being muted. It is a passionate and beautiful movement and is enjoyable for all. Mutes come off for the finale, which is a theme and variations; but in the first two variations the viola still clings to its prominence. The variations tend to become more difficult, reaching a slow-moving variation in six flats. Brahms's ingenuity then again comes to the fore as the opening material of the quartet reappears and combines with the variation theme.

## String Quintets (2 violins, 2 violas, cello)

These are both rich, mature works, rewarding to play but difficult. They sometimes display Brahms's tendency to thickness of the writing especially for the middle parts.

<u>Op. 88 in F (1883)</u>                                                27m; D4

A vigorous, rich and ebullient work, which Brahms thought one of his best. In the opening bars, the second violin will enjoy trumping the first by twice coming in an octave higher. There are three movements, the second combining the functions of slow movement and scherzo. It is long and outstandingly beautiful; the *Grave ed appassionato* slow sections are expressive and exquisite, giving wonderful opportunities to all players. The finale, which combines fugal and sonata forms, has almost the character of a *moto perpetuo* and ends with an exhilarating *Presto*.

<u>Op. 111 in G (1891)</u>                                               30m; D4

Brahms originally planned this to be his last composition, and it is certainly one of his greatest chamber works. It is in four movements, powerful but fresh, vigorous, outgoing and optimistic. There is a surprising controversy (first raised by Joachim) over the opening, where the four upper strings play a vigorous accompaniment above the tune in the cello, all parts being marked *forte*. But clearly the cello tune must come through: so, as in normal chamber-music discipline, the other players must moderate their dynamic to ensure this is so. The serious and moving second movement *Adagio* is in contrast with the rest; it is one of the composer's most profound conceptions. Near its end, the first viola is given a short cadenza of almost improvisatory freedom. The third movement (effectively an intermezzo) is relaxed and unlike the rest is technically quite easy. An exhilarating vigour fills the finale; its *animato* final section employs Brahms's favourite gypsy or Hungarian manner.

## String Sextets

The two sextets are the first chamber music for strings without piano that Brahms published. They are probably the most enjoyable to play of his string chamber music, being spacious, having a free and relaxed lyricism, and making relatively moderate technical demands. Perhaps Brahms could relax more because they had no classical precedent. Rather like the Mendelssohn octet, many string players have a special affection for them and will grasp any opportunity to bring together six instrumentalists to play them. The presence of two violas and two cellos allows many special pleasures to be offered to their players.

Op. 18 in B♭ (1862)                                                             38m; D4–

Written at a relatively contented period in Brahms's life, this work is relaxed and attractive throughout. Technically it is probably the easiest of all his string chamber works, and is the better of the sextets to approach for the first time. The second movement *Andante, ma moderato* is a set of variations. It starts without violins, and throughout its course it makes a point of exploiting textures available only to the string sextet grouping, with some memorable passages for two violas or two cellos together. The scherzo that follows is usually played rather more slowly than its *Allegro molto* indication might suggest, allowing the *animato* marking of the trio and the *più animato* of the coda to make these really fast. Again relaxed and radiant, the finale is a rondo.

Op. 36 in G (1866)                                                              39m; D4

This, too, is a spacious and beautiful work. Its general mood is serene, though it is more powerful and sometimes more intense than its predecessor – and correspondingly rather more complicated and technically demanding. Its emotional feeling is perhaps connected with Brahms's relationship with Agathe von Siebold, to whom he was for a time engaged before extricating himself. It has been suggested that the inclusion in the first movement (initially at bar 162) of a theme based on her name – AGAHE (in English musical notation AGABE) – was to ease his conscience. The second movement scherzo has a rollicking *Presto giocoso* middle section. Variations again form the slow movement, here coming third. The whole work is rewarding and a pleasure to play.

## Piano Trios

The three piano trios form a varied set, each with its own special pleasures.

Op. 8 in B (1854, 1891)                                                         38m; D4

Although this was Brahms's earliest published chamber work, much later he published a greatly revised version, refining it with all his mature mastery. The revision considerably shortened it, but it is still spacious, the largest of his trios and outstanding among piano trios for the breadth of its scope. The first movement of the four is particularly long. Along with its warm, expansive richness it has an ardent, youthful vigour. It is one of the composer's most loveable works, for some a favourite; the awkward key does not prevent it from being enjoyable to play.

Op. 87 in C (1883)                                                    30m; D4–

This trio is beautiful and again spacious. Much of it is relaxed and sunny, and never unduly heavy or complicated. The slow movement is a charming set of variations, in Brahms's characteristic gypsy or Hungarian mood. A mysterious scherzo follows, and then a cheery finale. The key helps to make this trio technically relatively easy, at least for the strings: it is probably the best to try first when approaching Brahms's trios.

Op. 101 in C minor (1887)                                            21m; D4

Much the most concise of the three trios. The outer movements are generally tough and dramatic, but there is also much in this work of elegant, wistful lyricism. Especially lovely is the *Andante grazioso* third movement. This is distinctive for its mixed time signature, combining 3/4 and 2/4: this is not in itself a difficulty, but this work is nevertheless in places not easy to play.

## Piano Quartets

Brahms's three piano quartets all date from the earlier years of his career. All three are wonderful, on a generous scale and broad in their scope: Brahms here appears at his most powerful and resourceful. The piano parts are demanding.

Op. 25 in G minor (1863)                                             40m; D4

This quartet is on a very large scale, bold, intense and full of vigour. It is one of Brahms's most famous and popular chamber works, particularly because of the finale, *Rondo alla Zingarese* ('rondo in gypsy style'). This is a memorable and compelling movement, but demanding – not least in the brilliant final section marked *molto presto*. The whole quartet is strenuous but highly enjoyable to play.

Op. 26 in A (1863)                                                   50m; D4

Even more expansive than its predecessor, this quartet is on a tremendous scale – by a considerable margin Brahms's longest chamber work. Every movement seems unhurried. As compared with the G minor quartet, it is much more relaxed and lyrical, less emotionally demanding. It might be thought Brahms's most Schubertian work. The long *Poco adagio* second movement is memorable for its exquisite lyrical beauty. Despite its length, of the three piano quartets this is perhaps technically the least difficult. Notwithstanding the popularity of the G minor, some players will enjoy this even more.

Op. 60 in C minor (1875)                                             35m; D4

This quartet occupies a special and personal position in Brahms's music. It originated in 1855, before the other two piano quartets, in the emotionally difficult years of his involvement with Robert Schumann and his wife Clara during Robert's breakdown and then death. Eventually in 1873 he returned to the work and revised it drastically (including changing its key from C♯ minor and composing two new movements). In his correspondence with his publisher, Brahms linked it to thoughts of suicide. Indeed, it has a tragic intensity and power rare in music. The first movement immediately and compellingly conveys the composer's inner tumult. The scherzo continues the sense of tragedy. However, the long, lyrical *Andante* provides heart-warming consolation, with memorable solos for the cello. The tragic mood returns in the finale.

Though more concise than the other two piano quartets, this is still a long work. Technically it is probably the most difficult of the three. Moreover, with its tragic qualities, it is not to be approached lightly; but played with understanding, it is rewarding.

## Piano Quintet (piano, string quartet)

Op. 34 in F minor (1865)                                          43m; D4

Notwithstanding the piano quartets, this is perhaps Brahms's most epic and monumental chamber work, exceptional for its power and drama. Only the beautiful slow movement offers relaxation. Otherwise all is immense; the third movement scherzo and the finale both pound inexorably to their conclusions. Technically it is perhaps a little easier than the piano quartets, but it is intense and gruelling.

Brahms originally wrote the work in 1862 as a string quintet with two cellos; but dissatisfied with this, in the next year he rewrote it as a sonata for two pianos (later published as op. 34b). In 1865 he converted it to its final form. (Some consequence of these remodellings seems to remain in the second violin part, particularly in the slow movement where it plays for only 60 of the 126 bars.) A reconstruction of the destroyed string quintet original has been published: groups who have played the Schubert quintet for that combination and are frustrated by the absence of other works of comparable stature may like to try it.

## Ensemble Works including a Wind Instrument

There are just three of these works, two involving a clarinet, one a horn. However, the serenade no. 1 in D, op. 11, though published by Brahms for orchestra, previously existed as a nonet for flute, two clarinets, horn, bassoon, violin, viola, cello and double bass. This is now available in a reconstruction, which some may wish to try.

Trio in E♭, op. 40 (1868) (violin, horn, piano)                  28m; D3+

Brahms played the horn in his youth; but the motivation for this work and particularly its tragic *Adagio mesto* was probably the death of his mother. The work is otherwise outgoing, and has delightful horn writing. Brahms intended that the natural horn could be used. Probably because of the constraints of this, the trio is for the other players technically perhaps the easiest of Brahms's chamber works. Alternatives to the horn are provided for viola or cello.

<u>Trio in A minor, op. 114 (1892)</u> (clarinet, cello, piano)                    25m; D4

Unusually for Brahms, this work was criticized by some early observers as weak. But today it is recognized as superb, even if somewhat overshadowed by the clarinet quintet that followed. It is mellow and beautiful, with exquisite opportunities for the cello and plenty of evidence of the delight that Brahms took in Mühlfeld's clarinet playing. The clarinet is in A. Brahms provided alternative parts for violin or viola instead of clarinet.

<u>Quintet in B minor, op. 115 (1892)</u> (clarinet, string quartet)                    38m; D4

One of Brahms's most popular and loveable works, considered by some his finest chamber composition. It is as expansive as the string sextets and is full of warmth. It exquisitely exploits the tone colour of the clarinet, which contributes to the mellow quality of the whole work. The difficulty of the string parts is perhaps rather less than in the string quartets and quintets. However, timing complexities, particularly in parts of the lovely *Adagio*, can cause some ensembles serious problems. The clarinet is in A. Brahms authorized a viola part as an alternative to the clarinet (a challenge to be attempted only by very capable viola players!).

## Duet Sonatas and another Duet

Brahms provided the finest sets of duet sonatas for violin and for cello since Beethoven.

*Violin*

<u>Op. 78 in G (1880)</u>                    27m; D4

A gracious and rich work, in three movements: spacious, lyrical, relaxed and mainly tranquil.

<u>Op. 100 in A (1887)</u>                    20m; D4–

The smallest in size and scope of all Brahms's sonatas, gentle and song-like through most of its three movements. It is easier to play than its companions, but the violin part is perhaps less enjoyable.

<u>Op. 108 in D minor (1887)</u>                    21m; D4+

In four movements, this is a powerful work of large scope. It has a very enjoyable combination of boldness and lyricism.

<u>'Sonatensatz' (1853)</u>                    5½m; D3

Brahms's earliest surviving chamber work: this scherzo in C minor was written (as mentioned previously) for the composite 'FAE sonata'.

## Cello

Op. 38 in E minor (1866)                                      26m; D4

This is a fine and powerful sonata, in three movements; but it is tough, with little that is light or elegant.

Op. 99 in F (1887)                                           29m; D4+

In four movements: expansive, ardent and beautiful. However, it is difficult. It has some memorable use of instrumental effects: tremolo in the first movement, pizzicato in the *Adagio affettuoso*.

## Clarinet

Brahms's two clarinet sonatas are sometimes referred to as 'clarinet or viola sonatas' because of the popularity of the viola alternatives. Brahms also approved a version for violin.

Op. 120 no. 1 in F minor (1895)                              23m; D4

In four movements, this is a singing, lyrical work. The third movement (*Allegretto grazioso*) is quite straightforward for both players and might be tried by those who find the whole sonata too demanding. The clarinet is in B♭.

Op. 120 no. 2 in E♭ (1895)                                   22m; D4

This is in three movements, the last a set of variations. Like its partner, it is predominantly relaxed and lyrical. The clarinet is in B♭.

# BRITTEN
## 1913–1976; England

Benjamin Britten was born in Lowestoft, Suffolk. He was a student at the Royal College of Music, but probably the greatest influence on him was the composer Frank Bridge, with whom he studied privately. From April 1939 he spent three years in America. After his return he settled in Aldeburgh, Suffolk, where he remained for the rest of his life. In 1948 he was a founder of the Aldeburgh Festival. His international prominence was principally established by his opera *Peter Grimes* in 1945, and following the death of Vaughan Williams in 1958 he became the pre-eminent British composer. In his last year he was made a life peer. His greatest achievement was in opera, but he also composed in many other genres including chamber music. He was concerned to remain in contact with the broad musical public and although his style is of its time, he retained a tonal basis and avoided the avant-garde.

## String Quartets

No. 1 in D, op. 25 (1941)                                          27m; D4+

This was written during Britten's American period, in response to a commission from Elizabeth Sprague Coolidge. All four movements have a distinctive character; perhaps most memorable is the first, where the slow sections have a texture of three very high sustained strings above the cello's low pizzicato. Although this quartet is difficult, it does not assume virtuoso technique: capable amateurs who are prepared to work can make something of it.

No. 2 in C, op. 36 (1945)                                          31m; D4+

Composed to commemorate the 250th anniversary of the death of Purcell, this is an impressive work. By far the longest of its three movements is the third, which is an explicit tribute, headed *Chacony*, the spelling of chaconne used by Purcell. It has a nine-bar ground followed by twenty-one variations; between groups of variations there are cadenzas for cello, viola and first violin. Again, though difficult, playing is possible for experienced amateurs.

No. 3, op. 94 (1975)                                               28m; D5

Thirty years passed after op. 36 before Britten wrote another string quartet; this is his last major work. Musically it seems to occupy a different world from its predecessors. It is in five movements, each with a title: *Duets*; *Ostinato*; *Solo*; *Burlesque*; *Recitative and Passacaglia* (*La Serenissima*). The last is a name for Venice, where Britten composed the movement, and its haunting main melody will remain in the memory. The treatment of the quartet medium is strikingly free, and includes effects such as sustained col legno and (for the viola) 'wrong side of bridge'. Some of it is seriously difficult.

---

Britten in his youth composed extensively for string quartet. The works dating from the years 1928 to 1936 (all without opus numbers) may interest those who enjoy his music: these are string quartets in F and D, a quartettino and (last, and contemporary with some of his first works that have opus numbers) a set of three divertimenti. There is also a phantasy string quintet (with two violas) from 1932, which won a Cobbett prize.

## Ensemble Work including a Wind Instrument

Phantasy quartet, op. 2 (1932) (oboe, violin, viola, cello)        13m; D4

A lyrical and enjoyable work, early but too good to be neglected. It was written for the Cobbett prize (which determined the single-movement form). It did not win, but it was one of Britten's first successes, soon receiving performances in Britain and abroad. It will be enjoyed by the oboist, but this instrument does not dominate to the exclusion of interest for the strings.

## Duet Sonata and other Duets

Suite, op. 6 (1934–5) (violin, piano)                                          16m; D5
Virtuoso.

_Lachrymae_, op. 48 (1950) (viola, piano)                                    14m; D4
The title means 'Tears'; it is a set of ten variations on a theme of the Elizabethan composer John Dowland. It is playable; in one variation, Britten provides an easier alternative in the viola part. The work is also known in a later version with string orchestra.

Sonata in C, op. 65 (1960–1) (cello, piano)                                  21m; D5
In five movements, this is the first of five major works Britten wrote for the great cellist Rostropovich. It freely exploits Rostropovich's technique.

_Temporal Variations_ (1936) (oboe, piano)                                   14m; D4
Following the first performance in 1936, this remained for some reason without opus number, unpublished and unperformed until after the composer's death. It seems attractive, a useful addition to the small repertoire for the medium.

# BRUCH
## 1838–1920; Germany

Max Bruch must be considered a secondary composer, since most of his music – including major orchestral and choral works – is largely forgotten. Part of his problem is that he is overshadowed by his contemporary Brahms. Moreover his music, structured on classical lines and emphasizing melody and beauty of sound, arguably suffers from a lack of adventurousness. Yet his first violin concerto (op. 26, completed in 1868) is a major monument of music, played perhaps as often as any other violin concerto. So at his finest, Bruch is a front-rank composer. At least two other works for solo instrument and orchestra also hold a place in the repertoire.

There is a further reason why Bruch's appearance here as a composer of chamber music may seem surprising. Until quite recently only a few chamber works were known, mostly early and showing precocious talent but of little importance. However, unpublished at his death were four further full-scale chamber compositions. These finally emerged only between 1988 and 2008. Three of them form a group, written at the end of his life when he was in his early eighties, in

Berlin in the time of and following Germany's defeat in the First World War. These three are on a quite different level from his other chamber works, and are surely masterpieces. Perhaps the only serious criticism of them is that, though written in the era of Schoenberg and Stravinsky, they are in the style Bruch had established by the late 1860s. As with all his music, they show an excellent understanding of string instruments. For players, they are splendid additions to the limited repertoires of the string quintet and string octet.

## String Quartets

No. 1 in C minor, op. 9 (1856)                                              28m; D4
Written at the age of eighteen, and immature. However, it contains some quite striking music, and signs of Bruch's personal style already seem recognizable.

No. 2 in E, op. 10 (1860)                                                   31m; D4–
Compared to its predecessor, this is more spacious and relaxed; it is also easier. The musical interest is well distributed.

## String Quintets (2 violins, 2 violas, cello)

No. 1 in A minor (1918)                                                     25m; D4
This splendid quintet was published in 1991. There is much in it that is vigorous, but also much that is meltingly lyrical. Its slow third movement derives from the composer's *Serenade on Swedish Folk Melodies*. The musical interest throughout is democratically distributed, and Bruch gives the first viola plenty of opportunities. However, the writing for the first violin is sometimes demanding.

No. 2 in E♭ (1918)                                                         19m; D4
For those who came to love the A minor quintet, there followed years of frustration when this second quintet was known of but was at first lost and then, after its whereabouts were known, inaccessible. When finally published in 2008, it did not disappoint, though it is remarkably different from its companion. There are again four movements, but in two pairs each to be played without a break. The first movement, *Andante con moto*, effectively an extended introduction, has a running semiquaver figuration that originally appeared in Bruch's first symphony and evokes the flowing waters of the Rhine. This material reappears in a slow introduction to the finale. The second and fourth movements are vigorous and again feature technically brilliant writing for the first violin.

## String Octet (4 violins, 2 violas, cello, double bass)

String octet in B♭ (1920)                                                  25m; D4
Publication in this case was in 1996. This is the finest string octet after that of Mendelssohn. The unusual instrumentation provides one of the rare chamber

opportunities for the double bass. Using a cello instead is possible, but much is lost. The work is in three spacious movements, the central one a deeply felt *Adagio*. The instrumental combination is resourcefully exploited, and all parts are enjoyable. As with the string quintets, the first violin part is technically demanding.

## Piano Trio

Op. 5 in C minor (1857)                                                                                      19m; D3
Another precocious early work, attractive and playable. The finale is mainly intense.

## Piano Quintet (piano, string quartet)

Piano quintet in G minor (1886)                                                                           28m; D3–
Written for an amateur ensemble during a period when Bruch was in Liverpool. It is pleasant but small in scope.

## Ensemble Works including a Wind Instrument

Eight pieces, op. 83 (1910) (clarinet, viola, piano)                                              37m; D3
Being for this rare but attractive instrumental combination, these pieces have retained some place in the repertoire. Charming and not unduly difficult, they are gratifying for both clarinet and viola, which are treated equally. The piano part, however, is always an accompaniment. Bruch regarded the pieces as independent and, at least in the concert environment, recommended performing a selection rather than the complete set. Clarinets in both B♭ and A are required. An alternative is provided for cello instead of viola.

In 1849 (at the age of eleven!), Bruch wrote a septet for clarinet, horn, bassoon, two violins, cello and double bass. It has been published and is occasionally played.

# BRUCKNER
## 1824–1896; Austria

Anton Bruckner is known for his great series of symphonies and for his religious choral music. He had a deep Roman Catholic faith, and in some ways was a simple man. Aspects of his music arguably illustrate these characteristics, but it has great originality and power. His style was strongly influenced by Wagner. He was a late developer, and his first representative work is perhaps the Mass in D minor, of 1864. He wrote just one important chamber work, but there also exists an early string quartet of 1862.

## String Quintet (2 violins, 2 violas, cello)

String quintet in F (1878–9)                                    43m; D4

This quintet is an impressive work, and has qualities comparable to those of the composer's symphonies, of which it was composed between the fifth and sixth. It is long, and it often makes its musical points at length and with multiple repeated phrases. Playing it requires commitment: for those unsympathetic to Bruckner's idiom, it can seem tedious. Tempi are never very fast, but notes can be awkward. Bruckner was a supreme composer of slow movements, and the long and profound *Adagio* is the quintet's musical summit. Instructions in the music are in German.

Bruckner also wrote an intermezzo as an alternative to the scherzo of the quintet; it is published separately.

# CHOPIN
### 1810–1849; Poland, France

Frédéric or Fryderyk Chopin was born in Poland of a Polish mother and a French father. He settled in Paris in 1831 and became a French citizen in 1835, but seems still to have regarded himself as Polish. He is the master-composer for the piano – predominantly solo piano. He composed very little chamber music, but his cello sonata is an important member of the repertoire of that instrument.

## Piano Trio

Op. 8 in G minor (1828–9)                                    29m; D3

As the composer's only concerted chamber work, players may be interested in trying this trio. But it is early and although some of it is attractive it is dull. Even the piano part, though not easy, is not very enterprising.

## Duet Sonata

Op. 65 in G minor (1845–6) (cello, piano)                    30m; D4

Unsurprisingly, the piano part is demanding; but so is the cello part. The third movement *Largo* is relatively straightforward, and is sometimes played separately.

# CORELLI
### 1653–1713; Italy

Arcangelo Corelli was one of the most important composers in the history of music, and arguably the outstanding figure of his time – more than a generation before Bach and Handel. He was also very important as a violinist, and in the development of violin technique. The greatest part of his life was spent in Rome, and he was notable for the success of his musical career: he died wealthy. His compositional output was relatively small, but very important: it was influential throughout Europe, and continued to be played and republished for many years after his death. He did not invent any forms, but the fine works he produced in existing forms demonstrated their potential, and became the *de facto* standards for them, copied by many other composers.

Six sets of works comprise the bulk of his output; five of these are chamber music. Although in classifying his works as either *sonate da chiesa* or *sonate da camera* he was following precedent, it was his works that established the typical character of the two types. Dates given are of publication. Stated numbers of movements may vary in different authorities, as there is sometimes ambiguity as to whether a section given a distinct tempo indication is actually a separate movement. The sets usually have about equal numbers of works in major and minor keys. Sets or works lacking an opus number have been allocated WoO numbers.

## Trio Sonatas

Twelve *sonate da chiesa*, op. 1 (1681) (2 violins, continuo)     4–7m; D2
All have four movements with the exception of nos 7 (three) and 10 (five).

Twelve *sonate da camera*, op. 2 (1685) (2 violins, continuo)     4–8m; D2
Most have four movements, but nos 2, 6, 9 and 11 have three, and no. 12 has just one, a chaconne.

Twelve *sonate da chiesa*, op. 3 (1689) (2 violins, continuo)     5–9m; D2
All are in four movements except for no. 12, which has six.

Twelve *sonate da camera*, op. 4 (1694) (2 violins, continuo)     4–9m; D2
Six of these have four movements, but no. 7 has five and the rest have three.

Six *sonate da chiesa* (WoO 5–10) (1714) (2 violins, continuo)     3–7m; D2
This set was published posthumously. Nos 2 and 6 have three movements; the rest have four.

## Four-Part Sonatas

*Sonata a quattro* in G minor (WoO 2) (1699) (2 violins, viola, continuo)     7m; D2
In five movements.

*Sonata a quattro* in D major (WoO 4) (1704) (trumpet, 2 violins, continuo)  7m; D2
This five-movement work offers a rare opportunity for a trumpet to play with a

small string-based ensemble.

## Duet Sonatas

These are all for violin and continuo, and were published as the twelve violin sonatas, op. 5 (1700). Of them, the first six are *sonate da chiesa* and the remainder are *sonate da camera*, but no. 12 differs from its fellows.

Op. 5 nos 1–6                                               10–12m; D5

These *sonate da chiesa* all have five movements. The violin parts are of virtuoso character.

Op. 5 nos 7–11                                             9–12m; D3

These *sonate da camera* are mostly in four movements, but nos 10 and 11 are in five. Unlike the *sonate da chiesa*, their technical difficulties are moderate.

Op. 5 no. 12 in D minor                                    11m; D4

This work has a popularity that continues to this day. It is a single movement, a set of variations on the ancient tune *La Folia* (or *Follia*).

# DANZI
## 1763–1826; Germany

Franz Danzi was a cellist and composer; he was German but his family had Italian origins. Born only a few years after Mozart (whom he came to admire), his formative years were spent at Mannheim, from which school his style derives. He was later a friend of Weber. His output includes symphonies, concertos, operas and much chamber music. Most of it is forgotten today, but his nine wind quintets are played, forming alongside those of Reicha the basis of the repertoire for the combination.

## Wind Quintets

Danzi's wind quintets are for the standard combination of flute, oboe, clarinet, horn and bassoon. All are in four movements and uniform in layout. Their style is classical and conservative for their time; they are cheerful, fresh and melodically attractive, but unadventurous. They sometimes show resemblances to Mozart or Weber. The leading part is the flute, sometimes shared with the oboe; but all players are given enjoyable opportunities. The horn parts were written with the natural horn in mind. Compared with the slightly earlier wind quintets of Reicha, Danzi's are on a smaller scale, musically less ambitious and technically easier. They are probably the best wind quintets for amateur ensembles to start on. Dates shown are of publication.

Op. 56 no. 1 in B♭ (1821)                                  16m; D3

The clarinet is in B♭.

Op. 56 no. 2 in G minor (1821)                                          15m; D3

This has been suggested as the best of Danzi's quintets. The trio of the minuet is a flute solo. The clarinet is in B♭.

Op. 56 no. 3 in F (1821)                                                23m; D3

The influence of Weber is noticeable. The clarinet is in B♭.

Op. 67 no. 1 in G (1823–4)                                              16m; D3

The clarinet is in A.

Op. 67 no. 2 in E minor (1823–4)                                        17m; D3

The clarinet is in A.

Op. 67 no. 3 in E♭ (1823–4)                                             17m; D3

This is one of the most lively and entertaining of these quintets. The clarinet is in B♭.

Op. 68 no. 1 in A (1823–4)                                              18m; D3

The trio of the minuet is a solo for oboe. The clarinet is in A.

Op. 68 no. 2 in F (1823–4)                                              23m; D3

The second movement is a set of variations. The clarinet is in B♭.

Op. 68 no. 3 in D minor (1823–4)                                        18m; D3

This final quintet is a more serious and substantial work than its fellows – though not noticeably more difficult. The clarinet is in B♭.

## Other Chamber Works

Danzi's works include nineteen string quartets, also string duos and string quintets with two violas. Works involving wind instruments include two sextets for two horns and strings (in one case with oboe alternative for a violin); three quintets for piano and winds; and trios, quartets and quintets for flute and strings. There are also several duet sonatas for wind instruments.

# DEBUSSY
## 1862–1918; France

Claude Debussy was one of the most important composers of his time, both for his music itself and for his influence. It was not until the early 1890s that he established his very distinctive and original style, to which the term 'impressionist' is often given. He is seen as having freed music from the limitations of classical harmony, leading to developments by others in the first decades of the twentieth century. His output was not large, but it includes chamber music, in which his contribution is important. The three works of the wartime years 1915–17, when he was ill, were all he lived to complete of a planned set of six sonatas 'pour divers instruments'. They are all in three quite short movements.

## String Quartet

String quartet in G minor (1893)                                                    25m; D4

Although composed relatively early in Debussy's career, this is a great and unflawed masterpiece, fully representative of his genius. It is also popular and often appears in concert programmes. Curiously, Debussy designated it as op. 10, though he never gave an opus number to any other work. Musicologists consider influences on it to have included the quartets of Grieg, Borodin and Franck. However, this was mainly structural: its sound-world is utterly its own. Instrumental tone colour is exploited to exquisite and sensuous effect. It is very playable. There are no major technical or rhythmical problems: those who can play middle-period Beethoven can play this.

## Ensemble Work including a Wind Instrument

Sonata for flute, viola and harp (1915)                                             16m; D4

The second of Debussy's set of sonatas, this is charming, light and whimsical in character. Technically there are no major difficulties, but fitting it together is not easy.

## Duet Sonatas

Sonata in G minor (1916–17) (violin, piano)                                         13m; D4

This is a fine sonata. For many amateurs it is playable, but not by sight-reading.

Sonata in D minor (1915) (cello, piano)                                             11m; D4+

Beautiful and very original, but technically demanding.

# DOHNÁNYI
### 1877–1960; Hungary

Ernő Dohnányi is always considered a Hungarian composer, although most of his music was published under the German form of his name, Ernst von Dohnányi; and from 1949 he made his home in America. He was conservative in his compositional style. He impressed Brahms in his early days, and he consistently followed Brahms in his adherence to classical forms and to romanticism. He has been overshadowed by his more progressive Hungarian contemporaries Kodály and Bartók, and now most of his music, which includes symphonies, concertos, choral music and operas, is neglected. However, he was at his best in his chamber music, and much of this is still sometimes played. Most frequently heard is the serenade for string trio, but most of his chamber works deserve attention. The first few show recognizable reminiscences of Brahms, but by soon after 1900 he had fully formed his own style, with a characteristic use of chromaticism and some definite if not strongly marked Hungarian characteristics.

Dohnányi left many juvenile compositions. A string sextet, written in 1893 and revised in 1896, may be of interest considering the shortage of works for this grouping.

## String Trio

Serenade in C, Op. 10 (1902)                21m; D4

There are five movements. As would be expected from the title, the character is generally light. However, this is a characteristic and fine work, excellently written for the instruments and rewarding to play. Dohnányi's chromatic writing makes the third movement scherzo technically difficult. This is surely the best string trio composed during the romantic period.

## String Quartets

Op. 7 in A (1899)                30m; D3

A charming and relaxed quartet, and relatively straightforward to play.

Op. 15 in D♭ (1906)               27m; D4+

This has long been the most popular of the three string quartets. It is a fine work, with a confident romantic lushness. It is in three movements, and is quite difficult. In the central *Presto acciacato* (effectively a scherzo), some ricochet bowing is called for. The finale is a complicated *Adagio*.

Op. 33 in A minor (1926)            27m; D4

A large work, but less serious in tone than its predecessors. It has a vigorous and fresh quality, more astringent than his earlier quartets. The second of its three movements is a set of variations.

## Piano Quintets (piano, string quartet)

Op. 1 in C minor (1895)          29m; D3 (piano harder)

A fine and powerful work, full of original and attractive ideas. However, Dohnányi had not yet found his personal voice, and this is Brahmsian in character. For the strings it is straightforward to play, but the rich and elaborate piano part is demanding.

Op. 26 in E♭ (1914)               24m; D4

The second piano quintet is one of the composer's finest achievements, sombre, powerful and beautiful. It is in three movements, the second and third complicated, with many changes of tempo. The viola is given good opportunities to display its distinctive tone colour.

### Ensemble Work including Wind Instruments

Sextet in C, op. 37 (1935) (piano, clarinet, horn, violin, viola, cello)          30m; D4
This is the composer's last chamber composition, for a very rare combination of instruments. It is a fine, outgoing and confident work, giving good opportunities to all the players. The lead role is mostly shared between violin and clarinet. The clarinet is in B♭.

### Duet Sonatas

Op. 21 in C♯ minor (1912) (violin, piano)                                        19m; D4
In three movements; the final coda returns to the material of the opening movement.

Op. 8 in B♭ minor (1899) (cello, piano)                                          27m; D4
Brahms's influence is evident.

# DVOŘÁK
### 1841–1904; Bohemia

Antonin Dvořák was born in what was then Bohemia in the Austro-Hungarian Empire, and is now part of the Czech Republic. He remained deeply attached to the country throughout his life, and became much loved as a national composer. He also in the course of nine visits became popular in England, and (as is well known) he spent three years in America. Chamber music was an important part of his output: his series of chamber works is exceptionally long for a major late romantic composer. However, he was late in reaching maturity. From his first substantial compositions around 1861 until about 1873 his style was largely influenced by German models, latterly particularly Wagner. He then changed direction towards a consciously national Czech or Slavonic style. His works are usually considered to be mature from about 1875 (the year of the popular serenade for strings). Many earlier chamber works still exist (although he destroyed some), but they are not discussed here. As a player, his preferred instrument was the viola.

Dvořák's thematic material is often folk-inspired, but he did not employ actual folk melodies. Characteristic Slavonic dance rhythms such as the *polka*, *furiant* and *sousedská* are used. He frequently made use of the form known as the *dumka*, in which elegiac, slow music alternates with fast and exuberant sections. Although he employed his national style throughout his maturity, his music from about 1881 to 1886 shows more German influence, mainly of Brahms. In the compositions of his period in America (1892–5), some influence of American (including African American) music may appear. After 1895 he abandoned absolute music and gave himself to symphonic poems and operas of national character.

The finest of the chamber works are superb, of remarkable freshness, originality and perfection. However, his output was uneven, and not all of his mature chamber compositions are of such high rank. His writing for string instruments is idiomatic, and they are often given gratifying opportunities. They can be quite difficult to play, though there are no virtuoso demands. He sometimes shows a striking freedom of rhythm. He composed for most of the principal combinations of strings and strings with piano, also for a few unusual combinations; but there are no works involving wind instruments. However, many wind players will be interested in his serenade in D minor, op. 44, for two oboes, two clarinets, two bassoons, three horns, cello and double bass.

Dvořák began numbering his works with op. 1 in 1861, but after a while ceased, resuming about 1873. Two chamber works from 1875 and 1876 have high opus numbers that belie their dates. A chronological numbering system now exists in the catalogue published in 1960 by Jarmil Burghauser; but these numbers have by no means ousted the opus numbers.

## String Trios

Terzetto, op. 74 (B. 148) in C (1887) (2 violins, viola)          20m; D4
For this surprising combination, Dvořák produced a charming work in four quite substantial movements: it was written for two violinist friends to play with him. Much of it is quite straightforward, but unfortunately some sections, especially parts of the last movement variations, are more difficult. The scherzo is a *furiant*, with characteristic cross-rhythms.

Miniatures, op. 75a (B. 149) (1887) (2 violins, viola)          14m; D3
These are not true chamber music, but they are attractive and can be useful. The *Terzetto* being too difficult for one of the violinists, Dvořák immediately went on to compose these four pieces, which are easier. However, the second violin and viola parts are almost entirely accompaniments. He then arranged them for violin and piano and published them as *Four Romantic Pieces*, op. 75. The original version was published in 1945.

## String Quartets

Fourteen full-scale string quartets are in existence, of which seven were composed before 1875 and are considered immature. The remaining seven are all fine works, though variable. Op. 96 in F is easily the most popular, and deservedly so. For some players, however, op. 51 in E♭ is the finest. The final two, opp. 105 and 106, stand alone in their scale and power, and some would consider these to be the greatest. Unfortunately, printed parts for Dvořák's quartets are only available singly.

(Of the early quartets, op. 9 in F minor, op. 12 in A minor and op. 16 in A minor, all of 1873–4, may be of interest. The slow movement of op. 9 in a later revised version is the Romance in F minor for violin and orchestra, op. 11. Some may also wish to investigate *Cypresses*, B. 152: these are string-quartet arrangements made in 1887 of twelve songs from his 1865 song-cycle of the same name.)

## Op. 80 (B. 57) in E (1876)                                      28m; D4

The late opus number was given on publication in 1888; Dvořák had intended op. 27. This is a beautiful and interesting quartet, serious in character, with a distinctive Czech flavour. Perhaps especially striking is the *Andante con moto* second movement. The work is technically fairly demanding, aggravated by the awkward key; but its quality makes it well worth playing.

## Op. 34 (B. 75) in A minor (1877)                                36m; D4–

One of the most enjoyable to play of Dvořák's quartets, and perhaps the best to start with. Its technical difficulties are moderate. The writing demonstrates the composer's understanding of string instruments, and gives gratifying opportunities to all. It is strongly Czech in character. The mood is serious and sometimes tragic, especially in the rapt and beautiful slow movement.

## Op. 51 (B. 92) in E♭ (1878–9)                                   32m; D4

In 1973, in the last concert of the then English String Quartet, this was the final work – because, as the leader (Nona Liddell) said, of all quartets this was their favourite. This illustrates the high esteem in which it is held by some. Not all would rate it so highly, but it certainly should be played. It was written in response to a commission for a quartet in Slavonic style, and its character is fresh and highly original. The second movement is a *dumka*; there is a *furiant*, and the last movement is a *skočná* (a fast dance in 2/4 time). It is gratefully written for the strings and enjoyable in all parts.

## Op. 61 (B. 121) in C (1881)                                     38m; D4+

Despite being one of Dvořák's mature works, this quartet is rarely played. It was commissioned by the Hellmesberger Quartet, Vienna's most important chamber ensemble, steeped in the classical repertoire. This perhaps influenced the composer to aim at a serious and impressive work of classical cast. It is long, complicated and technically difficult to play. On the other hand, many of its melodies could have been written by no-one but Dvořák, and there are many passages of haunting beauty. So though not one of his best quartets, it is too good to be ignored.

## Op. 96 (B. 179) in F ('American') (1893)                        27m; D3+

The most popular of Dvořák's string quartets; indeed, among the most popular of all chamber works. This goes for both listeners and players: the directness and simplicity of the writing is wonderful. Its intentions are lightweight rather than profound. It is full of melody and delightful rhythms. It was written during the composer's period in America, but despite the nickname nothing in either melodies or treatment is definitely American. Every instrument is given glorious opportunities. The viola has the quartet's opening melody – but is made to pay for the privilege by its unrelieved accompaniment in the *Lento* second movement. This movement is an almost unbroken song, in which the cello and first violin especially are indulged. Technically this is the easiest of Dvořák's quartets, though inexperienced players often have problems with some rhythmic figures and timing. A first sight-reading, therefore, can be frustrating: but these are not serious difficulties and can be avoided by looking at the work in advance.

Op. 106 (B. 192) in G (1895)         39m; D4

The two final quartets are dramatically different from the 'American'. They are large-scale, powerful and ambitious, and technically quite difficult. Although they perhaps lack the popular appeal of the 'American', they are splendid works and should certainly be played. Op. 106 is the larger of the two. Every movement is spacious. It is full of Dvořák's Czech character, and the thematic material shows remarkable originality – as is immediately illustrated by the opening. The second movement *Adagio ma non troppo* is of great power, and reaches a climax marked *fff grandioso*. The original and delightful scherzo has two trios, the second particularly eventful. Towards the end of the finale, there is an episode in which the opening of the first movement returns.

Op. 105 (B. 193) in A♭ (1895)         33m; D4

This quartet was begun before op. 106, but finished later. It too is a splendid, large-scale work, but it is mostly sunny in mood and more relaxed than its companion. Nevertheless it is equally fine, and every movement is on the same high level. Perhaps especially memorable is the second movement scherzo, another *furiant*. Also superb is the slow movement, with its very resourceful use of the instruments. The worst thing is the key, which adds awkwardness to what is already difficult, and makes this technically slightly the harder of the two quartets.

## String Quintets

There are two mature string quintets, for different combinations. (In addition, the composer's first chamber work, op. 1 in A minor of 1861, is a two-viola quintet – but even his devotees are unlikely to get much satisfaction from it.)

Op. 77 (B. 49) in G (1875) (2 violins, viola, cello, double bass)  34m; D4

Dvořák originally intended this to be op. 18, but a higher number was allocated when it was published much later. Although the earliest of his chamber works here considered, it is excellent. It does not attempt profundity: rather it is charming throughout, characteristic of the composer and excellently written for the instruments. The unusual medium makes for a distinctive sound, and the freedom that it offers for the cello is exploited generously – cellists will particularly enjoy this work. It is not easy in any part.

As published, the quintet has four movements, but there was originally also an intermezzo, which came second (and had originated in a movement of one of his early string quartets). Before publication of the quintet Dvořák removed it and arranged it for string orchestra as the Nocturne for Strings, op. 40. It is a beautiful movement, and in its quintet version it is today sometimes reinstated in its previous position.

Op. 97 (B. 180) in E♭ (1893) (2 violins, 2 violas, cello)                    33m; D4
Dvořák's wonderfully resourceful use of the ensemble in this quintet is gratifying for all. For example, both the first and second movements begin on unaccompanied second viola, while the first twenty-four bars of the *Larghetto* third movement belong almost entirely to the violas and cello. This quintet followed immediately on the 'American' quartet, some of the character of which it shares; but it is bigger, more complex, and more difficult to play. There are some tricky keys, especially the seven flats of much of the *Larghetto*. Overall it is splendid; but some may feel that the last page verges on vulgarity.

## String Sextet

Op. 48 (B. 80) in A (1878)                    35m; D4–
This is one of the most strongly Slavonic of Dvořák's works. The second movement is a *dumka* (though, unusually, it contains no fast music), and the third movement is a *furiant*. The last movement is a set of variations. Most of the sextet is relaxed, and it does not aim at profundity: but it is uniformly elegant and charming. The textures are delightful, and the writing is a remarkable contrast to that used by Brahms in his sextets. The cellos and perhaps even more the violas are treated generously. Much of it is not particularly difficult.

## Piano Trios

The four piano trios divide into two groups. The first two, both early in Dvořák's mature output, are not among his finest works. The other two are major masterpieces, though very different from each other.

Op. 21 (B. 51) in B♭ (1875)                    35m; D3
This trio is rarely performed professionally, and one can see why: it is rather colourless and lacks strong character. It also has few noticeably Czech features. However, it is well written for the instruments and not very difficult, so amateurs may well

enjoy trying it.

<u>Op. 26 (B. 56) in G minor (1876)</u>                                    32m; D4–

A much better work than its predecessor. Written following the death of the composer's eldest daughter, its mood throughout is of sombre beauty. However, it again has little national character. Cellists will enjoy their frequent prominence.

<u>Op. 65 (B. 130) in F minor (1883)</u>                                    40m; D4

This massive and tremendously powerful trio is among Dvořák's greatest chamber works. It was written after the death of his mother, and is deeply felt and sombre throughout. It is technically difficult, but very rewarding. As with its predecessor, the cello is treated with enjoyable freedom. Although it shows some national elements, much of it seems influenced by Brahms. However, this should not be seen as a drawback: this is a superb trio, and for capable ensembles it is one that sooner or later must be played.

<u>Op. 90 (B. 166) ('Dumky') (1890–1)</u>                                   33m; D4+

There is nothing else like this much-loved and highly regarded work. Its spirit is that of folk music, full of feeling, alternating between lyrical melancholy and energetic, high-spirited gaiety. The textures are highly original, often simple and open, with much of cello melody. It is unique in its form, a series of six *dumky* (plural of *dumka*). It seems divorced from any classical precedent, though arguably the first three *dumky* (which are linked, *attacca subito*) can be read as a first movement; the fourth is mainly slow; the fifth represents a scherzo; and the sixth indeed stands as finale. However, whether or not this was Dvořák's intention, it scarcely affects how the work is perceived or played.

Despite the apparent simplicity of the textures, it is difficult to play; sophisticated technique is assumed. A further difficulty is the many changes of tempo, which make sight-reading unlikely to give much satisfaction: advance practice is needed to know what is going on.

## Piano Quartets

There are two piano quartets for the normal combination. A further work is for a different and unusual grouping.

<u>Op. 23 (B. 53) in D (1875)</u>                                          35m; D3+

In three movements, but on a quite ambitious scale. However, it seems immature, with musical invention mostly at a low temperature. Best is the set of variations that forms the central movement. As a pleasant and relatively straightforward piano quartet, this has a place.

<u>Bagatelles, op. 47 (B. 79) (1878)</u> (2 violins, cello, harmonium/piano)     18m; D2

A most charming work, in five short movements. It is musically lightweight, but in its democratic distribution of the musical interest it is genuine chamber music.

It makes only modest technical demands, no doubt because it was intended for a broad domestic market. A piano is specified as an alternative to the harmonium (perhaps for commercial reasons), but this is unsatisfactory because of the extensive use of sustained chords. Much better is a suitable sound from an electronic keyboard.

<u>Op. 87 (B. 162) in E♭ (1889)</u>                                                                       36m; D4

Here we have a major work by Dvořák at the height of his powers; yet it is not very often played. In part this is because it is overshadowed by the popularity of the piano quintet. But its content is mainly stern and forceful; it rarely deploys the charm and beauty with which Dvořák often beguiles his players and listeners. Moreover it is technically difficult. Nevertheless, it is a fine work, a significant member of the limited repertoire for this combination, and is well worth playing.

## Piano Quintet (piano, string quartet)

Dvořák's piano quintet is one of the major monuments of the repertoire. There also exists an earlier work, op. 5 (B. 28), of 1872; like its successor, this is in A.

<u>Op. 81 (B. 155) in A (1887)</u>                                                                       40m; D4

A radiant, glowing, spacious and perfect work, one of Dvořák's finest creations. Its textures are utterly his own, and its melodies and rhythms are enchanting. The writing for the strings is wonderfully fresh and free, with opportunity after opportunity for all parts. Especially memorable is the opening viola melody of the long second-movement *dumka*; at various times this melody is given to every other player, but it most belongs to the viola. The use of the piano is relatively restrained. A good technique is demanded of all players; but given that, this is one of the most enjoyable works in the repertoire of chamber music including piano.

## Duet Sonata and other Duets

<u>Op. 57 (B. 106) in F (1880)</u> (violin, piano)                                        24m; D3

Although not well known, this sonata has much that is attractive; and it is playable by amateurs.

<u>Sonatina in G, op. 100 (B. 183) (1893)</u> (violin, piano)                        20m; D2

The last chamber work of the composer's American period, written for two of his children. It is a splendid gift to those of limited technical capability: fine music, yet relatively easy for both players.

———

Also for violin and piano are the *Four Romantic Pieces*, op. 75 (*see Miniatures*, op. 75a, above).

# ELGAR
## 1857–1934; England

Around the turn of the twentieth century it was Edward Elgar (from 1904, Sir Edward) who emphatically brought to an end the two long centuries since Purcell in which England had had no major native-born composer. He continues today to have a uniquely important position in English music, with a strong public following and frequent performances of his principal orchestral and choral works. On the international stage, however, he is less prominent. His music is firmly late romantic, showing influences derived from Wagner, and is untouched by modernist trends that were appearing elsewhere. He was an exceptional master of the orchestra. Nevertheless he was interested in chamber music. Only once, however, in 1918, did he fully give himself to the composition of large-scale chamber works, when in a concentrated burst of creativity he produced three. Unusually, they are all in only three movements. All are fine works that are enjoyed by those who appreciate Elgar's idiom; and the piano quintet is outstanding and should be played by all piano quintet ensembles.

Elgar composed many pieces for violin and piano; several are well known. He also, very early in his career, wrote much music for wind quintet (in this case, of two flutes, oboe, clarinet and bassoon), which has been published.

## String Quartet

Op. 83 in E minor (1918)                                            28m; D4

The first two movements are thoughtful and wistful, though the first movement reaches an emotional high point in a passage with Elgar's characteristic *nobilmente* marking. The second, marked *piacevole* ('agreeable'), is indeed a pleasure to play. A tougher fibre runs through the last movement. This is a fine quartet, of which appreciation grows with closer knowledge. Elgar was a supremely fine writer for strings, and all the instruments are given eloquent opportunities – though the violins sometimes need to exercise restraint to allow the viola or cello to be heard.

## Piano Quintet (piano, string quartet)

Op. 84 in A minor (1918–19)                                        37m; D4

This is a splendid work on a large scale and of wide musical scope – one of the half-dozen first-rank piano quintets. Although there are some loud and vigorous passages, most of it is gentler, and it is the latter that perhaps gives the work much of its power and distinctive character. Its core is the profound central *Adagio*. Elgar's writing for the piano is original and often delicate; this work is unusual among piano quintets for its restrained use of the piano. The writing for the strings also is fine: especially memorable is the viola part in the second movement. The cello is treated throughout with particular freedom (were the composer's thoughts already turning towards the concerto that was to follow?).

## Duet Sonata

Op. 82 in E minor (1918) (violin, piano)                                                   25m; D4
Large-scale and full of characteristic music; however, it is difficult for both players.

# FAURÉ
## 1845–1924; France

Gabriel Fauré is one of the most highly regarded French composers. By the time of his early thirties, he had developed an individual and attractive style, which is well displayed in his first two chamber works, the violin sonata in A major and the piano quartet in C minor. These are popular and are frequently performed. However, as his style continued to develop, it became more complex and subtle but also less immediately attractive. Like Beethoven, Fauré became increasingly deaf in his last two decades. Most of his chamber music was written in this period: six of his ten full-scale works date from the last eight years of his life. There are musicians who value them highly, but most of these later works are rarely played. Nevertheless, even if less obviously enjoyable than Fauré's earlier music, some of them deserve attention: the piano trio and the second piano quintet might be suggested.

Fauré also wrote many pieces for one instrument (mostly violin or cello) with piano. Of these, the Élégie for cello, op. 24 of 1880, is one of his best-known and most-loved works.

## String Quartet

Op. 121 in E minor (1923–4)                                                               24m; D2
Fauré's final work. Technically it is straightforward; but musically this is a problematic quartet. Its apparent blandness, lack of memorable melody and absence of contrast mean that on an initial sight-read most players dismiss it as not worth further attention. Nevertheless, there are some who argue for it.

## Piano Trio

Op. 120 in D minor (1922–3)                                                               19m; D3
Late as this trio is, it stays in the memory for its haunting melodies, especially in the central slow movement. The writing is unusual and distinctive, but not austere. The

piano part is sometimes demanding, but this is an enjoyable trio for the players.

## Piano Quartets

No. 1 in C minor, op. 15 (1879, rev. 1883)                                31m; D3+

This is certainly with both listeners and players Fauré's most popular chamber work. It is warm, sparkling, exquisite and never forceful. There are four movements. The texture and the whole atmosphere are different from anything else, and utterly Fauré's own. All the parts are gratifying, with many lyrical melodies for the string players.

No. 2 in G minor, op. 45 (1886)                                          34m; D4

A contrast to its predecessor: this is a tough and serious quartet. It lacks the obvious charm of the earlier work, but shows a power and depth rarely seen in the composer. Many consider it Fauré's finest chamber composition. Its textures are dense and it is fairly difficult. Nevertheless, it should be tried. The viola player, especially, may argue for it: many gratifying passages are given to that instrument.

## Piano Quintets (piano, string quartet)

No. 1 in D minor, op. 89 (?1887–1906)                                    31m; D3

In three movements, broadly consistent in mood, pleasant but rather colourless. Fauré worked on this quintet for many years; but it is perhaps the least played of his chamber works.

No. 2 in C minor, op. 115 (1919–21)                                      32m; D4

Large-scale and fine, in four movements. This quintet has much more contrast than has its predecessor, and contains much of real lyrical beauty. Like all Fauré's late works, it is relatively unknown, but it deserves attention. All the strings are given enjoyable opportunities. The piano part, whilst sometimes difficult, is varied in its textures.

## Duet Sonatas

Op. 13 in A (1875–6) (violin, piano)                                     27m; D4

An immediately lyrical and attractive sonata; but it is too difficult for many amateurs.

Op. 108 in E minor (1916–17) (violin, piano)                            23m; D4

A substantial work, but rather withdrawn in character.

Op. 109 in D minor (1917) (cello, piano)                                18m; D4

Modest but quite attractive.

Op. 117 in G minor (1921) (cello, piano)                                18m; D4

Similar in some ways to its predecessor, but greater in scope and feeling.

# FRANCK
## 1822–1890; Belgium, France

César Franck was born in Belgium but moved to Paris in 1835 and is regarded as a French composer. He became professor of organ at the Paris Conservatoire, and by his compositions he came to have a strong influence on French music. Unusually, all the works by which he is known today date from a period of major productivity in the last fifteen years of his life. Alongside the large orchestral, choral and operatic compositions of this period, he composed three major chamber works. His harmonic style was influenced by Liszt and Wagner; and his music sometimes has a heaviness that critics associate with his being an organist. He employed cyclic form – the unification of the movements of a work by a common theme or motif – which is used in each of the chamber works.

Not discussed here are four early piano trios dating from 1839–42.

## String Quartet

String quartet in D (1889–90)                                        44m; D4

Unlike the other two chamber works, this quartet is relatively infrequently performed. One reason is probably its length. Also sometimes criticized is its texture – rests are rare in all parts, and the result tends to be thick. Yet the music is splendid, the outpouring of a mature master-composer; and he gives excellent opportunities to all players. For most, this is a quartet to play – it is good, enjoyable playing throughout. There is nothing that competent amateurs cannot manage with practice.

## Piano Quintet (piano, string quartet)

Piano quintet in F minor (1879)                        35m; D4 (strings easier)

This work has taken its place as one of the great piano quintets. It is dramatic, passionate, emotional and intense throughout its three movements – these qualities are perhaps what make it popular. But it is certainly fine, well written and ingeniously planned in its cyclic form. It is technically demanding for the pianist.

## Duet Sonata

Sonata in A (1886) (violin, piano)                        28m; D4+ (violin easier)

A superb work, one of the most popular of all duet sonatas. The violin writing is excellent: idiomatic and straightforward. However, the piano part is seriously difficult. Franck approved a version for cello; the piano part is unchanged.

# GRIEG
## 1843–1907; Norway

Edvard Grieg developed a distinctive style influenced by the folksong of his country. In an era when Norway was subject to Sweden (independence was achieved in 1905), this was an expression of Norwegian nationalism and made him popular in the country; but with the best of his music he has come to be admired internationally. He was remarkably original, but is considered best as a miniaturist, as in his piano pieces and songs. A famous exception is the piano concerto, op. 16, dating from 1868, fairly early in his career; he never again composed an extended orchestral work. Nevertheless he produced several full-scale chamber works in his maturity. Though not quite mainstream repertoire, they are played both in the concert-hall and by amateurs.

## String Quartets

### Op. 27 in G minor (1877–8)
35m; D4

In some ways this is a charming, fresh and very original work. Structurally, it is the earliest significant string quartet to employ cyclic form – the theme presented in heavy unison at the beginning appears in some guise in every movement. The textures throughout are remarkably unorthodox: much playing of octaves and chords is called for, and counterpoint is limited. Some may not like this: but if played with sensitivity it is enjoyable, and the quality of the material will win many over. Once familiarity has been gained, the technical difficulties can be coped with.

### No. 2 in F (unfinished; 1891)
19m (two movements); D4

Grieg completed the first two movements but left only sketches of the other two. The completed movements (the second is a scherzo) were published in 1908, soon after his death. Their style of writing is very different from that of op. 27, and less idiosyncratic. They are vigorous, cheerful music, and many players will enjoy them; it is a pity the quartet is unfinished. Completions have been made of the remaining movements, which Grieg enthusiasts may wish to investigate.

## Duet Sonatas

All four of Grieg's sonatas are in three movements. Two are early works, two are mature.

### Op. 8 in F (1865) (violin, piano)
23m; D3–

Immature; but it is attractive and valuable for amateurs as a technically fairly straightforward romantic sonata.

### Op. 13 in G (1867) (violin, piano)
21m; D3

This is a finer work than its predecessor. Almost all its material is of Norwegian folk character.

<u>Op. 45 in C minor (1886–7)</u> (violin, piano)                                          25m; D4–

Of tremendous boldness and originality: surely Grieg's greatest chamber work. It is among the finest of all romantic sonatas for violin and piano.

<u>Op. 36 in A minor (1882–3)</u> (cello, piano)                                          27m; D4

In character comparable to the op. 45 violin sonata – passionate and vigorous and covering a wide emotional range.

# HANDEL
## 1685–1759; Germany, England

George Frideric Handel was born in Halle in Germany. From perhaps 1706 he spent several years in Italy. In 1712 he moved to London, where he remained for the rest of his life, becoming a naturalized citizen in 1727. He was highly esteemed in his adopted country, and at his death was buried in Westminster Abbey. The earlier part of his career was dominated by composition of operas, but from the 1730s he turned principally to oratorios, a form he did much to develop. He composed in other forms too, including chamber music. Most of his chamber works were published in his lifetime, but the publications do not seem to have had his involvement or approval. Partly because of this, and also because of his tendency sometimes to reuse earlier music, there is confusion among them. However, the appearance in 1978–86 of the *Händel-Werke-Verzeichnis* (HWV), the catalogue of Handel's works by Bernd Baselt, has provided a welcome basis for establishing clarity.

Handel's chamber works, especially the sonatas for one instrument with continuo, have long been popular with amateurs. They exist widely in editions from the nineteenth and earlier twentieth centuries, but these mostly suffer from editing of the melody parts and piano realization of the continuo that by modern standards are not good.

## Trio Sonatas

The trio sonatas are for two violins and continuo unless otherwise stated. Handel's output of trio sonatas consists essentially of two sets, op. 2 and op. 5, containing a total of thirteen works. There are also some others of doubtful authenticity, and some that are certainly spurious. The doubtful works include six for two oboes or oboe and violin with continuo, which have been thought to be Handel's earliest compositions, dating from about 1696 (when he was aged ten or eleven).

The six trio sonatas of op. 2 were published in 1733; most were probably composed about 1718. Some consider this the finer of the two sets – though Handel did not compose them as a set. All except one have four movements, in the normal slow-fast-slow-fast pattern of the *sonata da chiesa*. Confusingly, the Chrysander edition of 1879 gave them a different numbering within op. 2 (and also added several further questionable works, which are not discussed here).

Op. 2 no. 1 (HWV 386b) in B minor (flute/violin, violin, continuo)          12m; D2
The third movement is an accompanied solo for the flute/first violin. This sonata is sometimes referred to as op. 2 no. 1b; there also exists a variant (perhaps earlier) version in C minor, HWV 386a, first published in 1879, sometimes numbered op. 2 no. 1a.

Op. 2 no. 2 (HWV 387) in G minor          10m; D2+
This sonata is thought to be much earlier than the rest of the opus, dating from Handel's teenage years. It has an attractive simplicity.

Op. 2 no. 3 (HWV 388) in B♭          11m; D3–
Excellent throughout, with much enjoyable dialogue between the violins.

Op. 2 no. 4 (HWV 389) in F (flute/recorder/violin, violin, continuo)          12m; D3–
This work has five movements. Several of them give an enjoyable prominence to the flute/recorder/first violin part.

Op. 2 no. 5 (HWV 390) in G minor          11m; D2+
Beautiful and enjoyable playing throughout.

Op. 2 no. 6 (HWV 391) in G minor          9m; D3–
Another fine work.

---

The op. 5 set of trio sonatas was first published in 1739, unusually containing seven works. They differ considerably from those of op. 2. All have at least five movements. As in op. 2, they start with alternating fast and slow movements, but they depart from the *sonata da chiesa* format by including dances, often as their last two movements. They are more varied and perhaps more lightweight than those of op. 2. All are for two violins and continuo.

Op. 5 no. 1 (HWV 396) in A          8m; D2+
In five movements, the last a gavotte.

Op. 5 no. 2 (HWV 397) in D          9m; D3–
The surprisingly long third of its five movements is a musette. A march and a gavotte follow.

Op. 5 no. 3 (HWV 398) in E minor          11m; D2+
Attractive, mostly gentle music, in six movements.

Op. 5 no. 4 (HWV 399) in G                               14m; D3–

This sonata differs from the others in the opus: it is the longest in the set, and its musical character is different. Almost all the music is derived from various orchestral pieces by Handel, often associated with his operas. Particularly striking is the long passacaglia third movement. The Halle Handel Edition (Bärenreiter) provides an ad lib viola part for this work – a rare opportunity for a viola to participate in a trio sonata.

Op. 5 no. 5 (HWV 400) in G minor                      12m; D3–

One of the loveliest of Handel's trio sonatas. It has six movements.

Op. 5 no. 6 (HWV 401) in F                              12m; D3–

Very attractive music throughout. There is an alternative version of the minuet final movement.

Op. 5 no. 7 (HWV 402) in B♭                             10m; D3–

The fourth movement gavotte is an accompanied solo for the first violin.

## Duet Sonatas

All the sonatas accepted as authentic are with continuo. The majority have four movements, slow-fast-slow-fast, but others have from three to seven movements. Most were first published about 1727–30 (apparently in Amsterdam) as a set of twelve sonatas, op. 1, for various instruments. This was republished in 1732 in London by John Walsh in what was stated to be a more correct edition (but much that was incorrect remained!). The changes included the replacement of two of the original sonatas. The numbering in the 1732 edition is generally used today for these twelve sonatas. Sometimes added to them are the two displaced sonatas, and another, numbered as 13 to 15. Further sonatas also exist (five of which are sometimes numbered on from 16 to 20).

*Violin*

Editions of six Handel violin sonatas from publishers including Schirmer, Augener and Peters have been played and loved by generations of violinists; but views of these sonatas have been shaken by modern developments. Four of them are now considered of doubtful authenticity (because handwritten notes on a copy of the original edition say they are 'not Mr. Handel's'). In compensation, however, several further authentic violin sonatas have been added to the canon. Moreover, whether spurious or not, the doubtful sonatas should not be ignored: they have HWV numbers, are included in modern urtext editions, and are not obviously inferior to their fellows. All but one of the violin sonatas have four movements.

For those seeking a reliable modern edition of these sonatas, several are available. That of Henle, from 1971, includes one sonata additional to the six. The two-volume Peters urtext edition of 1981 and the Bärenreiter edition of 1982 include this sonata and a further two (along with fragments and other items).

Sonata 'no. 1' in A, op. 1 no. 3 (HWV 361)                          8m; D3

Sonata 'no. 2' in G minor, op. 1 no.10 (HWV 368)                    9m; D3
Doubtful.

Sonata 'no. 3' in F, op. 1 no. 12 (HWV 370)                         3m; D3–
Doubtful.

Sonata 'no. 4' in D, op. 1 no. 13 (HWV 371)                         12m; D3
Authentic, and believed to be Handel's last chamber work, dating from about 1750. Older editions have several cuts in the last movement (which derive from those made by Handel for his subsequent reuse of the music in the oratorio *Jephtha*).

Sonata 'no. 5' in A, op. 1 no. 14 (HWV 372)                         8m; D3–
Doubtful.

Sonata 'no. 6' in E, op. 1 no. 15 (HWV 373)                         9m; D3–
Doubtful.

Sonata in G minor, op. 1 no. 6 (HWV 364a)                           6m; D2+
Originally published for oboe, but Handel's autograph shows he wrote it for violin.

Sonata in G (HWV 358)                                               5m; D3
A strange work, in three movements; it is thought to be early, from about 1707. Handel did not indicate the instrument for which it is intended; violin is thought probable, though recorder is a possibility. Four startlingly high notes appear just before the end.

Sonata in D minor (HWV 359a)                                        8m; D3
Originally published as a flute sonata in E minor, op. 1 no. 1.

## Viola da gamba
A sonata in C major for viola da gamba and obbligato harpsichord, long believed to be by Handel, is now firmly considered spurious. However, a sonata in G minor, HWV 364b, first published in 1950, is regarded as effectively authentic. It is an arrangement of a violin sonata on the autograph of which, at the bottom of the first page, Handel wrote the first bar an octave below in the alto clef, with the note 'per la viola da gamba'.

## Flute
Handel's flute sonatas are important in the repertoire of the instrument; but there are questions over many of them, either because of doubtful authenticity or because

Handel did not intend them for the flute. The op. 1 set of sonatas included three for flute, but these were all originally composed for other instruments. However, there are other sonatas for flute that were not published in op. 1. Altogether eight sonatas are listed here, but further doubtful works exist – for example the 1995 Bärenreiter edition contains eleven sonatas.

Sonata in E minor, op. 1 no. 1 (HWV 359b)                                   8m; D3
Originally composed for violin. Sometimes called op. 1 no. 1b.

Sonata in E minor, op. 1 no. 1a (HWV 379)                                   13m; D3
The only flute sonata of which Handel's manuscript survives. However, it is a composite work using movements from other sonatas, two of them from op. 1 no. 1.

Sonata in G, op. 1 no. 5 (HWV 363b)                                         8m; D2+
Originally composed for oboe. In five movements.

Sonata in B minor, op. 1 no. 9 (HWV 367b)                                   15m; D3–
Originally composed for recorder. In seven movements, the longest of these sonatas.

Sonata in D (HWV 378)                                                       7m; D3–
Probably authentic; published only in 1979. Several fragments from other works are incorporated.

Sonata in A minor, 'Halle Sonata no. 1' (HWV 374)                          11m; D3–
This and the following two sonatas were published in 1730; their names come from a now discredited belief that they date from Handel's early years in Halle. They are considered of doubtful authenticity.

Sonata in E minor, 'Halle Sonata no. 2' (HWV 375)                          8m; D2+
Mainly put together from movements of other Handel works.

Sonata in B minor, 'Halle Sonata no. 3' (HWV 376)                          8m; D2+

*Oboe*
There are three authentic sonatas for oboe. Others are sometimes played, of which one is included here.

Sonata in B♭ (HWV 357)                                                      7m; D2+
In three movements.

Sonata in C minor, op. 1 no. 8 (HWV 366)                                    7m; D3–

Sonata in F, op. 1 no. 5 (HWV 363a)                                         8m; D2+
In five movements. It appeared in op. 1 arranged for flute. The final movement (a minuet) is well known in arrangements out of context.

Sonata in G minor, op. 1 no. 6 (HWV 364a)      6m; D2+

This was written as a violin sonata but published in op. 1 for oboe (despite the last movement including notes below the oboe compass! They are transposed up in modern editions).

## Recorder

Six recorder sonatas are considered authentic.

Sonata in G minor, op. 1 no. 2 (HWV 360)      8m; D2

Sonata in A minor, op. 1 no. 4 (HWV 362)      11m; D2+

Sonata in C, op. 1 no. 7 (HWV 365)      11m; D2+

In five movements.

Sonata in D minor, op. 1 no. 9a (HWV 367a)      15m; D3−

A seven-movement work. It was published as a flute sonata.

Sonata in F, op. 1 no. 11 (HWV 369)      8m; D3−

Sonata in B♭ (HWV 377)      6m; D2+

In three movements.

# HAYDN
### 1732–1809; Austria

Joseph Haydn is the earliest of the four great composers of the classical period, and played a major part in establishing the character of the period's music. Both Mozart and Beethoven knew him and were influenced by him. He was a relatively late developer: although he composed extensively in the 1750s and 1760s, arguably he did not produce works of real importance until past 1770. He played the keyboard and the violin to a good standard, but virtuoso performance played no part in his career. From 1761 to 1790 his life was centred on his employment by the Esterházy family, for most of the period as Kapellmeister. Through the publication of his works he gradually became widely known, and by the 1780s was the most famous composer of the day. His role as Kapellmeister required him to live at the Esterházys' palace far from Vienna, though he was able sometimes to visit the city. From about 1781 he enjoyed a friendship with Mozart, which including their playing string quartets together (Mozart playing the viola, the other players being Vanhal (cello) and Dittersdorf). After 1790, although an association with the Esterházys continued, residence was no longer required, and he was free to live elsewhere and to travel. In 1791–2 and 1794–5 he paid two eighteen-month visits to England.

Haydn did not invent the combination of two violins, viola and cello; his early years in the 1750s coincided with a period when many composers were beginning to write for it. However, with his works for the combination over the next three decades and more, it was largely he who established the string quartet as we know it, having four movements and with contents that make it a high art-form.

Haydn was a highly prolific composer. So were others of his time: but he was unique in producing such large numbers of major masterpieces. In chamber music, this applies above all to his string quartets. He is the earliest composer who today has a place in the string quartet repertoire, and it is still a supreme place. Concert programmes probably include a string quartet by Haydn more often than they do those of any other composer. This dominance applies even more to playing by amateurs, for as well as being superb music, they are playable.

He also produced an important series of piano trios.

For other groupings, too, he composed a great deal: however, most of this is early, and all of it is minor. There is also some confusion, and much of what is available is arranged from other music (sometimes not even by Haydn). Potential sources for arrangements include his numerous small chamber works involving the baryton (an obsolete string instrument, which was played by his employer Prince Nikolaus Esterházy). Having an opus number does not necessarily imply authenticity; and publications may not state that works are arrangements.

Cataloguing Haydn's music – a vast task – was undertaken beginning in the 1930s by the Dutch-born musicologist Anthony van Hoboken. Numbers from the Hoboken catalogue are widely used. Works are listed in groups: Group III is string quartets; XV is piano trios. Thus, for example, the string quartet op. 1 no. 1 is identified as Hob.III:1 (the exact form of presentation can vary, and Hob. is sometimes reduced to H). Numbering in each group is intended to be chronological. Continuing scholarship, however, has by now shown that the Hoboken lists are far from correct; nor does possession of a Hoboken number necessarily imply authenticity. Nevertheless, the Hoboken numbers identify works unambiguously.

## String Duos

Six sonatas (Hob.VI:1–6) (c.1769) (violin, viola)          11–14m; D3+ (viola easier)
These sonatas, also called duos, are minor but are attractive music. However, the violin part is essentially a solo and is quite technically demanding, whereas the role of the viola is entirely accompaniment.

—•••—

Also published are various arrangements of other works by Haydn, not made or authorized by him. Some are more equal in their distribution of musical and technical interest than are the authentic sonatas, so may be more enjoyable to play.

They include three sonatas for violin and viola, op. 93, and three duets for two violins, op. 99.

## String Trios

The only authentic string trios are minor works, dating from before 1767. Just one is for violin, viola and cello, all the rest being for two violins and cello.

String trio in B♭ (Hob.V:8) (violin, viola, cello)                                        14m; D2
This is a three-movement work, but of small musical scope. Most of its duration is occupied by the first movement *Adagio*, which is a set of variations. Little interest is given to the cello.

Seventeen string trios (Hob.V:1–4, 6, 7, 10–13, 15–21) (2 violins, cello)     7–21m; D3
Though again mostly modest, a few include some more musically significant material. Most are in three movements. Haydn was still thinking in the old trio sonata tradition, and their interest (and technical difficulty) is concentrated in the violins, particularly the first violin. The cello does little other than supply the bass. Many of these trios were originally published as members of sets opp. 3, 5 and 6.

•••••

Other published string trios, usually for violin, viola and cello, are all arrangements. Examples are three trios, op. 53 (arranged from piano sonatas) and three trios, op. 32 (which originated as trios for baryton, viola and cello).

## String Quartets

For many amateur ensembles Haydn's string quartets are the basis of the repertoire. Technically they can be quite demanding, especially for the first violin; but they are within the range or at least aspiration of all amateurs. Musically almost all of the mature quartets are superb. There are so many of them that few players can hold them all clearly in the memory: even after decades of experience a Haydn quartet may be put up that seems completely unfamiliar – but is usually a delight.

Traditionally, the number of Haydn's string quartets was given as eighty-three. The accepted number today, however, is sixty-eight. This number still includes early works, one oddity and one unfinished quartet.

Most of Haydn's quartets were written in sets of six. Each set has an opus number, or in some cases two, one for each half-set of three. Very helpfully – and remarkably, considering the typical confusion of opus numbers in this period – this numbering is entirely in chronological order. The opus numbers remain the normal way of identifying the quartets, even in modern scholarly editions. The Hoboken numbers are also often given, but for the string quartets they are not actually very useful – they still reflect the old total of eighty-three quartets.

Quartets are also sometimes referred to by chronological number, but since over the years these have changed they are potentially ambiguous and so best avoided. Some of the individual quartets have a nickname (never given by Haydn), as do some of the sets.

The first set of quartets that can be said unreservedly all to be masterpieces is op. 20. Every subsequent quartet, too, is a masterpiece with the possible exception of the singleton op. 42 and of op. 103 because it is unfinished. The total of these masterpieces may be put at forty-four. The earlier works nevertheless include much music of interest, and perhaps a few masterpieces.

A significant aspect of Haydn's writing for string quartet concerns the distribution of the musical interest among the instruments. Unlike most other great composers for string quartet, Haydn often gives most of the significant material to the first violin, the material for the other voices being mainly subsidiary. This is most marked in the early works. With op. 20 and subsequent sets Haydn treated the parts more equally, with a good distribution of musical interest to all players. Nevertheless, the tendency to dominance by the first violin still sometimes appears. Along with this dominance sometimes goes technical difficulty – so for amateur ensembles, a capable player of the first violin part is desirable.

When writing in sonata form (almost always the case in his first movements), Haydn often marked both halves – the exposition and the development with recapitulation – to be repeated. Mozart frequently did the same, but thereafter the second repeat was unusual.

A form of which Haydn was fond, and which remained largely his own, is that of alternating variations (also called double variations). This is a set of variations based on two contrasting themes, one in a minor key and the other in the major, which appear in alternate variations. Several quartets have a movement in this form; Haydn also used it in symphonies and other works.

In some non-urtext editions, several quartets include a movement with the tempo indication *Allegro spirituoso*. This is a rather laughable misspelling of Haydn's *Allegro spiritoso*.

In addition to the duration and difficulty indications for each quartet in the list that follows, two further parameters are given. The first indicates which volume of the four-volume Peters complete edition of the quartets in parts contains the particular quartet. (Some editions by other publishers including Kalmus and International also follow this layout.) These old editions are widely distributed and remain the cheapest way of purchasing the complete quartets – though more modern editions are now available from these and other publishers, which alongside other merits are organized more logically. An incidental factor is that the quartets included in the less expensive Volumes I and II of these old editions tend to be better known. The second parameter is a suggested indication of the value of the quartet in terms of musical quality and enjoyment of playing. This is from one to five stars (*****), where five is highest. The great majority of those from op. 20 onwards are given five stars.

---

The quartets of opp. 1 and 2 were probably composed in the second half of the 1750s, perhaps between 1757 and 1759. Their grouping as two sets of six under these opus numbers was subsequently carried out by publishers; there seems to be no reason to believe that the quartets of op. 2 were written later than those of op. 1. Moreover, three of these twelve works are now recognized as not really being string quartets at all, but arrangements (probably not by Haydn) of other works. However, one further genuine quartet belonging to these sets has been found, and is now known as op. 1 no. 0, or sometimes as op. 0. So Haydn composed ten quartets here. The three works that are not really string quartets are nevertheless included below, since they still appear in the older editions. They are not necessarily less enjoyable to play than their authentic fellows.

These works date from a time when many composers were beginning to write for four solo string instruments without continuo, but before the establishment of the string quartet as we now know it. It was also early in Haydn's career when, although a capable composer, he was not yet clearly a genius. So these are mostly pleasant but not great works. Haydn called them divertimenti (they are sometimes referred to as divertimento quartets); they are similar to other such works by Haydn and many other composers of the time for various instrumental combinations. They are all in major keys, have five movements, and mostly have the same layout. Their character is cheerful and lightweight and their scope is small, with little development of their material. The outer movements are fast, while the second and fourth are minuets. The third, central movement is normally slow and is often largely a first violin solo. Their texture is simple and lacks many of the features of later string quartet writing. Sometimes they are written in two parts, each played by two instruments in octaves. Interest is concentrated in the first violin part, often supported by the second violin. The viola and cello parts are less interesting; solos for the viola occur occasionally, but for the cello rarely.

Many players will play these quartets simply because they possess the parts, included in a complete edition. They are worth sight-reading through once, but that perhaps will be all. Moreover their texture, with limited interest for the viola and especially the cello, limits their interest for playing. However, they are perhaps the easiest quartets by any major composer, so they have a real value for those lacking experience or technical ability. In this they may be compared to the early Mozart quartets: these are easier, but they mostly fall short of Mozart's in musical quality.

Op. 1 no. 1 (Hob.III:1) in B♭                                    16m; D2; Vol. IV; *
Sometimes known, from the 6/8 first movement, as 'La Chasse' ('The Hunt'). This

is typical of these quartets: simple but attractive, sometimes with interest for all players, but more often uninspiring for the lower parts.

Op. 1 no. 2 (Hob.III:2) in E♭                                    18m; D2; Vol. IV; *
Again typical.

Op. 1 no. 3 (Hob.III:3) in D                                    15m; D2; Vol. IV; **
This differs from the usual layout in beginning with an *Adagio*, and having as its central movement a brief *Presto*. Musically this is one of the best of these quartets. The violins will enjoy the trio sonata-like duetting of the first movement. The trio of the second minuet, with its refreshing scoring giving full involvement to all (including the cello) is almost captivating.

Op. 1 no. 4 (Hob.III:4) in G                                    21m; D2+; Vol. IV; **
Some of this is quite attractive, especially the first two movements.

Op. 1 no. 5 (Hob.III:5) in B♭                                   14m; D3; Vol. IV; *
Not a string quartet: this three-movement work is what is known as 'Symphony A' (Hob.I:107), with the wind parts omitted. It may be enjoyed, mainly by the violins, but it is not excellent.

Op. 1 no. 0 (Hob.II:6) in E♭                                    17m; D2; Vol. N/A; *
Also referred to as op. 0 or as 'String Quartet no. 5', it is thought that early publishers replaced this by the spurious op. 1 no. 5. Its identity was rediscovered in 1931. It is typical, though the first and second movements are unusually democratic.

Op. 1 no. 6 (Hob.III:6) in C                                    18m; D2–; Vol. IV; *
Nothing special musically. The last two movements are best, with a fairly democratic distribution of interest. However, it is technically very straightforward, so suitable for beginners.

Op. 2 no. 1 (Hob.III:7) in A                                    17m; D2+; Vol. IV; **
This is one of the best of these early quartets. Interest is fairly well distributed, and all the movements are attractive; the *Poco adagio* is particularly beautiful.

Op. 2 no. 2 (Hob.III:8) in E                                    21m; D2; Vol. IV; *
Attractive, though interesting material for viola or cello is rare.

Op. 2 no. 3 (Hob.III:9) in E♭                                   18m; D2; Vol. IV; **
Not composed as a string quartet: it is really the divertimento for two horns and strings, Hob.II:21. However, this fact should not put one off: this is one of the more attractive works of the set. The horn parts in the original are generally unimportant, and the five-movement structure is almost the same as that of the works written for string quartet. It has, however, one surprising feature: after the trio of the second

minuet, three variations follow before the *Da Capo* is taken. Remarkably, the first variation is a viola solo.

### Op. 2 no. 4 (Hob.III:10) in F
20m; D2; Vol. IV; *

Generally typical. The F minor *Adagio non troppo* would be fine were its interest not so confined to the first violin.

### Op. 2 no. 5 (Hob.III:11) in D
15m; D2; Vol. IV; *

Not a string quartet: as with no. 3, this was originally a divertimento for two horns and strings (in this case, Hob.II:22). It is pleasant but unexceptional; it is not inferior to those members of the opus that are authentically for string quartet.

### Op. 2 no. 6 (Hob.III:12) in B♭
19m; D2+; Vol. IV; **

Like op. 1 no. 3, this starts with an *Adagio* (here a set of variations) and has as its central movement a *Presto* (in this case a scherzo, though not so named). This is one of the best of these quartets.

----

The six quartets of op. 3 are a very different matter. Since the publication of a paper about them in 1964, it has mostly been accepted that they are not by Haydn: the otherwise little-known Roman Hoffstetter is considered their probable composer. However, they remain widely available in older editions of Haydn's quartets; and some pre-1964 musicologists saw them as showing Haydn's progress since opp. 1 and 2. A dispassionate judgement might be that they are uneven, but the best are better than anything in opp. 1 and 2. Their character differs somewhat from those works. None have the five-movement divertimento plan; most are in four movements. Although most interest is given to the violins, the viola and the cello are a little more emancipated. They include one particularly popular movement (the Serenade in no. 5). So players who possess the sheet music should not ignore them. Hoffstetter was an avowed admirer of Haydn (and also an ordained monk): he deserves our admiration for apparently having composed works accepted for a century and a half as by the master!

### Op. 3 no. 1 (Hob.III:13) in E
16m; D2+; Vol. IV; *

The first two movements are quite good, but overall this is disappointing.

### Op. 3 no. 2 (Hob.III:14) in C
18m; D2; Vol. IV; **

Unpretentious but modestly enjoyable for all players throughout. There are only three movements, the first a set of variations.

### Op. 3 no. 3 (Hob.III:15) in G
18m; D2+ (first violin harder); Vol. II; ***

Excellent and entertaining. The writing gives good interest to all players, but there is some demanding figuration for the first violin. In the third movement, sometimes called the 'bagpipes minuet', the double-stopped bagpipes theme is given to the viola as well as to the first violin.

<u>Op. 3 no. 4 (Hob.III:16) in B♭</u>           10m; D2; Vol. IV; *
Strange; not worth attention. It has only two movements: might they be unrelated fragments put together by a publisher?

<u>Op. 3 no. 5 (Hob.III:17) in F</u>           16m; D2+; Vol. II; **
The second movement *Andante cantabile* was famous (often in arrangements) as 'Haydn's Serenade' – and it seems to have kept this celebrity despite the probable change of authorship. It is an attractive movement, but as entirely a violin solo with pizzicato accompaniment it is not delightful for the lower players. However, all parts in this movement (including the first violin) are technically very easy, so it is playable by beginners. The rest of the quartet is more democratic.

<u>Op. 3 no. 6 (Hob.III:18) in A</u>           16m; D2+; Vol. IV; *
Consistent, but nothing special. The fast dotted quaver-semiquaver figuration in the first movement will be found tricky by some.

---

About a decade elapsed between opp. 1 and 2 and Haydn's next set of quartets, op. 9, composed perhaps in 1769. Op. 17 followed probably in 1771. With these sets we enter a different world. Haydn's musical personality was developing rapidly, and these may be considered his first true string quartets. Nevertheless, they are transitional works in a development that we see in its fullest form only in the set following these two. All now have four movements, with fast outer movements, a minuet second and a slow movement third. However, unlike the *Presto* first movements of the earlier works, many of the opening movements are now *Moderato*. The scale has grown. The first movement is strong and lengthy, usually in sonata form, with a much more elaborate development section than has been seen previously. The other movements are correspondingly more weighty. Their content has grown in its emotional significance. Both sets include one work in a minor key – a pattern that became standard in most subsequent sets. This probably reflects the influence of the *Sturm und Drang* ('storm and stress') movement seen also in German literature of the period, which leads to more expression of emotion and sadness. In fact the minor-key works of these two sets are often considered the finest. Technically the writing has become a good deal more demanding. The first violin parts are more virtuosic in terms of speed, athleticism, and heights reached; the other parts, too, participate (to a lesser degree) in this development. However, the first violin continues to dominate, and especially in op. 9 there are some passages of showy technique. The freedom of the viola and cello parts is still limited.

The advances found in op. 9 appear more extensively in op. 17. Both sets are worth playing. But although they contain one or two very fine works, on the whole they are still to be regarded as immature.

Op. 9 no. 1 (Hob.III:19) in C                 22m; D3; Vol. III; ***

An excellent introduction to the opus. All movements are good, and although the first violin carries most of the responsibility, the increased emancipation of the lower parts is evident throughout.

Op. 9 no. 2 (Hob.III:20) in E♭      18m; D3 (first violin harder); Vol. I; ***

This, too, is a beautiful quartet, which all players will probably enjoy; but the distribution of musical interest to the lower parts is limited. The first violin part has some technically brilliant writing that many players will need to practise in advance.

Op. 9 no. 3 (Hob.III:21) in G              19m; D3; Vol. III; **

The first two movements are undemocratic and of limited musical interest; but the third and fourth movements are good. At two pauses in the third-movement *Largo*, ideally the first violin should improvise (or have prepared!) a cadenza.

Op. 9 no. 4 (Hob.III:22) in D minor      21m; D3; Vol. III; ****

Haydn's first quartet in a minor key, and surely the finest quartet he had yet written. It is powerful and sombre, and all movements are good. Moreover, it is more democratic than any previous quartet – especially in the first and last movements. It is not unduly difficult. Some hilarious tossing about of notes between the players in the finale is guaranteed to raise a smile – whether or not negotiated successfully!

Op. 9 no. 5 (Hob.III:23) in B♭          23m; D3; Vol. III; ***

One of the best quartets of this set: the music is good, and most movements offer some enjoyable independence for the lower parts. Unlike the usual pattern, the first movement is slow, in the form of variations. First violin agility is demanded in the last movement.

Op. 9 no. 6 (Hob.III:24) in A            18m; D3; Vol. III; **

There are some enjoyable sections but overall this quartet is not outstanding. The finale is strangely brief and trivial.

Op. 17 no. 1 (Hob.III:25) in E          22m; D3; Vol. III; ***

An attractive, mostly gentle quartet, with sufficient interest distributed to the lower parts to make it an enjoyable play.

Op. 17 no. 2 (Hob.III:26) in F          18m; D3; Vol. III; ***

Not of strongly marked character, but mostly an enjoyable quartet. However, the slow movement is almost entirely a first-violin solo and relatively dull for the others.

<u>Op. 17 no. 3 (Hob.III:27) in E♭</u>                    20m; D3; Vol. III; ***

Good music throughout. The first movement variations and the slow movement give the thematic material too exclusively to the first violin. But other sections are excellent for all: notably the trio of the minuet, with its remarkably original texture, and the hilarious final movement, with the material tossed about contrapuntally. This movement also demands some first-violin display.

<u>Op. 17 no. 4 (Hob.III:28) in C minor</u>                    22m; D3; Vol. III; ****

A fine C-minor work, perhaps the best of the set. Much of it gives good interest to the lower parts. Particularly striking are the first movement, the subtle and thoughtful minor-key trio of the minuet and the very contrapuntal finale.

<u>Op. 17 no. 5 (Hob.III:29) in G</u>                    19m; D3; Vol. I; ***

Perhaps not among the best of this set, but it is attractive and has interest. The slow movement is unusual, with sections marked 'Recitative' (which is sometimes used as a nickname for the quartet): the first violin takes the part of an operatic soloist, with the remaining players as the orchestra. Before sight-reading, first violins may be advised to look at some technical passages, especially in the outer movements.

<u>Op. 17 no. 6 (Hob.III:30) in D</u>                    19m; D3; Vol. III; ***

Musically gentle but delightful throughout. However, for the first three movements most interest is in the first violin part. The third movement *Largo* provides interesting accompaniments for second violin and viola throughout, but not for the cello. Amends are made, however, in the very contrapuntal finale which, for once in this set, has excellently distributed interest. The first violin has double-stopped passages in the slow movement that will be manageable by most – but to play them really beautifully would demand virtuoso technique.

---

The op. 20 quartets, known as the 'Sun Quartets' from the image on the title page of an early edition, were written in 1772. Though composed probably only one year after op. 17, they represent a dramatic advance from that set. (However, surprisingly, Haydn still called them *Divertimenti a Quattro*.) These are the first of Haydn's quartets that may be considered uniformly to be masterpieces. In their scale and aesthetic significance, they bring to the string quartet as a medium the qualities it has retained ever since. They have a new level of intellectual value and emotional meaning. The influence on Haydn of the *Sturm und Drang* movement here reached a peak. This is his only set of quartets to have two works in minor keys; and in these and other quartets of the set there are movements that display a remarkable intensity of emotion. They also include a greater emphasis than hitherto on counterpoint. This is seen throughout, and moreover three of the finales are full-scale fugues (a form that Haydn after this set only once again employed).

They also extend the exploitation of the different instruments with their distinctive characters, giving much-increased freedom and melodic use to the cello and viola. Alongside this, they largely abandon the technically brilliant writing for the first violin that sometimes appeared in the preceding sets. This new democracy is most evident in the first four quartets of the set. In layout, the main change is that in three quartets the minuet now comes third.

With hindsight, we can see that in his subsequent sets of quartets Haydn's writing developed a good deal further: but this does not make the op. 20 quartets inferior. They are fully part of the canon of Haydn's great string quartets.

### Op. 20 no. 1 (Hob.III:31) in E♭                    21m; D3–; Vol. IV; *****

This is, perhaps, not a quartet that will be popular with everyone: it is calm and its general dynamic is quiet; there is little passion or drama. But it is a very fine work: subtle, original and delightful. In this first work of op. 20, Haydn immediately shows the new, fully democratic texture he has reached, full of interest for every-one. Technically it is straightforward, though there are rhythmic complications in the finale. It also needs care over choice of tempo in order to realize its musical qualities (particularly in the slow movement, ambiguously marked *Affettuoso e sostenuto*).

### Op. 20 no. 2 (Hob.III:32) in C                    21m; D3; Vol. IV; *****

Again remarkably original in character. This applies especially to the *Adagio*, which is in the minor key and is intense and dramatic in an operatic manner, with power-ful unison passages. Also noticeable in the very democratic texture of this quartet is that the cello seems to be treated with special favour. Melodies are given to the cello in each of the first three movements; the last movement is a fugue, which by definition is democratic.

### Op. 20 no. 3 (Hob.III:33) in G minor              23m; D3; Vol. IV; *****

This is another excellent quartet. Its character is unusual and sometimes quirky, which perhaps explains why it is not one of the most popular among listeners. But the ensemble writing is excellent and it is highly interesting and enjoyable to play.

### Op. 20 no. 4 (Hob.III:34) in D                    24m; D3; Vol. II; *****

For some players, of all parts, this is the favourite of the set – and this seems true also with audiences. Every movement is of marked personality, as is illustrated by their unusual indications: second movement *Un poco Adagio, affettuoso*; third movement minuet *Allegretto alla zingarese* ('Allegretto in gypsy style'); and finale *Presto scherzando*. The slow second movement is a set of variations, and has remarkable heart-on-sleeve emotion. Cello and second violin will especially enjoy the variations given to them; the second violin variation also gives an important role to the viola. The trio of the minuet is another solo for the cello. In the finale, some hilariously disruptive comments are provided by the second violin.

### Op. 20 no. 5 (Hob.III:35) in F minor          22m; D3; Vol. II; *****

A powerful and sombre work; everything except the trio of the minuet and the slow movement is in the minor key. The finale is a fugue. Although most will find the excellent music makes it enjoyable to play, apart from the finale this quartet gives much less freedom to the viola and cello than do most others of the set. Second violin fares better.

### Op. 20 no. 6 (Hob.III:36) in A          18m; D3+; Vol. II; ****

The shortest quartet of the set. Much of it is light and humorous in character; the last movement is a fugue. Though musically good, in the first two movements Haydn disappointingly abandons his new-found democratic writing, and the viola and cello parts have little of interest. The first violin part in these movements is particularly demanding, and advance preparation will be essential for some. In the *Adagio cantabile* second movement the second violin has an enjoyable semiquaver accompanying role to the first violin soloist. The fugue is quite difficult for everyone.

---

Almost another decade elapsed before Haydn in 1781 produced his next set of string quartets, op. 33. These are nicknamed the 'Russian Quartets' (from their Russian dedicatee). Haydn described them as being written 'in a new and special manner'. By this he must have meant many things. There are structural innovations, including a perhaps more mature approach to sonata form. The title 'minuet' is replaced by 'scherzo' or 'scherzando' – though in many their minuet character has not changed. This movement still comes second in four of the quartets. Finales are often in rondo or variation form. But the most important aspects of the 'new way' are in the writing itself – especially in that counterpoint has become a natural part of the writing. There are no strict fugues here, or strict counterpoint: the art is concealed, but thematic material is more widely shared among the parts. Also gone is the frequent seriousness and emotion of op. 20: these quartets are shorter, lighter in character, and often use humour. Democracy continues, with interest frequently given to the lower parts. The style of writing established in these quartets largely continues throughout Haydn's remaining output.

These quartets are all unquestioned masterpieces. Mozart came to know Haydn personally about this time, and it was these quartets that stimulated Mozart to the composition of the great set of six quartets that he dedicated to Haydn.

### Op. 33 no. 1 (Hob.III:37) in B minor          18m; D3; Vol. IV; *****

An excellent quartet – powerful and consistent in its quality: all movements are equally good. It is also excellently democratic and is equally enjoyable for all players. The finale, driving single-mindedly to its B minor ending, makes considerable technical demands on the first violin.

Op. 33 no. 2 (Hob.III:38) in E♭ ('The Joke')                17m; D3; Vol. II; *****

The first three movements of this quartet are warm and beautiful. Especially fine is the *Largo sostenuto* third movement, which opens with its eight-bar theme presented by viola and cello alone. The finale, however, is entirely light and amusing in character – and it contains the joke, which hinges on the uncertainty as to when it will end. It never fails to raise a smile. This is an enjoyable quartet to play, though it is somewhat centred on the first violin.

Op. 33 no. 3 (Hob.III:39) in C ('The Bird')                19m; D3–; Vol. II; *****

Sunny throughout: this is one of the most charming of all Haydn's quartets. The nickname most obviously applies to the pervasive grace-note figures in the first movement, and to the chirpy duet for two violins that forms the trio of the scherzando; it can seem appropriate to the last movement too. The writing is democratic; and technically all four parts are unusually straightforward, making the quartet a delight to play for all and suitable for players of most standards. However, to achieve clean and accurate playing of the last movement at a real *Presto* speed is difficult.

Op. 33 no. 4 (Hob.III:40) in B♭                17m; D3; Vol. IV; *****

This is a rather quirky quartet, and some may be unconvinced by the first three movements, which are perhaps not very obvious in their musical attractions. However, with its perky energy, it is very consistent; and the hilarious comedy of the final movement is surely irresistible. Moreover, all movements give plenty of interest to all players. If at first you don't like this quartet, try it again!

Op. 33 no. 5 (Hob.III:41) in G                19m; D3; Vol. IV; *****

Sometimes known as 'How do you do?' from its polite two-bar opening. It is mainly vivacious and entertaining. It is not distinguished for its democracy, but enough interest is distributed that all will enjoy it. The *Largo* second movement, largely a first violin solo, is very beautiful. The third movement scherzo is the first fully to have a scherzo feeling. The finale is a modest but enjoyable set of variations on a *Siciliano* (and was probably the inspiration for Mozart's comparable movement in his D minor quartet).

Op. 33 no. 6 (Hob.III:42) in D                17m; D3; Vol. II; *****

Not very well known: it is mostly quiet, and has perhaps no especially distinctive features. But it is one of the most enjoyable to play. One factor is that it is so democratic, with every movement giving all players variety and plenty of opportunities to lead the ensemble. The very beautiful *Andante* second movement is, contrary to Haydn's frequent custom, not a first-violin solo. The scherzo, marked *Allegro,* is often played at minuet speed, but it also works well fast, when it is more fun and has more scherzo feeling. In the trio, tempo is the cellist's choice as it starts with a solo. The finale, though quite short, is in alternating variation form. More leadership comes to the cello in the two minor-key variations.

### Op. 42 (Hob.III:43) in D minor (1785)                    13m; D2; Vol. III; ***

A puzzle: a solitary work, small in its dimensions, technical demands and musical scope. The reason for Haydn writing it remains unknown, though it is possible that it was associated with a commission from Spain for three short quartets. That it was intended for beginners seems plausible. However, the writing is democratic, and it is worth playing.

Haydn's next set of six quartets is op. 50, which was written over several years and published in 1787. It is dedicated to King Frederick William II of Prussia who was an amateur cellist, perhaps quite capable; Mozart and Beethoven, too, both wrote works for him. No doubt with the dedicatee in mind, their cello parts are distinctly more free than hitherto – which also means they are sometimes more difficult. Some of this additional democracy extends also to the viola. The extra freedom is, however, much less marked than it was later to be in the quartets that Mozart wrote intended for the king. These quartets are generally longer than those of op. 33, and at least some are more ambitious and more serious. The designation 'scherzo' used in op. 33 has disappeared (never to reappear) in favour of a return to 'minuet': this movement is now always placed third. Of these very fine quartets, the last three are the best-known and perhaps the most striking, but from the point of view of players the first three are every bit as enjoyable.

### Op. 50 no. 1 (Hob.III:44) in B♭                    22m; D3; Vol. III; *****

Calm, gentle and mostly light-hearted: this quartet is a delight for the players. It is very democratic, and the additional attention given to the cello is noticeable. The second movement is a set of variations. The finale is full of Haydn's humour; a two-bar silence near the end may remind one of 'The Joke' (op. 33 no. 2).

### Op. 50 no. 2 (Hob.III:45) in C                    21m; D3+; Vol. III; *****

As with all of this set, the writing gives good opportunities to all players. It is mainly beautiful and thoughtful but not profound. The first movement is striking for its extensive counterpoint. The lovely second movement *Adagio* is far from being a violin solo: interest is distributed to everyone. In it, the direction to the first violin *a piacere* ('at pleasure') indicates where a cadenza might be played. The finale is playful and hilarious; but to work well it has to go fast, which makes it quite difficult.

### Op. 50 no. 3 (Hob.III:46) in E♭                    20m; D3; Vol. III; *****

Once again a quartet that is entirely charming for the players, and distributes the interest excellently. Particularly gratifying to the cello are the second movement variations: the cello presents the theme at the opening accompanied by viola alone, and there are several further solos. Towards the end of the third movement minuet there is even a pause where a cellist wishing to grasp every opportunity could improvise a short cadenza. The *Presto* finale dashes along with tremendous zest but is not actually very difficult; it has an amusing throw-away *pianissimo* ending.

<u>Op. 50 no. 4 (Hob.III:47) in F♯ minor</u>                    20m; D3+; Vol. III; *****
In its whole mood and character, this quartet in its unusual key is very different from its predecessors. It is a tough and very fine work, but there is little of light entertainment here. All parts again have excellent interest, but the key immediately makes it difficult to play. The second movement is a set of alternating variations, introduced to powerful effect by the cello. Also very fine is the minuet, in F♯ major, with a very contrapuntal trio in the minor. The finale is a fugue – Haydn's only string quartet fugue after those of op. 20. It remains minor to the end, and though short is uncompromising and powerful. Because of its technical and musical difficulty this quartet might be better avoided in sight-reading: playing it after some preparation can be more rewarding.

<u>Op. 50 no. 5 (Hob.III:48) in F</u>                    17m; D3; Vol. III; *****
This quartet is a great contrast to its predecessor: happy, gentle, innocent and charming. It is also the shortest of the set. It is excellent to play, with interest well distributed throughout. Some may find the fast triplet semiquavers in the first movement tricky – but they are not seriously difficult. The slow movement, with its continual, almost trance-like gentle movement, is known as 'The Dream', which is sometimes used as a nickname for the quartet.

<u>Op. 50 no. 6 (Hob.III:49) in D ('The Frog')</u>                    23m; D3+; Vol. I; *****
This is the best-known quartet of the set. It is powerful, very fine and strikingly original. It is also mostly serious. The writing is democratic: all instruments, especially perhaps the cello, make plenty of individual contributions. The second movement *Poco adagio*, in D minor and powerfully sombre, is particularly distinctive. Also strong and serious is the minuet, which has an unusually long trio. The bariolage effects in the finale (which give the quartet its nickname) are a part of the originality of its writing. Other than for the first violin, they are always on the same note, and one is usually an open string. Some viola players, therefore, will be dismayed to find that the last four bars have it on A, across the G and C strings – an awkward stretch. Since the part lies below two others also doing bariolage, a cheat may be permissible!

———

<u>Op. 51 (Hob.III:50–56) The Seven Last Words of Our Saviour on the Cross</u>
                    66m; D3; Vol. IV; ***
This comes next in the chronological sequence, is included in the old complete editions of the string quartets, and is listed in the string quartet section of the

123

Hoboken catalogue. However, it is not in any normal sense a string quartet or set of quartets. It was written in 1787 in response to a commission from Cádiz in Spain for a series of pieces to be performed at a service on Good Friday. For each of the 'words' (actually sentences), the words were pronounced, followed by a sermon; the applicable movement would then be performed. Haydn wrote it for orchestra, but then provided an alternative for string quartet. (He later produced a choral version as a sort of oratorio, and also approved an arrangement for piano.) The string quartet version is today perhaps the best-known. There are in total nine pieces, with the seven 'words' entitled sonatas, as follows:

Introduzione in D minor – *Maestoso ed Adagio*
Sonata I in B♭ (Hob.III:50) – *Largo*
Sonata II in C minor (Hob.III:51) – *Grave e cantabile*
Sonata III in E (Hob.III:52) – *Grave*
Sonata IV in F minor (Hob.III:53) – *Largo*
Sonata V in A (Hob.III:54) – *Adagio*
Sonata VI in G minor (Hob.III:55) – *Lento*
Sonata VII in B♭ (Hob.III:56) – *Largo*
*Il Terremoto* in C minor – *Presto e con tutta la forza*

These movements are very different from most Haydn string quartet slow movements. Their context is serious and deeply religious, and so is the music. They lack warmth; and that they were not conceived for string quartet sometimes shows. However, in their way they are fine, and in many sections their musical interest is well distributed among the players. It does not make sense to try to play this sequence of very slow movements as a single work. In order to explore them, just one movement might on occasion be played, alongside other music. All the slow movements are technically straightforward. The short final movement, *Il Terremoto* ('the earthquake'), is much more difficult mainly because of its speed, but it is manageable with advance practice.

The twelve quartets of opps. 54 and 55 (two half-sets) and 64, written between 1788 and 1790, are together known as the 'Tost Quartets', from their association with Johann Tost, a minor figure but a good violinist and a friend of Haydn. This seems to be responsible for several of them having a degree of virtuoso figuration in the first violin part. There are also a few movements in which the first violin dominates, but this is not a general characteristic. Indeed, some of these quartets are as democratic as any in op. 50. At least two – op. 54 no. 2 and op. 55 no. 2 – seem experimental in the unusual and surprising layouts of their movements. Two others revert to Haydn's earlier placing of the minuet second rather than third.

Op. 54 no. 1 (Hob.III:58) in G                    19m; D3; Vol. I; ****

This is not the best quartet with which to try to convert someone sceptical about Haydn's music. The first two movements in particular have repeated quavers that chug along almost continuously and can seem prosaic or unduly hearty. That said, however, this quartet is good music and is good to play. Much of it, especially the outer movements, distributes the interest well. The trio of the minuet is especially delightful, with entertainment for everyone and a most gratifying cello part.

Op. 54 no. 2 (Hob.III:57) in C                    20m; D3+; Vol. I; *****

An outstanding work: indeed, for many players a best-loved quartet. All movements are equally good, though very different. However, some of it is very unusual. The first movement is bold, vigorous and masculine; it is enjoyable for all, though much of the burden lies in the first violin part, which has some quite difficult notes. Hauntingly memorable is the following C minor *Adagio*. The lower instruments play a sombre but beautiful melody, over which the first violin has very free rhapsodic ornamentation of Hungarian or gypsy inspiration. Less experienced quartets may find this movement difficult, the problem being to coordinate the melody and the ornamentation. It is not a case of the first violin leading and the others following: the second violin leads the lower parts, and they and the first violin must mutually watch and listen in order to keep together. The minuet follows without a break – also excellent, with a plaintive C minor trio. Most extraordinary is the last movement. It is another *Adagio*, though it contains a short *Presto* section as if making a gesture towards what is expected of a finale. Some musicologists criticize this movement: but to most players (particularly cellists) it is especially delightful. What is unique is its texture, in which the cello continually plays rising legato arpeggio figures, some of them reaching high into the treble clef.

Op. 54 no. 3 (Hob.III:59) in E                    23m; D3+; Vol. I; *****

Although one of the less-known of Haydn's mature quartets, this is an attractive, vigorous and enjoyable work. Its first-violin part is more demanding than most, particularly in the complex triplet quaver figurations of the first movement. The *Largo cantabile* second movement is very beautiful, although it includes some remarkably florid ornamentation for the first violin. Nevertheless, all movements have plenty of interest for all.

Op. 55 no. 1 (Hob.III:60) in A                    17m; D3; Vol. III; *****

Attractive music throughout: an excellent example of mature Haydn. Plenty of interest is distributed to all players, and there is little exploitation of first-violin brilliance. Enjoyable features one may remember are the written-out cadenza for all four instruments in the *Adagio cantabile* second movement, and the fugato which adds to the entertainment of the finale.

Op. 55 no. 2 (Hob.III:61) in F minor ('The Razor')      26m; D3+; Vol. III; *****
A story that appears in varying versions explains the nickname. This quartet
again has many non-standard features. Most strikingly, it begins with a long slow
movement, *Andante più tosto Allegretto*. This is in Haydn's alternating variation
form, the two themes being in F minor and F major. It is enjoyable for everyone,
but perhaps especially the cello. The following movements, too, are good to play,
though they are not entirely easy. The minuet is unusual, starting in just two parts
with the theme in the viola, and then giving the theme in succession to each instrument. In the trio, the cello is again treated generously. The *Presto* finale is most
entertaining and original, though some of the figuration for first violin is difficult.

Op. 55 no. 3 (Hob.III:62) in B♭      20m; D3; Vol. III; *****
There is plenty of originality and interest in this quartet, but it is much more
normal than its predecessor. It is delightful throughout, exceptionally democratic,
and one of the most enjoyable for players. No movement has any significant technical problems of either notes or ensemble, and the first violin part is unusually
straightforward.

Op. 64 no. 1 (Hob.III:65) in C      20m; D3; Vol. III; *****
Not well known, and indeed some critics consider this quartet a failure – based not
on structural shortcomings but on lack of attractiveness. But many find it delightful – the more so players, because this is perhaps the most democratic quartet that
Haydn ever wrote. All movements give everyone multiple opportunities to lead the
quartet. It is technically straightforward, and there is no difficult brilliance for the
first violin. Instead of a real slow movement, there is an *Allegretto scherzando* in
the form of variations. The material of the finale is humorously trivial, but from it
Haydn constructs a highly entertaining movement.

Op. 64 no. 2 (Hob.III:68) in B minor      19m; D3+; Vol. I; *****
A fine and serious quartet. It is not as democratic as some, the first violin part
being prominent even though it eschews brilliance. However, plenty of interest is
provided for the other parts. It is difficult to play, partly because of the awkward
key of B major that is used for the very beautiful *Adagio ma non troppo* second
movement, the trio of the minuet, and the last section of the *Presto* finale. This
finale has several silences of two bars' duration; amusingly, yet another is written
after the last notes have been played – leaving any listeners unsure whether it really
is the end.

Op. 64 no. 3 (Hob.III:67) in B♭      22m; D3; Vol. I; ****
Another less well-known quartet. It is good fun to play and not particularly difficult; but some of its material is not as charming as Haydn's best. Also, though
the lower parts are not dull, much of the emphasis is on the first violin or (as in the
*Adagio* second movement) on the two violins together.

Op. 64 no. 4 (Hob.III:66) in G                                    18m; D3; Vol. I; *****

Although it has no particularly memorable features, this is an attractive quartet, lightweight and charming throughout. For the first three movements, however, most of the main musical interest is given to the first violin; the trio of the minuet is simply a first-violin solo with pizzicato accompaniment. Indeed, this is a quartet with which the first violin might show off, because though prominent the notes are never technically difficult. The helter-skelter last movement is more democratic. Moreover, although in the earlier movements the lower players mostly have subsidiary material, this is often enjoyable to play.

Op. 64 no. 5 (Hob.III:63) in D ('The Lark')                       18m; D3+; Vol. II; *****

This is among the most popular of Haydn's string quartets. Its nickname well describes the singing melody given to the first violin in the opening movement. However, this movement has two other principal themes, and is full of interest for all players. Indeed, though the second movement is mainly a melody for the first violin, most of this quartet is democratic and enjoyable for all. Technically hardest (at least, for amateurs) is the *Vivace* finale, which opens on the first violin with fast running semiquavers. To have its effect, it must indeed go fast. The semiquaver motion is almost continuous, but the movement is not just a *perpetuum mobile*: there is an exciting fugato, and everyone gets quite enough of the semiquavers!

Op. 64 no. 6 (Hob.III:64) in E♭                                   18m; D3–; Vol. II; *****

A quartet particularly valuable for amateurs because technically, for all players including the first violin, it is one of Haydn's easiest. Musically it is not one of the most striking but it is all good; its atmosphere is gently meditative. The part-writing is excellent, with the musical interest democratically distributed to all. The second movement *Andante*, for example, has sinuously interweaving melodic lines in quavers for all four players. Only in its short minor-key middle section does the first violin play a solo with accompaniment from the remaining parts. The dashing energy of the last movement is highly entertaining but still somehow matches the gentle atmosphere of the rest. This quartet is or was sometimes known as 'The Railwayman', a nickname that hardly seems appropriate.

---

The next six quartets, published as two half-sets, opp. 71 and 74, are known from their dedicatee as the 'Apponyi Quartets'. They were written in 1793 after Haydn, having been freed from his ties to the Austrian court by the death of Prince Nicholas Esterházy, had undertaken his first eighteen-month visit to London. They differ considerably from any that had gone before because, though given in Austria to Count Apponyi, Haydn wrote them also for Salomon in London, where they were to be publicly performed. During his visit to London he had for the first time seen chamber music played before an audience in a concert hall, rather than it being only for 'the chamber'. So Haydn made changes in his way of writing with suitability for this purpose in mind. Most obviously, the quartets all open with an introductory gesture to draw the attention of the listeners, ranging from a loud chord to an eight-bar introduction. He employed instrumental textures that have bold gestures, brilliant passage-work and multiple-note chords. It is also suggested that, in consideration of an audience who were not necessarily musical connoisseurs, they have a more 'popular' melodic style.

Some observers have considered the three quartets of op. 71 to be by Haydn's standards poor – but that view is not shared here. Indeed, from the player's point of view, all six of these quartets are particularly enjoyable. They perhaps lack the intimacy of some of Haydn's earlier quartets, but the outgoing vigour of their material has an exhilarating quality. Moreover, they are very democratic.

### Op. 71 no. 1 (Hob.III:69) in B♭            22m; D3; Vol. IV; *****

This is immediately an excellent quartet. The outer movements are vigorous, extrovert music, and all movements are most attractive and also democratic. Particularly charming is the way the material of the *Adagio* second movement is when recapitulated enriched by grace notes in all parts.

### Op. 71 no. 2 (Hob.III:70) in D            18m; D3; Vol. IV; *****

For some players, this is a favourite. Its material seems especially original and compelling throughout, and it is highly democratic. The first movement has a wonderful vigour and momentum, based on a falling or rising octave that is resourcefully tossed around among the players. The slow movement forms a very beautiful core to the work. In the minuet and trio, the originality of the trio is amazing – so simple yet so effective. Again striking is the finale, which starts gently, *Allegretto*, but reaches an exhilarating ending, *Allegro* and loud.

### Op. 71 no. 3 (Hob.III:71) in E♭            23m; D3; Vol. IV; *****

This quartet is quieter and gentler than most others of the six, and of less marked personality. Nevertheless, it has plenty of interest for all players. Most memorable is probably the long *Andante con moto* second movement, a set of variations. Both viola and cello are given an innings, and there is a passage of remarkable scoring where the three top instruments without cello play semiquavers high in their range.

### Op. 74 no. 1 (Hob.III:72) in C            23m; D3+; Vol. I; *****

The outer movements are vigorous and masculine – and also quite difficult, mainly because of the high-speed semiquavers that come not only to the first violin. Much gentler are the middle movements, especially the elegant and delightful *Andantino grazioso*, which has many passages particularly gratifying to the lower parts.

### Op. 74 no. 2 (Hob.III:73) in F            23m; D3; Vol. I; *****

More lightweight than most of its companions, but excellent. The outer movements are full of zest. It is very enjoyable for all players, and offers good opportunities to viola and cello. But second violinists in particular may remember it for their gratifying solo variation in the *Andante grazioso* second movement. This is in Bb minor. Amusingly, when the same five-flats key signature reappears for the trio of the minuet (this time signifying Db major), the second violin is again called on to play solo. First violinists, too, may appreciate this quartet because their part, despite at times sounding impressively bravura, is easier than most.

Op. 74 no. 3 (Hob.III:74) in G minor ('The Rider')        22m; D3; Vol. I; *****

This well-known quartet is generally agreed to be among Haydn's finest. It is serious and powerful. Both of the outer movements have urgency, the galloping motion of the finale giving the quartet its nickname. In the first movement, the main material follows the introductory bars not (as in the other quartets of the set) after a pause but after two bars' silence. In the splendidly serious *Largo assai* second movement, the demisemiquavers are to be played in time, not as unmeasured tremolo.

We now at last come to Haydn's final set of six string quartets, op. 76. It was commissioned by Count Joseph Erdödy and completed in 1798. It is often considered his greatest set, in which he brought the characteristics of his previous quartets to their highest perfection. In them, he occasionally reverts to styles he used earlier in his career, but with a new power and insight. The most obvious example is the minuet of op. 76 no. 2, which has stark two-part writing with each part played by two instruments in octaves, reminiscent of some movements in opp. 1 and 2. All the part-writing is resourceful and masterly, but these quartets are sometimes less democratic than some in earlier sets. The minuets show further development; those of nos 1 and 6, marked *Presto*, are scherzos in all but name.

Op. 76 no. 1 (Hob.III:75) in G        22m; D3; Vol. II; *****

A really excellent quartet to open the set: outgoing and vigorous, with all movements very fine and enjoyable to play. Though energetic, it is not technically difficult. The first is a movement of robust vigour; after the opening chords (reminiscent of the preceding set of quartets), the cello opens the proceedings in a fugato. The second movement is a very beautiful and serious *Adagio*, perhaps particularly memorable for the dialogues between cello and first violin. The third movement minuet demands a one-in-the-bar scherzo speed; the trio, however, must be much slower (though it is not so marked): it is an elegant solo for the first violin above pizzicato accompaniment. The finale has much rushing around in triplet quavers, with ingenious counterpoint. It is remarkable for being principally in G minor, turning only to the major and lightening the mood near the end.

### Op. 76 no. 2 (Hob.III:76) in D minor ('The Fifths')    21m; D3; Vol. II; *****

One of the most highly regarded quartets of the set; but not everyone likes it without reservation. No doubts arise concerning the beautiful and serious opening movement, in which the pervading motif of a falling fifth (sometimes inverted) gives the quartet its nickname. This is magnificent music, and all parts are fine and enjoyable. The following *Andante* in D major is a relatively lightweight movement in this dark-coloured quartet; it is mostly a first-violin solo, often with pizzicato accompaniment. The following minuet, known as the 'Witches' Minuet', is for its entire length a two-part canon with the upper and lower strings playing in octaves. It is inflexible, powerful and stark – for some, not attractive! Its effectiveness is reinforced by the remarkable D major trio. The finale is fine, too, in the minor key until moving to the major for the end; but again much of it is largely a first-violin solo.

### Op. 76 no. 3 (Hob.III:77) in C ('The Emperor')    26m; D3+; Vol. II; *****

The fame of this quartet is the slow movement, consisting of variations on the *Emperor's Hymn*, the tune that Haydn composed (or perhaps adapted) as the Austrian national hymn. (With different words, it has subsequently become the national anthem of Germany.) The treatment in the variations is delightful: each instrument in turn plays the tune unaltered, the variation being in the accompanying instruments. Also excellent is the rest of the quartet: confident, large-scale music, and fully democratic. However, it is difficult, and the democracy means that everyone encounters the difficulties. This ties with op. 55 no. 2 and op. 77 no. 2 as Haydn's longest quartet, and some may feel they must make it even longer by repeating the second half of the first movement, since towards the end appears the instruction *la seconda volta più presto*.

### Op. 76 no. 4 (Hob.III:78) in B♭ ('The Sunrise')    22m; D3; Vol. II; *****

This is deservedly one of Haydn's most popular and best-loved quartets. The writing is full of resource and interest throughout, and the treatment of the medium is perfect, with excellent interest given to all players. The nickname comes from the gentle, rising figure played by the first violin in the opening. When given soon after to the cello, it instead falls. All players have their opportunities with this theme, but bright, vigorous playing is also needed in the semiquavers that pervade the movement. There is a most lovely, thoughtful *Adagio*. The finale moves along happily at *Allegro ma non troppo* for much of its time, but then it steps up to *Più allegro*, in which the motifs are hilariously tossed between the players, and finally dashes to the finish at *Più presto*. None of this, however, is unduly difficult.

### Op. 76 no. 5 (Hob.III:79) in D    20m; D3; Vol. II; *****

The second movement *Largo* of this quartet is one of Haydn's very finest movements. Marked *Cantabile e mesto*, it is in the surprising key of F♯ major, and its serious and thoughtful music moves searchingly through further distant harmonic regions: it is difficult for intonation. Its themes are exquisitely beautiful, and all players have many opportunities to play them; a passage given to the viola perhaps most lingers in the memory. The other movements of this quartet, too, are good, often strikingly original; they distribute the interest gratifyingly to all voices. The first movement is for much of its length an *Allegretto siciliano*; but it then surprisingly moves to *Allegro*: this is not difficult, but some rhythms may cause accidents if come upon unawares. The third movement minuet has a strange, almost sinister trio in which the cello takes the leading role, moving in its lowest register. The finale offers some of Haydn's most high-spirited entertainment.

Op. 76 no. 6 (Hob.III:80) in E♭                                24m; D3; Vol. II; *****

This is the least popular quartet of the set: its general character is rather withdrawn, and its thematic material is curiously commonplace. Nevertheless, it is a fine work, and notably original. The first movement is a set of variations, with a gentle, rather bland quality. The second movement *Adagio*, entitled *Fantasia* (which is sometimes taken as a nickname for the whole quartet), is especially original. Remarkably Haydn gave the first half no key signature – not to define its key as C major or A minor but because the music is so chromatic. It is strange and reticent, but every part is interesting to play and it has a cool beauty. The minuet is marked *Presto*, and its character is strongly that of a scherzo – brilliant and enjoyable. The withdrawn character returns with the *Alternativo* that stands in place of a trio, in which almost the only material is a single-octave scale of E♭, up or down. Probably the most obviously attractive and enjoyable movement is the highly contrapuntal finale.

———•••———

In 1799, the year after he completed the op. 76 set, Prince Lobkowitz (best known for his patronage of Beethoven) commissioned Haydn to compose another set of six quartets. But Haydn was busy with other compositions – the Seasons, and the annual Masses he produced for the name-day of Princess Esterházy; moreover, he was now in his later sixties, and could not compose at his former rate. He completed two quartets during 1799, which we now know as op. 77. He began another in 1803, but was unable to finish it. Nevertheless, these works show no decline in his powers: some consider the two op. 77 quartets to be his crowning achievement in the medium.

Op. 77 no. 1 (Hob.III:81) in G                                24m; D3; Vol. I; *****

This is a quartet of masculine vigour, power and good spirits throughout. For much of the time the writing is dominated by the first violin, who has to work hard. However, the textures are excellent, so the other parts are interesting and enjoyable. The first movement is remarkable for being of march-like character. The *Adagio* is one of Haydn's finest; it is serious but not tragic. The so-called minuet is marked

*Presto* and once more is a scherzo in all but name. The trio continues at the same speed and with similar vigour: it is essentially for first violin, but the accompanying parts are far from relaxing. For the finale there is another *Presto,* again of tremendous energy; at the speed required the first violin part is sometimes very demanding.

Op. 77 no. 2 (Hob.III:82) in F                                    26m; D3+; Vol. I; *****

This last completed quartet is certainly among Haydn's finest, and some would claim it as the greatest of all. Its mood is luminous and the writing throughout is democratic. Unusually, the minuet is placed second, an order that he had largely abandoned for many years. Its character is entirely that of a scherzo, full of lively charm; relatively subdued but equally lovely is the trio. For some the slow third movement, quite unusual for Haydn in being an *Andante,* is an especial favourite. It opens delightfully as a duet for first violin and cello, and its wonderful main theme sings on and on. Both second violin and cello are given a long play of this theme; though the viola is not so favoured, the delightful part-writing makes that part equally enjoyable. The finale is in polonaise rhythm, brilliant and full of interest, but technically fairly difficult.

Op. 103 (Hob.III:83) in D minor                                   11m; D3; Vol. IV; *****

Unfinished: Haydn was able to complete only the two middle movements, an *Andante grazioso* and a minuet. (The key is sometimes given as B♭, which is that of the *Andante*; but the intended key of the work was probably that of the D minor minuet.) These are fairly gentle movements but they are masterly and beautiful, with excellent part-writing. The middle section of the slow movement is made quite difficult by its key of G♭ major. The minuet is a true minuet. There is only one shortcoming: the frustration of an incomplete work – and the sadness of knowing that, at the age of seventy, Haydn had finally reached the end of his long compositional career. It makes playing the D minor ending the more moving.

## String Quintet and Sextet

Haydn composed nothing significant in this category. The only work accepted as authentic is a quintet, Hob.II:2 in G, for two violins, two violas and cello. It is a cassation or divertimento in six movements, dating probably from 1753 – making it Haydn's earliest surviving instrumental composition, and also the earliest known work for this combination. Despite the interest this gives it, it cannot compensate for the fact that it is musically dull.

The so-called 'Echo' sextet, Hob.II:39, for four violins and two cellos, to be performed in two separate rooms, is of doubtful authenticity.

## Piano Trios

The piano trio is the only chamber medium other than the string quartet to which Haydn made a major contribution. Of a long series of works, a considerable number are early, dating probably from the 1760s (and must have been composed with the harpsichord in mind); these are rarely played, and are not considered here. However, almost thirty trios date from the years of his fullest maturity in the 1780s and 1790s. These were probably intended for the fortepiano and – with reservations – have an important place in the repertoire. Some are indeed moderate in their scope, but especially those composed in the 1790s are fine works.

As has already been discussed, the piano trio as employed by Haydn was very different from what it became soon afterwards in Beethoven's hands. Haydn's trios all have only two or three movements, and these movements are often quite simple in their structure. Ternary form, variations and minuets without a trio appear frequently; sometimes there is no movement in sonata form. The violin parts, though essential to the music, are limited in their freedom. The cello spends most of its time in the bass, often doubling the piano's left hand; in not one of Haydn's piano trios is it ever given a solo melody.

Nevertheless, the violin part frequently has thematic material, sometimes doubled by the piano but on other occasions alone. The cello part is never entirely redundant. It may play in a different octave from the piano left hand, add different notes, point the rhythm or move in a different rhythm. Occasionally it carries the bass alone; and it often holds long bass notes that, since the piano cannot sustain, may be prominent and essential. It is not always undemanding: when playing with the piano left hand it can be fast-moving, as also in unison passages for all the voices. Sometimes it parts from the piano and joins the violin. Although some cellists may find these trios frustrating, with an understanding of the nature of the role they can be enjoyable. These cello parts still need to be played well and with sensitivity to the others. It is not a good idea to grumble about the part but spoil the music by slovenly playing!

From the point of view of the pianist, these trios are not as difficult as much later piano chamber music, but they are far from trivial. To be on top of the notes, many pianists will need to practise. This is perhaps especially important in these relatively undemocratic works: if the pianist is struggling, the string players can hardly be expected to enjoy their roles.

It might be wondered whether these trios could be played without the cello – so effectively making them sonatas for violin and piano. After all, the modern piano has much greater tone and sustaining power than the instrument that Haydn knew. This can be done, and it can be musically pleasurable: but it is never entirely satisfactory, because the cello parts are not entirely redundant. Notes or rhythm are sometimes missing; and something is lost by the absence of cello tone. Essential bass notes may be lacking (with advance preparation, the pianist may be able to identify and play these). If it is tried, trios with the least independent cello parts should be chosen. An example might be the trio in B♭, Hob.XV:20 (RL.34 – *see* below).

There is much confusion over the numbering of the trios. Many were written as singletons, while others were composed in sets of three. Some early publications combined singletons into sets of two or three. Most of the sets (whether grouped by Haydn or by a publisher) were given an opus number; but, unlike the position with the string quartets, these opus numbers are confused and are not useful. They are not mentioned here. The Hoboken numbers identify the works unambiguously, and are now widely used. When a trio is today identified simply as 'No. x', this may mean the Hoboken number, properly written as Hob.XV:x. However, some of the many past published editions employ their own numbering. Still widely distributed is the old Peters edition, in three volumes, edited by Friedrich Hermann (1828–1907); many players may have access to it. For this reason, the volume and numbering in this edition are also given. Be aware, however, that this edition as still available today no longer follows that numbering.

Nevertheless, in the light of subsequent scholarship, the Hoboken order has errors and is not fully chronological. An updated chronological list of Haydn's piano trios was produced by the great scholar H.C. Robbins Landon for his complete edition of the trios published by Doblinger in 1970, and this order is used here, shown as RL.nn. To assist identification mainly for those with sheet music lacking modern numbers, an incipit from the violin part (in one case also showing the piano right hand) is provided for each trio.

As with Haydn's string quartets, a parameter of from one to five stars (*****), where five is highest, is shown as a suggested measure of musical quality and enjoyment of playing.

RL.18 (Hob.XV:5) in G (1784)　　　　　　　　　15m; D2+; Hermann III:28; **

Overall this is an unenterprising trio. Perhaps most enjoyable of its three movements is the opening *Adagio*.

RL.19 (Hob.XV:6) in F (1784)　　　　　　　　　13m; D3; Hermann III:25; ***

There are two movements. The first is quite lively. The second, a *Tempo di Menuetto*, has a beautiful central section in F minor, throughout which the violin has the melody and the piano accompanies; the rest is of less interest.

RL.20 (Hob.XV:7) in D (1785)　　　　　　　　　14m; D3; Hermann I:10; ****

This trio is charming throughout its three movements. The first two are both marked *Andante*; the first is a set of variations. The *Allegro assai* finale calls for some agility. In the second and third movements the cello very occasionally escapes from the piano and joins the violin.

RL.21 (Hob.XV:8) in B♭ (1785)          13m; D3; Hermann III:24; ***

A two-movement trio: the music is attractive but not outstanding. It is unenterprising in its use of the violin.

RL.22 (Hob.XV:9) in A (1785)          12m; D3; Hermann II:15; ****

Once more in only two movements, but both are very attractive. The long *Adagio* first movement almost from the beginning gives the cello significant material independent of the piano. Usually this is singing with the violin, but in one four-bar passage it has a completely separate and significant part. A little of this freedom is also found in the *Vivace* second movement.

RL.23 (Hob.XV:10) in E♭ (1785)         10m; D3+; Hermann II:20; ***

Again in two movements, neither of them slow. It is attractive, but the scope is modest. The *Presto assai* second movement is quite demanding.

RL.24 (Hob.XV:11) in E♭ (c.1788)         15m; D3; Hermann II:16; ***

Attractive, gentle music, in two movements. In the first, the violin enjoys a good deal of freedom; but less so in the following *Tempo di menuetto*.

RL.25 (Hob.XV:12) in E minor (c.1788)         16m; D3; Hermann I:7; ***

A musically attractive three-movement work, but the string parts are not very enterprising.

RL.26 (Hob.XV:13) in C minor (probably 1789)      18m; D3; Hermann II:14; ****

This two-movement work is one of Haydn's most attractive. The first movement is a set of variations: serious but beautiful. A lovely *Allegro spiritoso* follows. Gratifying parts are given to the violin throughout, including the principal role in three of the variations. Alas, the cello is given little of interest.

RL.27 (Hob.XV:14) in A♭ (1790)      21m; D3+; Hermann I:11; ****

In a key rarely used by Haydn, this is a fine three-movement work, musically on a larger scale than most. All the movements are good, and the violin part is often enjoyable. Most remarkable is the central section of the *Adagio* second movement, which is a piano solo with pizzicato string accompaniment, of remarkable rhapsodic freedom. This whole trio is quite difficult, its demands made greater by the sometimes awkward keys.

---

The next three trios were composed for piano, flute and cello for the London publisher John Bland. However, they have often been published as normal piano trios and are frequently played as such; they are included in the Hermann edition and the Robbins Landon list. Although naturally significant for flautists, in many respects they are little different from the other piano trios.

RL.28 (Hob.XV:16) in D (1790) (piano, flute, cello)      17m; D3; Hermann III:30; ***

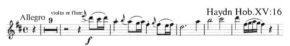

This trio is pleasant, mainly cheerful music, but not outstanding in the context of the other piano trios.

RL.29 (Hob.XV:15) in G (1790) (piano, flute, cello)      18m; D3; Hermann III:31; ****

An excellent trio, full of incident. All three of its movements are good. The first is quite long and substantial. The finale is highly entertaining: twice it gradually and amusingly comes to a complete halt; but eventually it dashes to the real finish.

RL.30 (Hob.XV:17) in F (1790) (piano, flute, cello)     13m; D3; Hermann III:29; ***

Attractive music, but in two movements and modest in scope.

---

RL.31 (Hob.XV:32) in G (c.1793)                    13m; D3; Hermann N/A; ****

This trio is a singleton; indeed it is something of an odd one out, being perhaps better known in its version as a sonata for violin and piano (*see* below). It has two movements, small in musical scope but very charming.

---

The next three trios form a set dedicated to Princess Maria Anna Esterházy. They were probably composed shortly before his second visit to London from February 1794 to August 1795, and with London in mind. With only one exception, the trios from this time onwards are of three movements and tend to show greater musical ambition than the earlier trios.

RL.32 (Hob.XV:18) in A (c.1793)                    16m; D3+; Hermann II:13; ****

Excellent: all three movements are good. The first is beautifully smooth and lyrical, and the second (*Andante*) is attractively plaintive, mainly in A minor. The finale with its syncopations has something of the exhilaration and verve of the famous 'Gypsy Rondo' movement (*see* RL.39 below).

RL.33 (Hob.XV:19) in G minor (c.1793)              16m; D3; Hermann II:17; ***

The first movement is a set of variations (the final variation being *Presto*), and there follows an *Adagio ma non troppo*. Both movements are rather subdued in character, and disappointingly their interest is largely confined to the piano part. The short *Presto* third movement, however, is lively and entertaining, and makes much better use at least of the violin.

RL.34 (Hob.XV:20) in B♭ (1794)                    14m; D3; Hermann I:9; ****

This is one of the most enjoyable of the trios for the pianist and violinist – though alas not for the cellist, who has scarcely any independent interest at all. But the music is delightful and fresh throughout the three movements, and the violin is given some entertaining playing, especially in the first two movements. Though less free in the last movement, there is a gratifying violin melody in its B♭ minor central section.

There now follows a set of three trios composed in 1794–5 and dedicated to Princess Maria Josepha Esterházy. All are in three movements.

RL.35 (Hob.XV:21) in C (1794–5)                    15m; D3; Hermann II:21; **

As well as having rather commonplace thematic material, the interest given to the strings is disappointingly limited.

RL.36 (Hob.XV:22) in E♭ (1794–5)                   20m; D3; Hermann III:23; ****

The first two movements are gentle and most beautiful, while the finale is much more lively. The string parts are fairly enjoyable.

RL.37 (Hob.XV:23) in D minor (1794–5)              20m; D3; Hermann II:22; ****

The first movement, a set of variations alternating between the major and minor keys, is outstandingly good. Also good are the remaining movements, though they cannot quite maintain the standard of the first.

The next set of three trios was composed during Haydn's second visit to England and dedicated to Rebecca Schroeter, a British amateur pianist and widow of a German musician, to whom Haydn gave lessons and formed a romantic attachment.

## RL.38 (Hob.XV:24) in D (1795)    14m; D3; Hermann I:6; \*\*\*\*

Beautiful, mostly gentle music. The long first movement is followed by two short movements, the second movement *Andante* being followed *attacca* by the *Allegro, ma dolce* finale.

## RL.39 (Hob.XV:25 in G (1795) ('Gypsy' or 'Gypsy Rondo')

16m; D3; Hermann I:1; \*\*\*\*\*

This is by far the best-known of Haydn's piano trios – and justifiably so. Its nickname comes from the last movement *Rondo all' Ongarese*; but every movement is excellent. The *Andante* first movement is a freely treated set of variations, full of beauty and interest. There follows a most lovely *Poco adagio, Cantabile*. The gypsy finale is brilliant, with a series of highly entertaining episodes. Although this trio remains within Haydn's normal treatment of the medium, it is more enjoyable than usual for the strings, and the cello is occasionally given some limited but significant freedom.

## RL.40 (Hob.XV:26) in F# minor (1795)    14m; D3; Hermann I:2; \*\*\*\*

A calm, gentle and sometimes serene work, thoughtful and never fast or brilliant. However, the unusual key sometimes makes for awkwardness. The violin part is limited in its independent contribution; on the other hand the cello is rather more free than usual.

---

The next two trios are singletons.

## RL.41 (Hob.XV:31 in E♭ minor (1797?)    12m; D3+; Hermann II:18; \*\*\*\*

This trio reverts to the two-movement layout. The *Andante cantabile* first movement is subdued but most lovely. The second movement *Allegro* is quite lively. The key makes this sometimes uncomfortable to play; and the second movement has some fast-moving notes that are not easy.

RL.42 (Hob.XV:30) in E♭ (1797?)  18m; D3; Hermann I:8; ****

An attractive and powerful three-movement work, with a beautiful, thoughtful central *Andante con moto*. The cello part of this trio has a little more freedom than some others.

---

Haydn's final three trios were dedicated to Theresa Jansen (Bartolozzi after her marriage in 1795). She had studied with Clementi and was a fine pianist – these are Haydn's only piano trios written for a professional. Nevertheless the piano parts are no more demanding than previously. The first trio perhaps suggests that the cello is to be treated with more freedom (after all, Haydn had probably by this time heard Beethoven's three piano trios, op. 1) – but the trend is not sustained.

RL.43 (Hob.XV:27) in C (1797)  18m; D3+; Hermann I:3; ****

In three movements, all very attractive and original. Though never allowed a solo melody, the cello quite often moves independently.

RL.44 (Hob.XV:28) in E (1797)  17m; D3; Hermann I:4; ****

This trio shows remarkable originality. The first movement has much variety; it also gives some noticeable freedom to the cello, but this does not continue in the subsequent movements. The second movement is mostly quiet and mysterious, with an almost unbroken, inexorable tread of steadily moving legato quavers; after the unison of the opening bars, the strings are silent for a long period. This movement is marked *Allegretto*, but it is difficult to decide a good tempo: what at first seems surprisingly slow perhaps works best musically. The finale is rarely forceful, but it is delightful and often unexpected.

RL.45 (Hob.XV:29) in E♭ (1797)  17m; D3; Hermann I:5; ****

A lyrical and charming work. Especially striking perhaps is the first movement, but all are good.

## Ensemble Works including Wind Instruments

Haydn wrote many works that include wind instruments; but disappointingly, hardly any are important. Most are early, from the 1760s or before, and of divertimento type – mainly lightweight entertainment music. Some were perhaps intended for outdoor performance. Many surveys do not admit these early divertimenti (of Mozart as well as of Haydn) to the classification of chamber music: but there is much music here that may be played and enjoyed. The works address a number of different instrumental combinations, both for wind instruments alone and with strings. Many of the latter are similar in character to the string quartets of opp. 1 and 2. Haydn also in his mature years composed a few further works involving wind instruments, but these too are minor.

Most of these works are here called divertimenti, but they often have alternative titles such as Cassation, Parthia (a variant of Partita) or Feldparthie. Many have five movements, and (like the string quartets opp. 1 and 2) usually have a central slow movement and a minuet second and fourth. Where bass is listed among the instruments, this is usually in practice a cello. Alternatives are double bass, bassoon or both cello and double bass. It is not usual with these works to employ a harpsichord for a *basso continuo*. With the early works, those with the ability could perhaps add ornamentation.

Some of these works were not published until the second half of the twentieth century. Those discussed here are not all that may be played. Others, however, are generally of doubtful authenticity, arrangements of uncertain origin, or smaller pieces or fragments; but some further authentic works may exist.

### Early works for wind and string instruments

All these works probably date from the 1750s or 1760s. The larger works in nine parts are excellently written to give plenty of interest to all the players. The strings too, including the violas, will enjoy playing these; only the bass parts are unenterprising.

Divertimento in G (Hob.II:9) (2 oboes, 2 horns, 2 violins, 2 violas, bass)     19m; D3
There are five movements. The central *Adagio cantabile* is for strings alone.

Divertimento in F (Hob.II:20) (2 oboes, 2 horns, 2 violins, 2 violas, bassoon)
19m; D3
This is another five-movement work. Oboes and horns are silent in the central slow movement.

Divertimento in C (Hob.II:17) (2 clarinets, 2 horns, 2 violins, 2 violas, bass)
28m; D2
This long work is in six movements.

**Divertimento in G (Hob.II:G1)** (2 oboes, 2 horns, 2 violins, 2 violas, bass)  16m; D2
Another attractive work in five movements. Oboes and horns are silent in the trio of the first minuet, and in the central *Adagio*.

**Divertimento in D (Hob.II:8)** (2 flutes, 2 horns, 2 violins, bass)  19m; D3
Also in five movements. The flutes are given plenty of interest and may particularly enjoy the central slow movement.

**Divertimento in E♭ (Hob.II:21)** (2 horns, 2 violins, viola, bass)  18m; D2
The horn parts are mostly subordinate, and of the five movements they are silent in the central *Adagio*. In a version that dispenses with the horns, this is the string quartet op. 2 no. 3.

**Divertimento in D (Hob.II:22)** (2 horns, 2 violins, viola, bass)  15m; D2
This is similar to the preceding work, and also exists as the string quartet op. 2 no. 5. The horns have only occasional prominence and do not play in the trio of the first minuet or in the slow movement, which is largely a solo for the first violin.

**Divertimento in G (Hob.II:1)** (flute, oboe, 2 violins, cello, double bass)  23m; D3+
This is an attractive, four-movement work. The flute player has much to enjoy, but the oboe's role is more subordinate. The last movement is a set of variations giving solo opportunities to everyone except the double bass. Some solos are difficult, especially perhaps those for cello.

**Divertimento in C (*The Birthday*) (Hob.II:11)** (flute, oboe, 2 violins, cello, double bass)  23m; D4+
This is a concertante work; many will find it too difficult. The flute, oboe and cello parts are identified as obbligato, but all players except double bass are given solos, often technically demanding. The cello part in particular is frequently high-lying. The second movement, entitled *Man and Wife*, however, is for strings alone and is not difficult; it is effectively in only two parts, with the violins playing in octaves (presumably representing the wife) and the cello and double bass also in octaves. The last movement is a set of variations, in which the first five are solos for each of the five higher instruments.

**Divertimento in E♭ (Hob.IV:5)** (horn, violin, cello)  9m; D3 (horn harder)
The parts for violin and cello have quite good interest, but this is a horn show-piece. There are two movements, the first a set of variations; the second provides an opportunity for a horn cadenza. It is difficult to play on a modern horn; to play it on the specified *corno da caccia* (hunting horn) must be a formidable feat.

---

Six three-movement quartets for flute, violin, viola and cello, op. 5, are not authentic. They are arrangements, not by Haydn, of various early works.

## Early works for wind instruments alone

These works, although (with one exception) in five movements, are all short in duration – even though almost all of their material is repeated. They are enjoyable, straightforward music, and not difficult.

Divitimento in F (Hob.II:15) (2 oboes, 2 horns, 2 bassoons)                   8m; D2
Although the oboes predominate, enjoyable opportunities are given to all.

Divertimento in F (Hob.II:23) (2 oboes, 2 horns, 2 bassoons)              10m; D2
Alternatively entitled Parthia. There also exists a version of this work in G.

Divertimento in C (Hob.II:7) (2 oboes, 2 horns, 2 bassoons)              10m; D2
Also called Feldpartie or Feld-Parthie.

Divertimento in G (Hob.II:3) (2 oboes, 2 horns, 2 bassoons)              10m; D2
This divertimento has the alternative title of Parthia.

Divertimento in C (Hob.II:14) (2 clarinets, 2 horns)                   5½m; D2
Particularly short as this work is, Haydn still squeezes in five movements. The clarinets are in C.

Divertimento in B♭ (Hob.II:46) (2 oboes, 2 horns, 3 bassoons, serpent)      10m; D2
Probably the best-known of all the wind chamber music associated with Haydn, because Brahms used its second movement, entitled *St. Anthony Chorale*, for his orchestral *Variations on a Theme by Haydn*. However, it is now considered spurious (the composer may have been Ignaz Pleyel). Also called Feldparthie, it is in four movements and is attractive and enjoyable. The serpent part is usually played by a contrabassoon.

## Late works for wind and string instruments

Six divertimenti (Hob.IV:6–11) (1784) (flute/violin, violin, cello)      6–10m; D2
These are pleasant but very minor works, all in three movements; the flute part predominates. Haydn incorporated much music from elsewhere, including his opera *Il mondo della luna*. (The violin part has double-stops and goes below the flute range, so these trios cannot be played with two flutes.)

Four London trios (Hob.IV:1–4) (1794–5) (2 flutes, cello)              4½–11m; D2
Attractive music but again of small scope. The first and third trios are in three movements, the others in one movement only.

———◦•◦———

Much more substantial are the three trios (Hob.XV:15–17) for piano, flute and cello. However, they are similar to Haydn's many trios for piano, violin and cello and are often played by that combination. They appear above as RL.28–30 of the piano trios.

## Duet Sonatas

Essentially Haydn wrote no duet sonatas. However, there exist publications of works described as sonatas for violin and piano; the best-known is of a set of eight by publishers including Peters and Kalmus. They are arrangements. Five of the eight are of piano sonatas (and in their arranged form are of 'piano sonata with the accompaniment of a violin' type). Two are of the great string quartets op. 77, with the minuets omitted. Haydn did not make or authorize these arrangements. Just one, however, no. 1 in G in this set, may have been arranged or composed by Haydn. It also exists as a piano trio (RL.31 (Hob.XV:32) – *see* the section on piano trios).

# HUMMEL
## 1778–1837; Austria

Johann Nepomuk Hummel is widely recognized as an excellent composer, yet not quite in the first rank. He spent part of his life in Vienna, was a contemporary of Haydn, Mozart, Beethoven and Schubert, and knew all four, especially Mozart (with whom he studied) and Beethoven. But although he outlived them all, his style remained essentially classical, and the scope of his works never extended beyond those of Haydn and Mozart. His music is charming and entertaining, but rarely profound. He had an undoubted melodic gift and a distinctive voice, and his technical skill was excellent. He was famous in his lifetime as a pianist as well as for his compositions, and the piano writing in the large ensemble works is brilliant and demanding.

Some of Hummel's music remains in the repertoire, most famously the trumpet concerto. Several of his chamber works, too, are regularly performed – especially the two septets. For amateurs, the less well-known compositions, too, are worth attention: he left a substantial body of chamber music, covering a variety of genres. Some works are valuable because they are for unusual combinations, notably the clarinet quartet and the viola sonata. All are playable, musically attractive and of good quality. Most of his chamber works were published in his lifetime and have opus numbers, which are in fairly good order; but a few works have either a misleading opus number or none.

## String Trios

Two four-movement trios for viola/violin, viola and cello of 1799 and 1801 have been published, but they are unimportant.

## String Quartets

Hummel's three string quartets were composed shortly after the appearance of Beethoven's op. 18 quartets. They inhabit a simpler world, but they are charming, full of melody, and give an excellently democratic distribution of the musical interest. All are in four movements. They offer an enjoyable foray into music comparable to but distinctly different from the usual earlier classics. (Publishers of the parts include S.J. Music in the UK.)

Op. 30 no. 1 in C (c.1804)                                                      25m; D3

This is a consistent and attractive quartet. A short *Adagio* introduction leads into the first movement *Allegro non troppo*. The third movement, *Adagio e cantabile*, beautifully maintains its thoughtful mood throughout.

Op. 30 no. 2 in G (c.1804)                                                      25m; D3+

For some, this quartet is the favourite of the three. The first movement has some triplet figures made especially awkward by their unexpected slur patterns. Perhaps most memorable is the delightfully infectious melody of the trio of the minuet, in which the viola joins the first violin in playing a prominent part. Unusually, Hummel directs that after the normal *Da Capo* of the minuet, this trio should be played again, and with repeats!

Op. 30 no. 3 in E♭ (c.1804)                                                     27m; D3

The beautiful *Andante* second movement surprisingly contains a quotation of 'Comfort Ye' from Handel's *Messiah*. (It has been suggested that, at the time, this 'archaic' reference would appeal to the musically knowledgeable.) The third movement, an *Allemande* with *Alternativo*, has a distinctive personality. A *Presto* finale ends the quartet in high spirits.

## Piano Trios

Hummel's seven mature full-scale piano trios form an excellent series, and are well worth playing. They all have three movements, and their emotional tone is generally entertaining and lightweight. Op. 83, however, stands out as being on a larger scale and serious in its content. In their scale and technical demands, most are comparable with the trios of Haydn and Mozart, but they have an advantage in that their texture is fully democratic.

Op. 12 in E♭ (c.1803)                                                           22m; D3

An attractive trio, with a simple but immediately engaging opening.

Op. 22 in F (1799)                                                              14m; D3

Though it is short, much enjoyment is to be had from this trio. The cellist may especially appreciate the many lyrical opportunities in the *Andante con variazione*. The finale is an entertaining *Rondo alla Turca*.

Op. 35 in G (probably c.1811)                                          15m; D3

A *Tempo di menuetto* serves as the central movement. The last movement has an enjoyably rollicking character.

Op. 65 in G (c.1814)                                                   16m; D3

Entertaining and energetic throughout. The central *Andante grazioso* offers lyrical opportunities for all, and the finale dashes along with plenty of contrapuntal ingenuity.

Op. 83 in E (1819)                                                     30m; D3+

This splendid trio is much longer than its predecessors, and of greater musical scope. It is full of beauty and richness; good opportunities are given to all three players. The piano writing is more demanding than generally in the trios.

Op. 93 in E♭ (1821)                                                   27m; D3

Despite its publication date, this is said to have been based on a work originally written in the late 1790s. Its musical character is typical of Hummel's lighter vein, but it is on a larger scale than most of the trios.

Op. 96 in E♭ (1824)                                                   21m; D3

This trio is humorous and sparkling in its material throughout. It is delightfully written, and the cello in particular has many enjoyable opportunities. The finale is a *Rondo alla Russa*.

## Piano Quintet (piano, violin, viola, cello, double bass)

Op. 87 in E♭ (1802)                                  22m; D3 (piano harder)

Despite its high opus number, this is a relatively early work. It is delightful, in four movements (though the short *Largo* third movement leads straight into the finale). Good melodic opportunities are given to the violin, viola and cello. The piano part employs Hummel's most brilliant writing.

---

Hummel also arranged his Septet, op. 74 (*see* below), for the same combination. This arrangement is frequently played and is perhaps better-known than op. 87. He also produced a piano quintet arrangement of his 'Military Septet', op. 114, in this case for piano and string quartet.

## Ensemble Works including Wind Instruments

Clarinet Quartet in E♭ major, WoO 5 (1808) (clarinet, violin, viola, cello) 29m; D3+

A characteristic, highly attractive and entertaining work. The clarinet is integrated as a member of the ensemble rather than used as a soloist. There are four movements. The fast and quirky second movement, *La seccatura* (*the bother*), is written with each part in a different time signature – at first bewildering! The clarinet is in B♭.

<u>Septet in D minor, op. 74 (c.1816)</u> (piano, flute, oboe, horn, viola, cello, double bass)                                                    39m; D3 (piano harder)
This work, for its unusual combination, is Hummel's largest chamber composition, and arguably his finest. It is charming and excellent, in four movements. Good opportunities are given to most of the players, though the viola and double bass have more supporting roles. The piano part is brilliant and demanding.

Hummel provided an alternative piano quintet version of this work (*see* above).

<u>Adagio, Variations and Rondo in A, op. 78 (c.1818)</u> (piano, flute/violin, cello)
15m; D3 (piano harder)
Charming and deservedly popular.

<u>Septet in C major, op. 114 ('Military') (1829)</u> (piano, flute, clarinet, trumpet, violin, cello, double bass)                                30m; D3 (piano harder)
The 'Military' nickname refers to the inclusion of the trumpet; this instrument is, however, treated with discretion, and is not allowed to play at all in the *Adagio* second movement. The work has four movements. Despite the nickname, its character is generally lyrical and gentle, and the finale ends *pianissimo*. There are many enjoyable melodies, for which the clarinet and violin are perhaps particularly favoured. The contributions of the trumpet give a distinctive quality to the whole. The clarinet is in B♭, the trumpet in C.

This septet, too, was arranged by Hummel as a quintet for piano and strings (*see* above).

## Duet Sonatas

Hummel's six duet sonatas are spread through his career. Usefully, they include sonatas for viola, cello and flute as well as for violin. All are in three movements and are relatively small in scope, though a progression is evident through them. The earlier sonatas are comparable in character and technical demands to Mozart's duet sonatas. They are quite easy to play, and their piano parts are much less demanding than those of the larger concerted chamber works. The later sonatas are somewhat more difficult.

<u>Op. 5 no. 1 in B♭ (c.1798)</u> (violin, piano)                                    21m; D3–

<u>Op. 5 no. 2 in F (c.1798)</u> (violin, piano)                                     17m; D3–

<u>Op. 5 no. 3 in E♭ (c.1798)</u> (viola, piano)                                    22m; D3
Charming: for those seeking a sonata for this instrument, it is well worth playing.

| | |
|---|---|
| <u>Op. 104 in A (1824)</u> (cello, piano) | 22m; D3 |
| <u>Op. 50 in D (c.1810–14)</u> (flute/violin, piano) | 19m; D3 |
| <u>Op. 64 in A (c.1814)</u> (flute/violin, piano) | 13m; D3 |

# JANÁČEK
## 1854–1928; Czechoslovakia

Leoš Janáček was born in Moravia; he was interested in the folk music of his homeland. He is remarkable in that almost every work by which he is known dates from late in his life. Two factors came together to stimulate an extraordinary outpouring of music through his last decade. In 1917 he began an intense but unrequited love affair with a younger married woman, Kamila Stösslová; and in 1918 independent Czechoslovakia (which included Moravia) was established. His greatest concentration was on opera, but he also composed orchestral and chamber music. The chamber works are of great originality and power. Unusually, most have a programme or at least an extra-musical inspiration. Janáček had developed a remarkably original and personal style, which, despite his being at this period in his sixties and early seventies, is 'modern' to the time. His approach to harmony was novel (though not atonal). He did not identify works by key, and in the later works ceased to use key signatures. His forms are unconventional, and there are often abrupt changes of dynamic, tempo and character. The music is frequently built on short melodies or melodic fragments. A fragment may be repeated rapidly as an ostinato, and there are sharp interjections. His music does not make virtuoso demands, but the complication of the timing and the strangeness of his style may be obstacles at least until familiarity and understanding have been gained.

## String Quartets
Both of Janáček's two quartets have four movements, but they otherwise ignore all classical precedent. The forms are unconventional, and there is nothing that can be identified as a slow movement or scherzo. All movements have multiple tempo changes, sometimes going to both fast and slow extremes. The textures include little counterpoint; instrumental solos or sometimes duets are accompanied by figurations or ostinati. Effects such as tremolo and sul ponticello are employed. All instruments are treated equally.

<u>String quartet no. 1 (*Kreutzer Sonata*) (1923)</u>      18m; D4+
The name is confusing. The work was inspired by the Tolstoy novella of this name, which had itself been inspired by Beethoven's sonata for violin and piano bearing that nickname. Janáček first wrote it in 1908–9 as a piano trio, later reworking it as

this string quartet. It is tremendously powerful and original. It is difficult to play, both in the notes and in fitting the parts together. Sight-reading is not practicable: but with practice some capable amateurs should find it manageable.

<u>String quartet no. 2 (*Intimate Letters*) (1928)</u>                              26m; D4+

The name, given to it by Janáček, refers to the letters he exchanged with Kamila Stösslová – hence its intensity of feeling. The writing is similar to that of the previous quartet but perhaps sometimes even more awkward. Advance study and practice are pre-requisites.

## Ensemble Work for Wind Instruments

Only one work comes in this category; however, two others may be mentioned, though neither is really to be considered as chamber music. The concertino for piano with clarinet, horn, bassoon, two violins and viola was written in 1925. It is a substantial work in four movements: but the piano dominates and the other parts are very subordinate. Much more democratic is the capriccio for piano left hand, flute, two trumpets, three trombones and tuba, of 1926, also in four movements.

<u>Wind sextet *Mládí* (*Youth*) (1924)</u> (flute, oboe, clarinet, horn, bassoon, bass clarinet)                                                                          17m; D4+

This is a suite in four movements, melodically charming and youthfully light-hearted. It is difficult; both timing and notes are complicated. The clarinet is in B♭. The flautist is asked to play piccolo in one of the movements.

## Duet Sonata and another Duet

<u>Sonata for violin and piano (1914–22)</u>                                      17m; D4
Characteristic and beautiful.

<u>*Pohádka* (*Fairy-tale*) (1908–23)</u> (cello, piano)                          12m; D4
After a Russian story: quite substantial, in three movements.

# MENDELSSOHN
### 1809–1847; Germany

Felix Mendelssohn is one of the most important composers of the early romantic period, and a major composer of chamber music. He is also remarkable for being the greatest child-prodigy composer in musical history – his achievements in this respect exceeding even those of the young Mozart. He completed his octet for strings, a supreme work in his output and a major monument in music, in October 1825, at the age of sixteen years and eight months. Through the remaining years before he was twenty-one, several further chamber-music masterpieces followed;

arguably he never achieved anything greater than these. However, the former view that the quality of his music declined as he grew older is no longer generally held. Rather, his style changed: he became less adventurous in form and harmony, and more interested in emotional feeling. Some may prefer his earlier works, but those from the later years of his sadly short life are also fine.

During his lifetime, Mendelssohn rapidly achieved popularity across much of Europe and particularly in Britain, to which he paid altogether ten visits. After his death, however, his music gradually fell from the high esteem in which it had previously been held – a process influenced in the late nineteenth and earlier twentieth centuries by the fact of his Jewish ethnicity. Since the Second World War, his reputation has recovered, and his position as a major composer is secure.

Mendelssohn's music is not without profundity, but the more frequent characteristics are charm and vigour, and this often means that it is fast. His writing is always democratic, giving good interest to all. Technically, it is not unduly difficult: Mendelssohn played the violin and viola and his writing for string instruments is highly idiomatic. But the speed required can sometimes be problematical for amateurs. All commentators recognize the brilliance and originality of Mendelssohn's scherzos: probably no other composer has so excelled at this form. Most often they are fast and exhilarating; but such was his inventiveness that he could equally effectively write a scherzo that is slow (as in the string quintet in B♭, op. 87) or tragic (as in the string quartet in F minor, op. 80).

Mendelssohn's opus numbers are not all in good order. This particularly applies to those from 73 upwards, which were allocated posthumously; and some works, late as well as early, lack any opus number.

## String Quartets

Mendelssohn left six complete, mature string quartets, forming an excellent, consistent set. Op. 12 in E♭ is probably the most popular. However, many would argue that the finest is either the earliest, op. 13 in A minor, or the last, op. 80 in F minor, both of which are serious in character. The others are mostly more relaxed, with more emphasis on charm. Notice that because the opus numbers of the first two quartets are out of order, the second (op. 12 in E♭) usually appears first in a complete edition.

In addition to these six, there are two other works. One is early; it is again in E♭ (and is not usually included in a complete edition). The other is a collection of fragments. Both are worth playing.

<u>String quartet in E♭ (1823)</u>                                   26m; D3–

Although this early quartet is fairly unadventurous, most of it is very attractive and characteristic of the composer. Interest is given to all the players. Only perhaps the trio of the minuet is uninspired enough to try the patience. The finale is a full-dress fugue. This quartet is much easier than any of his later quartets, making it a valuable possession for amateurs.

## Op. 13 in A minor (1827)
30m; D4

Written two years after the octet, this is another miraculous work from Mendelssohn's teenage years, in fact one of the most extraordinary quartets in the repertoire. Almost uniquely among nineteenth-century string quartets it takes up the challenge of Beethoven's late quartets and makes a clear and personal response. Mendelssohn probably came to know Beethoven's op. 132 in A minor shortly before composing it. The writing throughout is of remarkable complexity, and is both strongly contrapuntal and harmonically daring. Structurally it has its own type of cyclic form. Earlier in the year, Mendelssohn had written a *lied* (song) called *Frage* (*Question*), op. 9 no. 1, which includes the words 'Is it true that you are always waiting for me in the arboured walk?'. The quartet opens with an *Adagio* introduction based on this, and finally it concludes with a more extended statement of the same.

Although technically quite demanding, there are no serious problems. With its contrapuntal nature, it is generous to all four players. Moments that may be remembered include the several fugatos started by the viola, and some long, slow counter-melodies on the cello.

## Op. 12 in E♭ (1829)
24m; D4–

This quartet is as popular with players as it is with audiences. It is both technically and musically less demanding than its predecessor – indeed, this is the easiest of Mendelssohn's mature quartets. Any influence of Beethoven here is not of the late quartets but of the middle period – the slow introduction resembles that of Beethoven's op. 74 (also in E♭). Structurally there is again much originality. A subsidiary subject in the first movement, usually played by the second violin, reappears in the last movement, again on second violin. The coda that ends the quartet is almost identical to that of the first movement.

Especially popular is the *Canzonetta* second movement, with its central *più mosso* section of dancing semiquavers for the instruments in pairs. After this section, Mendelssohn neglects to tell us where to return to the original tempo. Usual practice is to do this not at the return to the original key, but twelve bars later at the return of the opening theme.

## Op. 44 no. 1 in D (1838)
31m; D4

Actually the last composed of this set of three quartets; Mendelssohn seems to have placed it first because he was particularly pleased with it. It is very classical in its form, and uniquely among Mendelssohn's mature chamber works it has a minuet instead of a scherzo – a charming movement. Plenty of interest is distributed to all players. The first and last movements are very fast, and musically do not work if taken too slowly; however, they are so well written for the instruments that they are not unduly difficult. Playing them can be exhilarating!

### Op. 44 no. 2 in E minor (1837)                                        28m; D4

Another favourite, almost as popular as op. 12. It is full of energy, yet it is most memorable for its mellifluous lyricism. This applies to all movements, even the scherzo. This scherzo is one of the composer's most brilliant, dashing along at *Allegro di molto*; yet its most haunting moments are the two occasions when motion is suspended and the viola sings a slow, soulful melody, the second time in extended form. The *Andante* bears a warning in German that it must not be dragged (presumably because too slow a tempo would make for excessive sentimentality); for much of it the second violin has a running semiquaver accompaniment, which, however, is grateful to play.

### Op. 44 no. 3 in E♭ (1838)                                            33m; D4

This is the largest, most ambitious and most serious quartet of the set. Again, it has a particularly fine scherzo. A memorable moment comes near the end of this movement, when the contrapuntal texture converges into a unison at pitch – still moving as fast as ever – before the parts spread out to bring the movement to a close. Also very fine is the *Adagio non troppo*. This quartet is in most respects no harder than the others of the opus: but it is challenging to play the semiquavers of the finale, articulated as marked and at the speed indicated.

### Op. 80 in F minor (1847)                                             25m; D4

Mendelssohn's sister Fanny (*see* Appendix I), to whom he was very close personally and musically, died in May 1847. He was severely afflicted, and this string quartet that he composed shortly afterwards must be his response to her death. It is intense and tragic throughout, utterly unlike any of his other quartets. Some echoes of Beethoven are apparent, most obviously from op. 95 in the same key; but this is nevertheless a strongly individual quartet. Even its scherzo is powerful, tough and completely without charm. This is less popular than many of Mendelssohn's quartets, but most will recognize its quality. It is strenuous and not easy to play. Some may find the semiquaver scrubs that are prominent in the first movement stressful for their bow arms.

### Four movements for string quartet, Op. 81                             21m; D4

Though problematical for the concert hall, for players this is a valuable opus that should not be neglected. The movements were gathered together for publication after the composer's death. The first two – an *Andante sostenuto* theme and variations in E major and a scherzo in A minor, both written in 1847 – are almost certainly the middle movements of another quartet that Mendelssohn was prevented by death from completing (was he planning another set of three?). Viola players will particularly enjoy the variations. The scherzo, his last piece in this form at which he excelled, is one of his finest: brilliant and zestful. Then comes a *Capriccio* in E minor, which has an introduction followed by a splendid fugal movement. It was written in 1843, when his correspondence shows that he was planning a set of pieces for string quartet; but as far as we know only this was written. It seems possible that he had abandoned the idea of the pieces and planned to use this as the finale of the intended new quartet. Its key is appropriate to follow the variations and scherzo, and it makes an excellent conclusion. So these three movements can well be played together.

As published, however, there follows a fugue in E♭ from 1827, probably written only as an exercise. In character it is completely unlike the other movements, and its key does not fit them well. Performances of the whole work sometimes place this fugue third and the capriccio fourth so that the latter serves as finale, and this order may be preferred. Alternatively, it may be thought better to treat the fugue as a separate item: it makes a pleasant play, technically much easier than the rest.

## String Quintets (2 violins, 2 violas, cello)

<u>Op. 18 in A (1826, 1832)</u>                                                     31m; D4

Written in its original form in 1826, this quintet has a wonderfully fresh brilliance of invention and contrapuntal virtuosity: it is a splendid youthful masterpiece in a comparable spirit to the octet of the previous year. Originally, however, it had no slow movement. In 1832, as a memorial to Mendelssohn's violin teacher and close friend Eduard Rietz who had just died, he wrote the present *Andante sostenuto* intermezzo second movement. The scherzo that had stood second was moved to third, displacing from the work a minuet and trio. The intermezzo, which is serious and beautiful but not tragic, admirably adds weight to this otherwise outgoing work. The whole quintet is a delight to play, but it is not easy, demanding plenty of agility!

The displaced minuet and trio has been published and can be played as an interesting curiosity.

<u>Op. 87 in B♭ (1845)</u>                                                      29m; D4–

Some critics have compared this quintet unfavourably with op. 18. Indeed, Mendelssohn himself was dissatisfied with the finale, and perhaps held the work back from publication pending a revision he did not live to carry out. However, although the central movements are perhaps the finest, the vigorous and dramatic outer movements are exhilarating to play, and their material stays in the mind. Overall, the work is technically easier than op. 18.

The first movement has passages with much quaver triplet figuration or semiquaver scrubbing. First violinists should appreciate that many of the triplet quavers in their part – especially the arpeggios across the strings – are only ornamentation and must be played discreetly! The second movement, *Andante scherzando,* is a slow scherzo, delightful yet technically straightforward. The third movement *Adagio e lento* is the emotional heart of the quintet, full of passionate and serious feeling. One may especially remember the long, high cello solo.

## String Octet (4 violins, 2 violas, 2 cellos)

Op. 20 in E♭ (1825)                                                                                    32m; D4

This octet, written at the age of sixteen, seems a miracle. No more perfect work exists. Its total command of his personal voice, its freshness and its originality seem the more startling when we realize that when it was written both Beethoven and Schubert were still living. It is unique and wonderful. As befits its youthfulness, it is glowing and extrovert, untouched by any shadow of sadness.

An opportunity to play it is a special pleasure. The part-writing throughout is superb: despite there being so many players, each one is treated generously. It is not easy, but for reasonably capable amateurs there are no major problems in either notes or ensemble. In any case, shortcomings of execution in this context are usually part of the fun. Every movement is strongly characterized. The third is the earliest of Mendelssohn's magical scherzos – mostly *pianissimo*, rising at maximum to *piano*. The finale is hilarious – opening with a fast-moving fugato that starts ungratefully on the C string of the second cello. The later tossing around of repeated minims among the violins is likely in sight-reading to collapse in hilarity. An aspect of this work is that each part has its own individual character, which once known can be a particular enjoyment. Everyone has the opportunity on different occasions to play a different part – for those who play both violin and viola, six are available!

## Piano Trios

The two piano trios are easily the finest of Mendelssohn's concerted chamber music with piano.

Op. 49 in D minor (1839)                                                    29m; D4– (piano harder)

One of the most popular of all piano trios, this is a large-scale work in four movements. Its popularity applies to domestic players as much as to the concert hall: but it depends on the pianist's ability to handle Mendelssohn's brilliant piano writing. The work is mellifluous throughout, full of memorable tunes, and musically delightful but undemanding. The writing gives both string players much enjoyable material, frequently taking the lead, but is technically playable by amateurs of reasonable attainment.

Op. 66 in C minor (1845)                                                                              29m; D4

Though less often played than its predecessor, this trio is not a lesser work: but it is more ambitious, larger in its scope and more varied in its character. The last pages of the finale are sometimes criticized for their bombastic forcefulness; but not all will agree. The string parts are more difficult than those of op. 49, though still within the range of capable amateurs.

## Piano Quartets

It is curious that Mendelssohn's first three published works are piano quartets. All are early, two of them very early. Only the third is really of interest.

Op. 1 in C minor (1822)                                                    29m; D3–
Perhaps fun to play once, but the material is too humdrum to maintain long-term interest. Most enjoyable is the trio (not so marked) of the scherzo, engagingly scored for viola, cello and piano left hand.

Op. 2 in F minor (1823)                                                    27m; D3
A great improvement on its predecessor – some of the themes have real magic; but there is also much uninspired passage-work. Most distinctive is the third movement *Intermezzo*.

Op. 3 in B minor (1824–5)                                    33m; D3 (piano harder)
Completed in January of the year that later saw the composition of the octet. This quartet is a major advance on its predecessors, and is almost a great work: but not quite. Perhaps it is too ambitious, trying to be an important and serious composition when the fifteen-year-old composer had not the emotional capacity for that. Nevertheless, given a pianist who can handle it, this is an enjoyable quartet to play.

## Piano Sextet

Op. 110 in D (1824) (piano, violin, 2 violas, cello, double bass)

31m; D3 (piano harder)
An immediate attraction of this early sextet is the unique instrumental combination: so it is fun to play. But it is not good. The piano works hard much of the time, while the use of the strings is unenterprising. Musically it is mostly gentle.

## Ensemble Works including Wind Instruments

Konzertstück in F minor, op. 113 (1832) (clarinet, basset horn, piano)      8½m; D4

Konzertstück in D minor, op. 114 (1833) (clarinet, basset horn, piano)       9m; D4
These two concert pieces are similar, both in three short movements and played without a break. Their scope is modest. They have no virtuoso display, and interest is shared between all three parts. The clarinet is in B♭, the basset horn in F. Arrangements for alternative instruments are published, including for two clarinets and piano, or with the basset horn replaced by bass clarinet or bassoon.

## Duet Sonatas and other Duets

There are six sonatas to be considered. Three are early, and are disappointing. The remaining three are a different matter. The two sonatas for cello and piano (together with the two other works for this combination) are an important contribution to the cello repertoire. All the sonatas except the second cello sonata are in three movements.

Op. 4 in F minor (1823) (violin, piano)                                                22m; D2
Insipid.

Sonata in F (1838) (violin, piano)                                                     25m; D4+
Strangely, this fine sonata from Mendelssohn's maturity remained unpublished until 1953. It is still not well known. Unfortunately it is technically difficult, especially the finale with its pervasive fast semiquavers.

Sonata in C minor (1824) (viola, piano)                               29m; D3 (piano harder)
Musically weak, and its treatment of the viola is unenterprising. It is playable, and viola enthusiasts may be keen to try it: but limited satisfaction will result. It was published in 1966.

Op. 45 in B♭ (1838) (cello, piano)                                                      24m; D4
Gratifying playing throughout. The whole sonata is of excellent, beautiful music; but its scope is moderate.

Op. 58 in D (1843) (cello, piano)                                                       26m; D4
Larger and more ambitious than its predecessor; all four movements are fine but particularly notable is the very original, Bach-inspired *Adagio*.

*Variations Concertantes, op. 17 (1829)* (cello, piano)                                 10m; D4+
Excellent – as is usual with Mendelssohn in variation form. As befits the name, the work is technically quite demanding.

*Song Without Words* in D, op. 109 (1845) (cello, piano)                                4½m; D3
This charming piece is the final work in Mendelssohn's important output for cello and piano.

Sonata in E♭ (1824) (clarinet, piano)                                                   23m; D3
Not a masterwork, but easily the best of the early sonatas: modest but attractive music throughout. It has a particular value in that, having probably been written for an amateur (Baron von Kaskel), it is technically undemanding. The clarinet is in B♭.

# MOZART
## 1756–1791; Austria

Wolfgang Amadeus Mozart stands with Haydn, Beethoven and Schubert: the four great masters of the Viennese classical period. Of them, Mozart is the only one to have produced multiple supreme masterpieces in every major genre. Opera, choral music, the symphony, the concerto, piano music, chamber music: he is indispensable to all. He was a consummate and peerless master. But more than that: for some, he is the most loved of all composers. His music has a natural inevitability, a 'God-given perfection', that is unique to him. His genius could create the sublime from the seemingly simple or commonplace. He had an apparently infallible command of form.

Mozart's chamber music is in some ways unmatched by that of any other composer. The number of works is large, though it falls well short of that of Haydn; but unlike Haydn, Mozart wrote major works for a wide range of instrumental combinations, including combinations that involve wind instruments. Some of them, such as the string quintets, the piano quartets and the works for one wind instrument with strings, are the first significant works for their medium, and in many cases they arguably remain the most important. He also made major contributions to the more standard combinations of string quartet, piano trio and sonata for violin and piano.

Another quality valued by amateurs is that his chamber music is playable. He avoided virtuoso writing. Of course, this does not mean that it is easy to play well. For all, including professionals, performing Mozart beautifully is a major challenge. Mozart's writing for chamber ensembles is often ideally democratic. Among the strings Mozart played the viola, and many of his works that include that instrument show the pleasure he took in writing for it.

Mozart's life was remarkable, but ultimately tragic. Born in Salzburg, from an early age he was a child prodigy as both performer and composer. His first known compositions date from when he was five years old. The years from 1762 to 1773 were dominated by lengthy journeys in which he and his sister Nannerl were taken by their musician father Leopold to be displayed as prodigies to the courts of Europe, generally to great acclaim. When he was no longer a child this could not continue. From 1773 to 1781 he lived in Salzburg as a musician at the court of the Prince Archbishop, but was frustrated by the limitations of this life. In 1781 he settled in Vienna to make his way independently. In 1782 he married. For a time, as composer and performer, he was successful. However, this did not last. Circumstances changed; the interest of the public seemed to waver. Through the later 1780s, now with family responsibilities, things went from bad to worse. New works brought him small return. His life became a struggle, begging and borrowing, desperately hoping that new compositions would solve his problems.

He became demoralized and his compositional output slowed. Then, late in 1791, he fell ill of a malady the nature of which is still unclear, and died. He was thirty-five.

Mozart's earliest compositions are of little interest to us. However, by 1772, at the age of sixteen, he was composing music some of which is highly valued and frequently played today. There is no dividing line between the early Mozart and the accomplished master: he developed throughout his life; but he might be considered as having reached full maturity by around 1778 or K. 300.

Some of Mozart's compositions were originally published under opus numbers, but these numbers are not useful and are rarely used today. Works are normally designated by their number from the catalogue of Ludwig von Köchel, originally published in 1862 – the first important catalogue of a composer's works. Its numbers were intended to be chronological. Inevitably, however, Köchel's original catalogue had errors and omissions. Later editions have introduced corrections, most recently in the sixth edition, of 1964. In this, Köchel's original numbers are retained as far as possible; but where their chronological sequence is incorrect, new numbers have been allocated, identified by having a letter added to them. Thus Mozart's first string quartet, in G of 1770, is usually known as K. 80, the number allocated to it in 1862; but its modern designation is K. 73f. Some works omitted from Köchel's original catalogue appeared subsequently in an appendix (Anhang, abbreviated Anh.). Thus the flute quartet no. 3 in C (still considered of uncertain authenticity) was first catalogued in this way as K. Anh. 171. These appendices have, however, subsequently been integrated into the catalogue, and this work now appears as K. 285b. For works that have changed number, however, the original number still uniquely identifies the work, and can continue to be used (and frequently is). Where two numbers are applicable, both are given in the descriptions below.

## String Duos

In his two duos for violin and viola, Mozart gave us the finest compositions that exist for the combination. Despite the small forces, these are fine and meaningful works, in which Mozart deploys all his skills. Both have three movements. Their distribution of the musical interest between the instruments is excellent. They contrast with all other works for the medium: the viola part is not simply an accompaniment to the violin; they are not relatively minor works (as are others of the late eighteenth and early nineteenth centuries); and (unlike some virtuoso works of the nineteenth century) they are playable.

K. 423 in G (1783) (violin, viola)                                      16m; D3

A confident and masculine work, with at its centre a beautiful *Adagio*. It is remarkable how democratic the whole work is, how fully the interest is shared. There is much vigorous and equal interplay between the instruments, and the viola is often given the melody, accompanied by the violin.

<u>K. 424 in B♭ (1783)</u> (violin, viola)                                    20m; D3+

This is the more graceful and relaxed of the two duos, but slightly the more difficult. Its final movement is a delightfully fresh set of variations. Though still beautifully written for the instruments, it does not have the almost miraculous equality between them of the companion work. In particular, in the *Andante cantabile* middle movement the viola accompanies throughout, largely in double-stops.

---

Other works for string duo published under Mozart's name are arrangements. The twelve duets for two violins, op. 70, first published in 1800, originated as various other chamber works (mostly either piano sonatas or sonatas for violin and piano). Also available in string arrangements are the twelve duos for two horns, K. 487/496a.

## String Trios

Mozart wrote one major work for string trio; but there is other music of interest too.

<u>K. 266/271f in B♭ (1777)</u> (2 violins, cello)                              10m; D2

This little-known work is in just two movements. Nevertheless, it is beautiful and makes an enjoyable short play. The violins are treated equally. The cello part (specified by Mozart in the manner of the time as basso) mainly provides support, but it has some interest too.

<u>Four preludes with fugues, K. 404a (1782)</u> (violin, viola, cello)    Each 6–9m; D3

These, too, are relatively little-known. They were unpublished until 1938. Though very probably Mozart's work, their authenticity has been questioned. They date from a period when Mozart was very interested in the music of Bach and Handel. Only the preludes are original works. The fugues are arrangements, and transposed to new keys: three are by J.S. Bach (from the *Well-Tempered Clavier*); the fourth is by Bach's eldest son Wilhelm Friedemann. They are enjoyable and interesting to play: the preludes (which are all *Adagio*) are beautiful, and the fugues are excellent. They make valuable additions to the small repertoire for the medium.

Included with these in at least one published edition are two further similar arrangements. In these, however, the preludes, too, are arrangements of movements by J.S. Bach. (Mozart also made some arrangements for string quartet of J.S. Bach fugues: they are K. 405.)

<u>Divertimento in E♭, K. 563 (1788)</u> (violin, viola, cello)          45m; D3+

It is surprising that Mozart gave this trio the title Divertimento – which though appropriate in that there are six movements seems otherwise misleading, since this is not lightweight entertainment music. Mozart here composed something special and monumental. It is a major masterpiece, widely considered the finest string trio ever written. It is also Mozart's longest chamber work. Everything about it is tremendous. Particularly memorable, perhaps, is the magnificent, powerfully beautiful *Adagio* second movement. There are two minuets, the second of which has two trios. The fourth movement is a set of variations. The distribution of the musical material between the parts is remarkably equal. In consequence the viola and cello parts are especially gratifying – what opportunities they are given! But they are also quite difficult by Mozart's standards: such powerful, large-scale music in such a small medium is demanding to play.

## String Quartets

Mozart's string quartets fall neatly into two quite different groups. Between 1770 and 1773, in his teenage years, he composed thirteen quartets (and also three other works often played as string quartets). A gap of nine years followed before he wrote the first of his ten great quartets. It is the latter group that are well known and a staple of the repertoire, but the early quartets are valuable too, both musically and because they are technically relatively undemanding.

For each quartet, in addition to the indications of duration and difficulty, a suggestion is given (as with Haydn's string quartets and piano trios) of value in terms of musical quality and enjoyment of playing. One to five stars (*****) are awarded, five being highest.

Not discussed is *Eine Kleine Nachtmusik*, K. 525, of 1787. This is for string orchestra, though it can be played by a string quartet.

<u>K. 80/73f in G (1770, 1773)</u>          16m; D3; **

This first quartet is a singleton, composed in Italy and in Italian style under the influence of Sammartini. The almost equal treatment of the violins comes from the trio sonata tradition. Nevertheless, the viola and cello parts are not without interest. Originally in three movements, Mozart returned to the quartet probably in late 1773 and added a fourth. This is a modest work but makes enjoyable playing.

---

The next three works are not really string quartets. They were written early in 1772, when Mozart was sixteen. Little is known about his intentions for them, but they were almost certainly to be played by multiple strings. They are often known as divertimenti because that heading appears on the manuscripts – but not written there by Mozart. It is appropriate to their light, entertainment character; but divertimenti normally have at least five movements and include minuets, whereas these are in three movements with no minuet. They are sometimes called 'Salzburg symphonies'. Concert performances are usually by a string orchestra. However, these works (especially the first and third) are highly popular and are frequently played by string quartets – they are staples of the 'wedding music' repertoire used as background music for social gatherings. They do not have a normal string quartet texture: their melodic interest is predominantly in the two violins, which are treated almost equally and are kept very busy. Their parts are moderately difficult, while the viola and cello parts are less interesting and are mostly undemanding.

'Divertimento' in D, K. 136/125a (1772)          13m; D3 (viola and cello easier); ****
Delightful music; the outer movements (*Allegro* and *Presto*) are brilliant and ebullient.

'Divertimento' in B♭, K. 137/125b (1772)          12m; D3 (viola and cello easier); **
Good, but less popular than its companions. Its charm is not quite so infectiously enjoyable. It opens with an *Andante*, followed by two fast movements.

'Divertimento' in F, K. 138/125c (1772)          10m; D3 (viola and cello easier); ****
Completely delightful. Perhaps most exquisite and memorable is the central *Andante*.

Within a year of the previous works, in Italy at the end of 1772 and beginning of 1773, Mozart composed his first set of six string quartets. Mostly written in Milan, they are known as the Milanese quartets. They all have three movements, are in major keys, and show Italian influence. They belong to that early period of quartet writing before Haydn had established the medium in its four-movement form and weightiness of content. They delightfully exhibit the young Mozart's growing natural genius. Their material has a fresh and compelling originality; and Mozart soon establishes an excellent true string quartet texture, with interest given democratically to all. They are not all unflawed masterpieces, but much enjoyment is to be had from them. Being musically charming, with the interest distributed to all parts, yet without being technically difficult, they are among the best quartets for inexperienced players to try.

K. 155/134a in D (1772)          9m; D2; **
Pleasant, but not musically one of the best of the set. Little independent interest is given to the cello until the very brief last movement.

K. 156/134b in G (1772)          13m; D2+; ****
This is Mozart's first string-quartet masterpiece. Textures are excellent, with at last real freedom and participation for the viola and cello. Every movement is fine.

Perhaps most impressive is the powerful and deeply felt central *Adagio*, in E minor. The delightfully fresh finale, a *Tempo di Menuetto*, is notable for the almost complete equality of the parts, especially in the trio section. This quartet is not difficult, but inexperienced players may have problems in the *Adagio* with the passages of quavers displaced a semiquaver from the beat. In the finale, bar twenty-four gives second violins a lesson in confident assertiveness by their *forte* entry from nothing.

<u>K. 157 in C (1772–3)</u>                                                    12m; D2; \*\*\*

Another good quartet. Mozart continues to distribute the interest through the parts (though not quite to the extent of the previous quartet). The three movements are well-balanced; the central *Andante* in C minor is beautiful and gently sad.

<u>K. 158 in F (1772–3)</u>                                                    15m; D2; \*\*\*

The central slow movement, again in a minor key (A minor) and with a series of canonic entries, is beautiful and enjoyable. However, the outer movements are rather quirky and capricious. The final movement is a *Tempo di Menuetto*.

<u>K. 159 in B♭ (1773)</u>                                                    13m; D2; \*\*\*

The first two movements are excellent and enjoyable to play; but the quartet as a whole is uneven. The *Andante* first movement is delightful. It opens with eight bars of second violin solo before the first violin enters; but a first violin who relies on instinct rather than counting carefully will come in wrongly! In the recapitulation, much the same happens, but this time after seven bars. The central movement surprises by being an *Allegro*: it is in G minor, serious and purposeful. After these, the final rondo is disappointing, with a rather trite main theme.

<u>K. 160/159a in E♭ (1773)</u>                                                    11m; D2; \*\*\*

Perhaps more conventional than most members of this set; but it is attractive, enjoyable to play and consistent in its three movements.

—••••—

Only about six months after completing the previous set, in Vienna in August and September 1773, Mozart followed it with another. There is immediately a difference in character: Mozart must have seen Haydn's quartets of opp. 17 and 20 (published respectively in 1771 and 1772) and been knocked sideways by them. In these quartets he attempted to assimilate what he had seen. Many of the changes are obvious. Instead of three movements, all now have four. As some of Haydn's finales are fugues, so are two of Mozart's. Haydn's sets included at least one quartet in a minor key: Mozart includes one in his set. However, it is often suggested that in this immediate response, apparently written in haste, the influences are ill-digested. Only as Mozart continued to develop did he fully absorb into his style the implications of Haydn's innovations.

Nevertheless, these quartets have much that is fine and well worth playing. They are of greater musical ambition than their predecessors, and much of that ambition is achieved. Their new emphasis on counterpoint adds a fresh dimension. They are a significant step along the road towards his mature quartet masterpieces. They are certainly uneven, but they are good at least in parts. As compared with the previous set, they are longer and a little more difficult to play.

K. 168 in F (1773)                                                14m; D2; ****

An excellent start to the set. All movements except the first are highly contrapuntal, and the last is a fugue. Musically, too, every movement is good.

K. 169 in A (1773)                                                16m; D2+; **

Overall this is not good. The trio of the minuet is brief and trite; and so short is the rondo finale that one feels that Mozart had lost interest and only wanted to move on to the next quartet. This is a pity, since the first two movements are well written for all and have a real breadth and power.

K. 170 in C (1773)                                                15m; D2+; **

This quartet, though largely consistent in character, is rather lacklustre by Mozart's standards. Also disappointing is its concentration of musical interest in the first violin. Whilst sometimes shared with the second violin and occasionally with the viola, it hardly ever reaches the cello.

K. 171 in E♭ (1773)                                               16m; D2+; ***

A quartet of ambitious seriousness in the *Adagio* sections that frame the first movement, and in the very contrapuntal *Andante* in C minor. Every movement is good, and all parts are enjoyable.

K. 172 in B♭ (1773)                                               16m; D2; ***

Although the *Adagio* second movement is perhaps the most beautiful in this quartet, disappointingly it is entirely an accompanied violin solo. Likewise there is little democracy about the first movement, though here both violins share the main material. Much better in their distribution of interest are the third and fourth movements.

K. 173 in D minor (1773)                                          17m; D2; ****

Powerful and serious: perhaps the finest quartet of the set. The first movement is sombre and mostly subdued. Only the relatively lightweight slow second movement is in the major key. The last movement is an impressive fugue.

---

Nine years elapsed before Mozart again composed for string quartet – though during this interval he composed several quartets for flute or oboe with strings. It was perhaps in late 1781, soon after he moved to Vienna, that he first met Haydn in person; certainly by 1785 they had become friends. Also in 1781 or 1782 Mozart encountered Haydn's op. 33 – the first new set of quartets by Haydn since Haydn's op. 20 that had so impressed him nine years before. This set, composed 'in a new and special manner', again deeply affected Mozart and he was stimulated to compose new quartets of his own, the first late in 1782. Five more followed over rather more than two years. They were published in 1785 (as op. 10) with a long and celebrated letter of dedication to Haydn, in which Mozart described them as 'the fruit of long and laborious endeavour'. Unlike what had happened in 1773, Mozart arguably this time went beyond Haydn's achievement and composed string quartets that are even greater, and in their character are fully personal to him. These six are the first of Mozart's ten incomparable quartet masterworks.

### K. 387 in G (1782)                                                                29m; D3+; *****

This very impressive quartet is long – the longest quartet to date by any major composer. It is also utterly democratic. In both the first and second movements, a chromatic scale is employed as a theme with the surprising device of alternate notes being *piano* and *forte*. The finale is exhilarating, with much fugal writing. It goes fast, and quavers are very fast (some accompanying quavers in the second violin involving string crossing are difficult). Though marked *Molto allegro*, it should not be so fast as to become a scramble! The nickname 'Spring' is sometimes used for this quartet.

### K. 421/417b in D minor (1783)                                                     27m; D3; *****

A magnificent, sombre and serious work. All movements are wonderful; and there are excellent opportunities for all players. Just the F major *Andante* that comes second offers relief from the seriousness. The finale is a set of variations; apart from one in D major it remains in the minor key to the end. Characteristically for Mozart, a variation is given to the viola.

Playing Mozart well can be difficult technically as well as musically. The triplet semiquaver figure that is tossed from player to player in the *più allegro* coda of the variations offers an example: even some of the best professional quartets fail to play it cleanly.

### K. 428/421b in E♭ (1783)                                                          27m; D3; *****

A warm and beautiful quartet. For the most part its melodies are not obviously singable, but everything is lovely to play, and its material is delightfully distributed to all voices. The core is perhaps the long and thoughtful *Andante con moto*.

Although this was the third quartet composed of the set, and is printed third in most editions, Mozart for some reason inscribed it on the manuscript as the fourth and the following 'Hunt' as the third.

### K. 458 in B♭ ('The Hunt') (1784)                                    27m; D3–; *****

The nickname alludes to the opening theme of the work. In keeping with that character, the outer movements are vigorous, outgoing and hearty. Within this cheery framework, however, the slow movement is the only one in this set of quartets marked *Adagio*; it is solemn and lovely, and has some memorable solos for the cello. Technically the whole work is straightforward – the least demanding of all Mozart's mature string quartets.

### K. 464 in A (1785)                                                   33m; D3; *****

Perhaps the least popular quartet of the set; some find it austere, withdrawn and unattractive. But when known really well, it can come to seem among the most beautiful of all. Much of it is highly contrapuntal. It is Mozart's longest quartet, and part of the reason for this is the *Andante*, which is a remarkable and lengthy set of variations. Particularly striking is the sixth and final variation, where the cello has a prominent and fascinating figure in semi- and demisemiquavers (from which this quartet is sometimes referred to as 'The Drum'). In the coda, this figure continues and is passed through all the other instruments before finally returning to the cello. Second violinists are warned that, in the final movement from bar 122, there is a running quaver passage that, if sight-reading, many fail to execute successfully!

Note that the *Andante* is the third movement: some editions (including the widely used Peters, originating in the late nineteenth century) wrongly print it second.

### K. 465 in C ('The Dissonance') (1785)                                31m; D3; *****

The nickname comes, of course, from Mozart's harmonic procedures in the *Adagio* introduction: once controversial, this introduction now seems a magical start to a wonderful work. Of all Mozart's quartets, this is perhaps the best-loved: rich and glowing, full of exquisite and imaginative details. An enjoyable feature is the many distinctive passages given to the cello. Both outer movements bear some resemblance to Haydn in having quite demanding semiquaver passages for the first violin.

The heart of the quartet is the exquisite *Andante cantabile* second movement. Especially memorable is the oft-repeated little four-note figure that first appears as a duet between first violin and cello. A curious point arises concerning bars 26 and 75. These bars begin a series of imitative entries, and might be expected to have the initial entry on the first violin: yet for the one bar that part is silent (*see* illustration below). Many, including eminent past musicologists, have considered this a musical nonsense and that it should be 'corrected'. So some editions insert a first violin entry (even the modern Bärenreiter urtext edition offers it as an alternative). Yet Mozart was unambiguous: both in his autograph manuscript and in the first edition (which he supervised), in both places, the first violin does not play.

### K. 499 in D ('The Hoffmeister') (1786)    28m; D3; *****

A singleton quartet, named after its publisher who was a friend of Mozart's. This is a further masterwork that broadly follows in the mould of the previous set. It is highly enjoyable for all to play – its interest could hardly be spread more demo-cratically. It is not particularly difficult, but everyone is thoroughly exercised by the fast triplet quavers of the last movement, which are not always straightforward.

### Adagio and Fugue in C minor, K. 546 (1788)    7½m; D3; *****

The splendid fugue was composed in 1783 for two keyboards (K. 426) – a culmina-tion of the period of Mozart's interest in fugue and the music of J.S. Bach. In 1788 he arranged it for four strings, and composed an equally masterly *Adagio* intro-duction for it. Mozart's score indicates that he envisaged performance by a string orchestra; but it is more frequently played by string quartet. It is good to play: a powerful and intense work, among Mozart's finest achievements. The cello's role in the *Adagio* is remarkably bold.

---

The remaining three quartets are the outcome of a visit Mozart made in early 1789 to King Frederick William II of Prussia in Berlin, hoping it might lead to some financial relief. The king was an enthusiastic cellist, and Mozart returned with a commission for a set of six string quartets. However, he found composing them difficult, and having completed three by June 1790 – in a time of his worst money troubles – he did not complete the king's commission but instead sold them for publication to raise some immediate cash. Nevertheless, their character being strongly influenced by the intended dedication, they are known as the 'Prussian' or 'King of Prussia' quartets. They are very different from any of Mozart's previous string quartets. The cello is given prominent solos. In doing this, however, Mozart could not leave his quartet style otherwise unchanged: the other parts, too, have solos. When published in 1791, they were described as 'concertante quartets'. They have a lighter, more open texture, and their material is more obviously melodious. Although some critics have considered them inferior to the set dedicated to Haydn, most would rank them equally highly: these again are masterpieces. For players, provided they can cope with the notes, they are especially delightful. Technically, they are rather more difficult to play – particularly for the cellist, whose solos are sometimes high-lying. But the many solo opportunities for all make these quartets a unique pleasure.

### K. 575 in D (1789)    24m; D3+ (cello harder); *****

The extent to which the cello is favoured is very marked in this quartet, rather more so than in the subsequent two. The high cello solos in the trio of the minuet may particularly be remembered. A capable cellist, or one who is well prepared, is necessary. But there are also many solos for second violin and viola. The whole quartet is sunny and melodious. The many triplet quavers in the *Allegretto* finale include some (in all parts) that are awkward.

<u>K. 589 in B♭ (1790)</u>                           23m; D3+ (cello harder); *****

This quartet is perhaps less obviously attractive than its predecessor; but when well known it can become a favourite. Cello prominence is most marked in the first two movements; in the *Larghetto* second, it is given some outstanding cantabile melodies. At bars 38–9, even capable cellists unfamiliar with the work may lose their composure: but these bars are unaccompanied and may be treated flexibly. The minuet is exceptional. With its numerous semiquavers, it has a vigorous, athletic quality. The extraordinarily long and complex trio is even more energetic, culminating in a workout by the first violin that needs to be seen in advance. By contrast, the very contrapuntal finale is straightforward and quite short.

<u>K. 590 in F (1790)</u>                           28m; D4–; *****

Mozart's last quartet: and a splendid work. The cello emphasis continues, but rather less than in the previous quartets; much of the writing is so completely democratic that all voices have roles as prominent as that of the cello. Indeed, the generous treatment of the viola is noticeable: it has the leading role in much of the recapitulation of the first movement, and also the last word in the finale. The slow movement is meditative and lovely. There is ambiguity about its tempo indication, and editions differ. The first edition (published shortly after Mozart's death, probably not checked by him, and usually considered unreliable) shows *Allegretto*. Mozart's autograph has *Andante*, and this is to be preferred. There is a quaver passage in the minuet that some first violinists will need to practise. This is technically Mozart's most difficult quartet, especially because of the finale, which is complicated and is rarely without energetic semiquaver movement in at least one part.

## String Quintets

Mozart left us six string quintets, all for two violins, two violas and cello. He was not the first to write for the medium (Michael Haydn, Boccherini, Sammartini and others preceded him), but he was the first to write major masterpieces for it. Indeed, his example established the medium and its distinctive character.

Mozart's first string quintet dates from his early period. But in his tragic final years of money troubles, he returned to the combination and composed four supreme works, in two pairs just over three years apart. We do not know why he wrote them. A theory has been advanced that he planned a set of six for the King of Prussia, but there are good reasons for doubting this. The last two were possibly commissioned by Johann Tost (who later commissioned string quartets from Haydn). But it may be that Mozart turned to composing string quintets simply out of artistic necessity. Whatever the reason, they did not solve his financial problems.

In addition to the works described below, several other string quintets are published under Mozart's name. None is of much interest. They are either derived from incomplete fragments or are spurious arrangements. That identified as K. 46 in B♭ was produced by an unknown arranger from four movements of the seven-movement Serenade ('Gran Partita'), K. 361/370a, for wind instruments.

### K. 174 in B♭ (1773)          25m; D2+

Although under the shadow of its great successors, this early quintet is an outstanding work that should not be neglected. Written in December 1773 shortly after Mozart had composed two sets of six string quartets within a year, it is remarkably fine and delightful throughout. It is technically straightforward to play. The leading material is continually tossed between the players, giving frequent moments in the limelight to everyone; this includes the cello, though to a lesser degree. The first viola has additional prominence as effectively a second leader.

Shortly after initially completing the quintet, Mozart completely rewrote the trio of the minuet and the finale. The first versions of these are printed in some editions: but other than out of curiosity there seems little reason to play them.

### K. 515 in C (1787)          35m; D3

An expansive, magisterial and confident work: one of Mozart's finest achievements. All movements are long, especially the first. Technically it is straightforward throughout, and makes enjoyable playing. The opening movement starts on cello, and continues to give plenty more for cellists to enjoy. The *Andante* is remarkable for being predominantly a rapt duet between first violin and first viola – a special pleasure for viola players. However, though in this movement the other parts are mostly subsidiary, Mozart maintains interest for all.

Confusion may be encountered about the order of the movements. This has arisen because Mozart's autograph was rebound at a later date with the *Andante* incorrectly placed second. The correct order has this movement third.

### K. 516 in G minor (1787)          34m; D3

An excellent quintet, beautifully written for the ensemble, enjoyable for all and not particularly difficult. Of all Mozart's string quintets, it has a particular celebrity, which probably derives from its key of G minor and the character that Mozart gave to all his mature works in this key. This quintet is often considered mainly in emotional terms, as expressing tragedy. Undeniably much of it is sombre, and it reaches a remarkable peak of intensity in the G minor *Adagio* introduction to the finale. Some critics, therefore, have considered as an anticlimax the apparently cheerful G major rondo that follows. But this is surely the wrong way to consider Mozart's music: the rondo is a very fine movement, long and resourceful, a splendid conclusion to a great work.

<u>K. 406/516b in C minor (probably 1788)</u>                                    23m; D2+

Mozart arranged this from his serenade for wind octet, K. 388/384a, of about 1782. This was perhaps done as a quick way of completing the set of three quintets which in 1788 he offered on subscription hoping to bring in some immediate money. It is good; Mozart's arrangement gives plenty of enjoyable playing for all. But it is not the equal of the companion quintets: compared with them it is short, stern in character, and still somehow sounds like arranged wind music. It is also technically easier than they are. The particular interest that Mozart in 1782 took in strict counterpoint is illustrated by the *Menuetto in Canone*, which has a *Trio al rovescio* (an inversion canon, in which the imitating voice moves in contrary motion to the leading voice).

<u>K. 593 in D (1790)</u>                                                        28m; D3+

A superb work. This and its following companion quintet show the significantly different style of Mozart's final years. Its texture is fresh and open, and all parts are very gratifying. For some, this (rather than the G minor) is the favourite among Mozart's string quintets. The pensive *Larghetto* introduction, which reappears near the end of the movement, is hauntingly beautiful. The *Adagio* is among Mozart's most exquisite and profound slow movements. Technically the brilliant, contrapuntal finale is quite difficult.

A curious consideration applies to the finale (*see* illustration below). All older editions (based on the first publication of 1793) have the opening theme on the first violin beginning with a stepwise diatonic descent (a). However, from 1956, authentic editions instead have a chromatic descent (b), which appears in Mozart's autograph manuscript. The difference affects all parts in many passages throughout the movement. Editors considered the stepwise form an unauthorized alteration by an unknown person. But in a reassessment, the editors of the 2010 Henle edition argue persuasively that the alteration may well be Mozart's, and print both versions as alternatives. So – for those who can choose – the stepwise version, which it is possible to feel is musically better, may be preferred.

<u>K. 614 in E♭ (1791)</u>                                                       25m; D4

This is Mozart's last full-scale chamber work. It shows him at his most spirited and cheerful – a glowing and outgoing work. It is energetic and dancing, and this makes it technically the most difficult of these quintets. It glories in its contrapuntal ingenuity, especially in the last movement. The whole work is full of grateful opportunities for every player: provided the notes can be handled, everyone will enjoy playing this – perhaps the first viola most of all.

## Piano Trios

Mozart composed six piano trios: one is early and of minor interest, but the remaining five date from his last years. Nevertheless, they are perhaps not quite the best of Mozart's chamber music. It has been suggested that the last five, composed in the period of his financial problems, were written mainly to make money and with less personal involvement. Whether or not there is any truth in this, they include much that is exceedingly fine. Unlike Haydn's piano trios, those of Mozart, after the first, have a cello part that is musically essential. At times it carries the melody or takes part in dialogue on equal terms with the other players. Nevertheless, as has already been remarked, there are limits to its freedom, presumably because Mozart was still influenced by the conventions of the time. In the last two trios, however, the cello's freedom increases. All six trios have three movements.

Often also included in complete publications of the piano trios is the clarinet trio, K. 498 (which is discussed in a later section).

Players seeking another Mozart piano trio in addition to those described here might try what is known as the piano trio in D minor, K. 442. This is a quite convincing assembly and completion, originally due to Mozart's friend Maximilian Stadler, from three unrelated, unfinished movements probably of about 1783. Alternative completions also exist.

Divitimento in B♭, K. 254 (1776)          21m; D2+

The title is a puzzle: this is a normal work in three movements. The texture is the same as Haydn's (yet to be written) mature piano trios: the violin part though somewhat subsidiary is interesting, but the cello part has scarcely any freedom. As music it is pleasant, but little more. However, being quite easy in all parts, it may be valuable to inexperienced amateurs.

K. 496 in G (1786)          26m; D3

This is a fine trio, with attractive and fresh music throughout. The final movement is a set of variations, in one of which the cello plays the leading role.

K. 502 in B♭ (1786)          23m; D3+

A beautiful work, characteristic of Mozart at his most inventive and delightful. Perhaps especially beautiful is the long, rapt central *Larghetto*. Throughout the work the pianist is given much energetic figuration.

K. 542 in E (1788)          19m; D3

Another unreservedly beautiful trio; and compared with its predecessor the piano part is less dominant and has less bravura. There are some for whom this is their favourite Mozart piano trio.

K. 548 in C (1788)          21m; D3

A charming and excellent trio, though some critics have considered it musically inferior to its predecessors. This is debatable; moreover, from the point of view of players it has some major advantages: its key is comfortable, and the writing is particularly democratic. The piano does not greatly dominate, and the cello part is gratifying – in the very beautiful *Andante cantabile* it is as free as the violin.

K. 564 in G (1788)                                                                                         17m; D2+

This final trio differs considerably from the others: it is shorter and seems more straightforward musically and technically. It was probably intended for beginners. It is nevertheless charming, and the more generous treatment of the cello noticeable in the previous trio is continued. The central movement is a set of variations (one being for cello). This trio is worth playing by all, but it is especially suitable for relatively inexperienced amateurs.

## Piano Quartets

This combination as chamber music was unknown before Mozart. Although both Beethoven and Schubert dabbled in the medium, these two great works stood largely unrivalled until the early romantic period. Both are splendid examples of Mozart at his best. They are in three movements.

K. 478 in G minor (1785)                                                                                26m; D3

Powerful and serious, as would be expected of Mozart in this key. The seriousness continues into the slow movement in B♭ major; and the impressive G major rondo finale is an appropriate conclusion. The ensemble is often used antiphonally – strings together against piano; the string parts, including that for cello, are good and enjoyable. Particularly gratifying material sometimes comes to the viola. Though technically interesting, the string parts are straightforward, but the piano part is quite demanding.

K. 493 in E♭ (1786)                                                                                     18m; D3

In its use of the ensemble, this quartet closely resembles its predecessor. However, it is a contrast in its mood, being warm, relaxed and full of engaging incident. It is hard to decide on a preference between the two quartets.

## Piano Quintets

Mozart wrote no piano quintets. However, when he composed his first Vienna set of piano concertos in late 1782 and early 1783, he said they could be performed with full orchestra or 'a quattro', which is taken as meaning with string quartet. These concertos are no. 11 in F, K. 413/387a, no. 12 in A, K. 414/385p, and no. 13 in C, K. 415/387b. They have been published in this form (with an optional double bass shadowing the cello an octave below). Some others of the piano concertos, too, have been made available for this grouping.

*See also* the Adagio and Rondo in C minor, K. 617, below.

## Works for one Wind Instrument with Strings

These works for a variety of different combinations are much valued especially by players of the respective wind instruments. All are singletons except that there are four quartets for flute and strings (which, however, are rather an uneven and curious group). The finest work is the great clarinet quintet.

Sonata for bassoon and cello in B♭, K. 292/196c (?1775)                13m; D3
This modest but attractive three-movement work gives the melodic role to the bassoon throughout. However, the cello part, though accompanying, is enjoyable. Several questions hang over the work, one being the possibility that Mozart wrote the cello part as a basso continuo.
    Arrangements are also published for many other pairs of instruments.

Flute quartet in D, K. 285 (1777) (flute, violin, viola, cello)    14m; D3 (flute harder)
This is the finest of the flute quartets. The flute part is mainly treated as a solo, which makes it demanding for amateur flautists. But Mozart is resourceful in his use of the strings, which have quite interesting parts; he even contrives a few solos for the viola. The centrepiece of the three movements is the *Adagio*, an exquisite flute solo with pizzicato accompaniment – though even this accompaniment moves and has some interest.

Flute quartet in G, K. 285a (1778) (flute, violin, viola, cello)                10m; D3–
Relatively minor, with only two movements: but it is still charming music. It is more democratic than its predecessor, and easier for all parts.

Flute quartet in C, K. Anh. 171/K. 285b (?1781) (flute, violin, viola, cello)    16m; D3
Some scholars, though not all, doubt the authenticity of this quartet. However, no matter: it is modest but charming and seemingly very Mozartian. Another version of the second of its two movements (a set of variations) appears in the Serenade ('Gran Partita'), K. 361/370a.

Flute quartet in A, K. 298 (probably 1786) (flute, violin, viola, cello)        11m; D3
This quartet (of which the Köchel number is now considered inaccurate) is a light-weight entertainment work, perhaps an occasional piece. As themes Mozart used tunes by other composers that were popular at the time, probably with an intention of parody. The result is without subtleties but offers enjoyable playing to all. There are three movements.

Oboe quartet in F, K. 370/368b (1781) (oboe, violin, viola, cello)
                                                                14m; D3 (oboe harder)
A fine work in three movements. It was designed to show off the oboe, and as with the flute quartets the strings are subsidiary, but Mozart gives them plenty of interest. It several times exploits the ability of the oboe to play high F, which was new at

the time (and is still not necessarily easy!). There is a remarkable (and demanding) passage in the 6/8 finale where the oboe alone goes into 4/4.

Horn quintet in E♭, K. 407/386c (1782) (horn, violin, 2 violas, cello)

17m; D3– (horn harder)

This is a warm and charming three-movement work. Mozart chose the unusual string combination no doubt to produce a rich middle-register sound to match the horn. This is predominantly a showpiece for the horn, for which it is difficult. However, the strings are given plenty of good interest, especially in the lovely central *Andante*.

Clarinet quintet in A, K. 581 (1789) (clarinet, string quartet)        32m; D3

Among Mozart's works this is one of the greatest and most loved. It is a masterly, spacious, four-movement work of gracious beauty. The clarinet, with its warm, mellow tone, is often used as soloist, but at other times it blends into the texture of the ensemble. All players have gratifying parts; that for the clarinet, whilst it exploits the instrument's range and agility, does not make virtuoso demands. In the *Larghetto*, just the two violins are muted. The third movement minuet has the unusual feature of two trios; the first is for strings alone. The finale is a delightful set of variations; perhaps especially memorable is the plaintive melody for the viola in the third variation. The clarinet is in A.

## Works including Piano and one or more Wind Instruments

Quintet in E♭, K. 452 (1784) (piano, oboe, clarinet, horn, bassoon)        25m; D3

This outstanding work is a splendid possession for wind players, one of the finest things in the repertoire of music for wind. It is exquisitely beautiful throughout, and its treatment of the ensemble seems ideal. The piano is never unduly dominant, and the use of the wind instruments is utterly democratic: every player is given many delightful opportunities. There are three movements. The clarinet is in B♭.

Clarinet trio in E♭, K. 498 (1786) (piano, clarinet, viola)        20m; D3

Sometimes referred to by the nickname 'Kegelstatt', after a story that Mozart wrote it while playing a game of skittles – but this seems to trivialize what is one of Mozart's most masterly and exquisite works. He composed it to play the viola part himself with close friends. This probably explains its special warmth and sense of shared pleasure. It is entirely democratic (the free use of the viola contrasts with the rather constrained cello parts in the piano trios composed shortly before and after); and the writing is idiomatic to the characters of the instruments. All three movements are wonderfully distinctive. The minuet has a long and complicated trio, notable for the extensive triplet-quaver passages for the viola. The rondo finale has much singing melody for the clarinet; a declamatory section belongs mainly to the viola. This is a perfect work, a special joy for those who play it.

<u>Adagio and Rondo in C minor, K. 617 (1791)</u> (armonica, flute, oboe, viola, cello)

12m; D3–

Mozart's last chamber work. Strictly it does not include piano. The armonica, or glass harmonica, was invented in 1761 and had a short-lived vogue in the late eighteenth century. It is quiet, lacks attack and its sound, though sustained, is vague. Its music is written on two staves and resembles piano music. A few instruments and players exist, but even professional performances mostly use another instrument, usually piano. Alternatives include organ, harp, celesta or electronic keyboard. The work is beautiful and worth playing.

Sheet music is also obtainable for other instrumentations: piano and wind (with clarinet for viola and bassoon for cello), or piano and string quartet.

## Divertimenti and Serenades including Wind Instruments

Mozart (like Haydn) composed many works in this category. As with Haydn, the majority date from the earlier years of his career. Most of them are charming entertainment music; they are not really chamber music. However, they can be played domestically for pleasure and may be much enjoyed, although some may feel that most of them have insufficient interest for repeated playing.

### Divertimenti for wind and string instruments

These works are mostly for two horns with four string instruments. They make no attempt at being democratic, and in all of them the principal musical burden lies with the first violin, with considerable interest coming also to the second violin (where present). Most of them need a very strong first violinist. The cello part (identified as basso) may alternatively be played by double bass, or perhaps both. The horn parts are usually subsidiary and have few solos.

These divertimenti are sometimes played with multiple string players to a part – a small orchestra. Some include a march movement, which may be played first, last, or both. Mozart also composed many other works (often called serenade) for larger numbers of players, which are not discussed here. Also not considered, and certainly not chamber music, is *A Musical Joke*, K. 522, for two horns and four string instruments.

<u>Divertimento in D, K. 205/167a (1773)</u> (2 horns, violin, viola, cello, bassoon)

18m; D3

As usual, the violin part dominates, in this case supported by the viola: both have busy, entertaining but quite demanding parts. Cello and bassoon are specified, but they play the same line. There are five movements.

<u>Divertimento in F, K. 247 (1776)</u> (2 horns, string quartet)

31m; D3 (first violin harder)

Very entertaining and attractive music; there are six movements.

<u>Divertimento in D, K. 251 (1776)</u> (oboe, 2 horns, string quartet)

25m; D3 (first violin harder)

Thought to have been written for the twenty-fifth birthday of Mozart's sister Nannerl, this divertimento is distinctive for including an oboe. The oboe part is enjoyable, but is still mainly subsidiary to the first violin. There are six movements.

<u>Divertimento in B♭, K. 287/271H (1777)</u> (2 horns, string quartet)

39m; D3 (first violin virtuosic)

Another charming six-movement work. It perhaps gives the horns more interest than do some others. However, some of the first violin part is like a violin concerto and demands virtuoso playing.

<u>Divertimento in D, K. 334/320b (1779–80)</u> (2 horns, string quartet)

44m; D3 (first violin harder)

This last of these divertimenti is the longest and the closest to true chamber music. Its character is often less directly tuneful and more thoughtful than most of its predecessors. There is also rather more distribution of musical interest, sometimes including the horns, though most of the principal material is still given to the first violin. It has six movements.

### Divertimenti and serenades for wind instruments alone

These, too, are mainly lightweight entertainment music, in this case probably intended for outdoor performance, and not really chamber music. Most are sextets for two oboes, two horns and two bassoons. Compared to the works for wind and strings, these are more enjoyable for the wind players: they are democratic, with plenty of interest given to all parts – although in the sextets the first oboe is the leader and usually has most of the melodic material. Most have four movements and are short and modest in their musical scope. However, the series ends with two serenades that in both scale and character dwarf all their predecessors, and may surely be considered true chamber music.

In addition to those listed, there exist further works of doubtful authenticity – including another divertimento for two oboes, two horns and two bassoons, K. 289/271g. Also not discussed are several works for more than nine players, outstanding among which is the Serenade for thirteen instruments, K. 361/370a ('Gran Partita').

Also worthy of mention are the twelve charming duos for two horns, K. 487/496a, of 1786. (It has been suggested that they were intended for basset horns, but this seems doubtful.) Arrangements have been published for many other instruments, including two violins.

<u>Divertimento in C, K. 188/240b (1773)</u> (2 flutes, 5 trumpets, timpani)    9m; D2

In six short movements: simple both musically and technically. Three of the trumpets are in C, two in D.

Divertimento in F, K. 213 (1775) (2 oboes, 2 horns, 2 bassoons)    10m; D3

Divertimento in B♭, K. 240 (1776) (2 oboes, 2 horns, 2 bassoons)    13m; D2+

Divertimento in E♭, K. 252/240a (1776) (2 oboes, 2 horns, 2 bassoons)    11m; D2+

Divertimento in F, K. 253 (1776) (2 oboes, 2 horns, 2 bassoons)    15m; D2+
This divertimento is particularly attractive. It has only three movements, and is dominated by its opening movement, a theme and variations.

Divertimento in B♭, K. 270 (1777) (2 oboes, 2 horns, 2 bassoons)    12m; D2+
Returning to the four-movement standard, this is another attractive work, and one that shows Mozart's gradual advance through these works to a richer and more sophisticated treatment.

Serenade in E♭, K. 375 (1781–2) (2 oboes, 2 clarinets, 2 horns, 2 bassoons)  25m; D3
Mozart first composed this in 1781 for sextet, but the next year he rewrote it to add clarinets, which is the form in which it is usually played. It is in five movements, of relaxed, happy and exquisitely beautiful music: a delight for all players. The principal role is shared between first oboe and first clarinet. The clarinets are in B♭.

Serenade in C minor, K. 388/384e (1782 or 1783) (2 oboes, 2 clarinets, 2 horns, 2 bassoons)    24m; D3
This serenade is sometimes called 'Nacht Musik'. However, unlike its predecessor, it is a stern and serious work, not obviously of serenade character. It has four movements. Mozart shows his particular interest at the time in the counterpoint of J.S. Bach by including a *Menuetto in Canone*, with as its trio an inversion canon (the imitating voice moving in contrary motion to the leading voice). The last movement is a set of variations. The chamber-music character of this work is illustrated by the fact that Mozart later arranged it as a string quintet (K. 406/516b: *see above*).

## Duet Sonatas and other Duets

These are all for violin and keyboard. Not addressed here are sixteen sonatas (six of them for violin/flute) that were written in Mozart's first decade: though remarkable as the achievement of so young a child, they are of little interest. He returned to the form in his more mature years and completed a further sixteen works that are still today a major part of the repertoire. For these, Mozart clearly had the fortepiano in mind, not the harpsichord. There are also two sets of variations. (Not discussed are several further sonatas that were left incomplete, some of which have been completed by others.)

Still widely distributed are old editions of these sonatas not indicating their

Köchel numbers. Incipits of the violin part (occasionally also showing the piano right hand) are provided here to assist in identification.

Mozart did not in these sonatas follow the convention sometimes adopted at the time that the violin part was only an optional accompaniment to the piano. The violin is absolutely necessary and often has gratifying solos. Nevertheless, the first dozen of these sonatas show some influence of that practice: although the musical responsibility is usually well shared, the violin sometimes for considerable periods has subordinate or accompanying material.

There is some progression from the smaller and technically easier first group of sonatas to larger and more demanding works in the second set. The final three major sonatas are larger again; they are also fully democratic.

Especially in the earlier sonatas, neither part is difficult to play; even the later sonatas are often straightforward enough for sight-reading by reasonably capable amateurs. Musically they are delightful. For playing by amateurs, these are perhaps the ideal duet sonatas.

Various arrangements exist, usually for flute or other wind instruments instead of the violin.

The first group, known as the Mannheim Sonatas, has seven works. They comprise six that were published as a set, and one singleton (K. 296). The first five were written in Mannheim, the last two in Paris. Most are in two movements.

### K. 301/293a in G (1778)                                13m; D2

### K. 302/293b in E♭ (1778)                               11m; D2

The touchingly simple melody of the *Andante grazioso* rondo second movement remains in the memory.

### K. 303/293c in C (1778)                                10m; D2

### K. 305/293d in A (1778)                                15m; D2+

The second movement is an excellent set of variations.

K. 296 in C (1778)                                                                 17m; D2+

In three movements; perhaps not as attractive as some.

K. 304/300c in E minor (1778)                                                      15m; D2

A most beautiful minor-key work, one of the finest of the set and excellent to play.

K. 306/300l in D (1778)                                                            23m; D3–

In three movements, long and ambitious in its musical character; its seriousness contrasts with the charm of most of these sonatas. It is also more difficult, especially in the piano part.

* * *

The next group comprises five sonatas, mainly composed in 1781. They were published as another set of six by the inclusion of K. 296 from the previous group. These are generally more difficult and on a larger scale than their predecessors; all except K. 379 have three movements.

K. 378/317d in B♭ (1779)                                                           20m; D3

A large-scale work, bold in character and musically superb. The equality of the two parts seems ideal. Both are sometimes technically quite challenging.

K. 379/373a in G (1781)                                                            20m; D3–

In only two movements, but large-scale and fine. A long *Adagio* introduction is followed by a powerful *Allegro*, which is in G minor. The second movement is a set of variations: most are good, but violinists may be frustrated by their secondary role in the last three variations.

K. 376/374d in F (1781)                                                    17m; D3–

K. 377/374e in F (1781)                                                    19m; D3

The first two movements are fine, especially the magnificent second movement, a set of variations in D minor. But the finale is disappointing, particularly for the violinist.

K. 380/374f in E♭ (1781)                                                    18m; D3

All three movements are excellent. Some of the work, especially the restless first movement, has an almost Beethovenian character.

The final four sonatas are singletons. They all have three movements. The first three are his supreme achievements in the medium. The fourth, however, is not. (Also included in some old editions is K. 570 in B♭: this is a piano sonata to which a violin part has been added, probably not by Mozart.)

K. 454 in B♭ (1784)                                                        22m; D3

A splendid, large work, and totally democratic. Is this the most perfect and lovely of all these sonatas?

K. 481 in E♭ (1785)                                                        24m; D3

This, too, is an excellent, large work. Perhaps especially fine is the long, serious *Adagio*.

K. 526 in A (1787)                                                         25m; D3

Often considered the greatest of these sonatas, this is a serious and impressive work. However, it is quite difficult and has less Mozartian charm than some.

K. 547 in F (1788)                                                                                                   19m; D2+

Mozart described this as being for beginners: but even as such it is disappointing. The pianist cannot be a beginner; and the violin part is sometimes boringly dull, yet (at least for a beginner) it is in places awkward.

Variations on *La bergère Célimène*, K. 359/374a (1781)                                    15m; D3
Twelve variations: enjoyable. The theme is a French song.

Variations on *Hélas, j'ai perdu mon amant*, K. 360/374b (1781)                       11m; D3
In G minor; also excellent. This theme, too, is a French song.

# POULENC
## 1899–1963; France

Francis Poulenc was born in Paris and died there. He first came to prominence in the years around the end of the First World War, and in 1920 he was one of the group of young composers who became known as *Les Six*. (The others were Auric, Durey, Honegger, Milhaud and the female composer Tailleferre.) His compositions in this period were lightweight, high-spirited and occasionally irreverent; they sometimes show the influence of Stravinsky, whom he admired. Poulenc also displayed a melodic gift, and as he matured he developed a distinctive, mainly lyrical and melodious style; though flavoured by twentieth-century dissonance, it is basically diatonic, comprehensible and attractive. Through the 1930s, his compositions became more serious, and in these and subsequent years his output included religious music, many songs for voice and piano, and the well-known concerto for organ, strings and timpani. He composed chamber music throughout his compositional life. Most of it is for wind instruments; he said that he felt uncomfortable writing for solo strings, though his output includes duet sonatas for violin and for cello. The chamber works fall chronologically into three groups. The first three sonatas and the trio date from between 1919 and 1926, and are short and mainly bright. The three works of the 1930s and 1940s are more substantial, lyrical and sometimes serious. Between 1956 and 1963 he composed three duet sonatas for wind instruments. (A further sonata, for bassoon, was to follow; but like Saint-Saëns and Debussy in their comparable series of late sonatas, death prevented him from completing all he had planned.)

Poulenc did not use opus numbers. Recent publications give FP numbers, from the catalogue of Poulenc's works by Carl Schmidt, published in 1995. With the exception of the cello sonata, all the chamber works are in three movements.

## Ensemble Works for Wind Instruments

Sonata for two clarinets, FP 7 (1918, rev. 1945)                    6½m; D4
The central of its three short movements is gently beautiful, but the outer move-ments are brilliant, dry and sometimes humorous. One clarinet is in B♭, the other in A.

Sonata for clarinet and bassoon, FP 32 (1922, rev. 1945)                    8m; D4
Naturally the bassoon accompanies for much of the time, but Poulenc gives it plenty of interest. The clarinet is in B♭.

Sonata for horn, trumpet and trombone, FP 33 (1922, rev. 1945)                    9m; D4
This is a straightforward and remarkably melodious work. The trumpet plays the tune for most of the time, but melodic opportunities also come to the horn though not usually to the trombone. The trumpet is in C.

## Ensemble Works for Piano and Wind Instruments

Trio for oboe, bassoon and piano, FP 43 (1926)                    12m; D4
Perhaps the first of Poulenc's chamber works to be considered mature. It is full of verve and originality but is especially memorable for its many distinctive tunes. The writing for all parts is excellent, and melodic material is given to the bassoon almost as much as to the other players.

Sextet, FP 100 (1932, rev. 1939) (piano, wind quintet)                    18m; D4
This may be Poulenc's best-known and most popular chamber work. Much of it is in his most brilliant vein, vigorous and energetic; but equally, much of it is slower and lyrically beautiful. It is a true sextet, not dominated by the piano, and all parts are given much gratifying material. The clarinet is in B♭.

## Duet Sonatas

Sonata for violin and piano, FP 119 (1942–3, rev. 1949)                    18m; D4+
A fine and serious sonata, composed in occupied France and dedicated to the memory of the Spanish poet Federico García Lorca, who had been killed in the Spanish Civil War.

Sonata for cello and piano, FP 143 (1940–8)                    22m; D4+
In four movements, an impressive and beautiful work of broad scope.

Sonata for flute and piano, FP 164 (1956–7)                    12m; D3+
This is a popular and well-known sonata, direct in its musical appeal and fairly straightforward technically.

Sonata for clarinet and piano, FP 184 (1962)                    14m; D4

A fine and memorably attractive work. The clarinet is in B♭.

Sonata for oboe and piano, FP 185 (1962)                    14m; D4

Beautiful but sombre, this sonata was dedicated to the memory of Prokofiev; the outer movements are respectively *Élégie* and *Déploration*.

# PROKOFIEV
## 1891–1953; Russia

Sergey Prokofiev stands alongside Dmitri Shostakovich as the greatest and best-known of post-romantic Russian composers. Following the October Revolution of 1917, he left Russia and for most of the next two decades was based in Paris. However, after several visits to Russia, he returned permanently in 1936. In his student days he gained a reputation for his avant-garde harsh dissonance. However, he soon afterwards found his distinctive style, which remained based on tonality (keys are assigned to his works) and in which he adhered to classical forms. He had a gift for lyrical melodies, and though he sometimes employs astringent or percussive effects, his music is usually attractive and not hard to understand. He wrote a considerable number of chamber works, some of them in response to commissions. Although mostly quite difficult to play, they do not make virtuoso demands.

## String Duo

Sonata in C, op. 56 (1932) (2 violins)                    15m; D4+

In four short movements, in slow-fast-slow-fast layout, like a baroque *sonata da chiesa*. Some of it is readily playable but there are some very difficult passages.

## String Quartets

Both string quartets have three movements.

No. 1 in B minor, op. 50 (1930)                    23m; D4

The first two movements of this quartet are quite wayward and sometimes surprising, but they are full of interest. The emotional high point is the *Andante* final movement, which is varied but deeply felt throughout. Although challenging to sight-read, with practice most experienced amateurs will be able to play and enjoy this work. Musical interest is well distributed to all.

No. 2 in F, op. 92 (1941)                    22m; D4+

When Nazi Germany invaded Russia in 1941, Prokofiev along with other musicians and artists was evacuated to the Caucasus. There he heard the Kabardino-Balkar folk music of the region, with its oriental character, and he made extensive use of it in this quartet. The result is a powerful, atmospheric and delightful work, considered by some the finer of the two quartets – but it is also probably the more difficult. Sometimes the writing imitates Caucasian instruments. Instrumental techniques including ricochet bowing, sul ponticello and col legno are called for. The cello is sometimes sent very high, and has a cadenza in the last movement.

## Ensemble Works including Wind Instruments

<u>Overture on Hebrew themes, op. 34 (1919)</u> (clarinet, string quartet, piano)    9m; D3
This popular, lightweight work was written to a commission; Prokofiev was given a notebook of tunes from which to select. Curiously, the origin of the themes is unclear, but they certainly have a strong and attractive Jewish character – especially the opening theme, which plays an important role throughout. The clarinet part is prominent, but there is interest for all. It is not difficult to play. The clarinet is in B♭.

<u>Quintet in G minor, op. 39 (1924)</u> (oboe, clarinet, violin, viola, double bass)

20m; D4+

This rarely played work originated in a commission for music for a ballet, *Trapèze*, the subject being a circus. From this music, Prokofiev made six short movements into this quintet. Though entertaining, the music is abrupt, dry and impersonal, without any warmth. Not everyone will find it enjoyable to play; moreover some of it is very difficult. The third movement, *Allegro sostenuto, ma con brio*, is in a complicated 5/4 metre; a simplified alternative is offered – but some will still have problems! Oboe and clarinet share much of the musical interest, but the others have their opportunities, including unaccompanied solos for double bass. The clarinet is in A.

## Duet Sonatas

<u>Op. 80 in F minor (1938–45)</u> (violin, piano)                          29m; D4+
Usually referred to as 'Violin sonata no. 1', this is a fine and beautiful four-movement work, serious and sombre in character. Technically it is out of reach for most amateurs.

<u>Op. 119 in C (1949)</u> (cello, piano)                                  25m; D4+
This fine work again has much of Prokofiev at his most beguilingly lyrical.

<u>Op. 94 in D (1943, 1944)</u> (flute/violin, piano)          23m; D4 (violin harder)
A year after its composition for flute, at the encouragement of the violinist David Oistrakh, Prokofiev arranged it as 'Violin sonata no. 2'. The piano part is common to both. It is lyrical, warm and sunny – one of Prokofiev's most popular works. There are four movements, very classical in form. Some technically demanding additions in the violin part may be attributed to Oistrakh's involvement; trying the flute version could be an option for amateur violinists.

# PURCELL
## 1659–1695; England

Henry Purcell, one of the finest composers of his age, is generally considered the greatest native-born English composer before Elgar. He was highly regarded during his lifetime, but it was then not until the twentieth century that his importance was again appreciated and his music widely performed. He spent his entire life in London, and held important positions including organist of Westminster Abbey. Purcell's works are now usually identified by their number in the catalogue of 1963 by Franklin B. Zimmerman.

Most of Purcell's output is church music, incidental music to plays, and music dramas. *Dido and Aeneas* is his only opera. He also wrote music for small forces, but not all of it can be considered as chamber music. His works for viol consort are admired; principal among them is the series of fantasias (or fantazias), most of which are in four parts, the others being in three or five. They may be enjoyed in published editions for string quartet (or trio or quintet). Memorable among them is the *Fantasia On One Note*, Z745: when played by a two-viola quintet, the second viola plays C (on the G string) throughout! Another well-known work that can be played by a string quartet is the *Chacony in G minor*, Z730.

## Trio Sonatas

Twelve trio sonatas, Z790–801 (2 violins, continuo) 4–7m; up to D3–
These sonatas were published in 1683, and probably written shortly before that time. The publication describes them as 'Sonnata's of III. Parts', and indicates that the continuo is for organ or harpsichord. They are in an earlier style than the trio sonatas of composers such as Corelli and Handel. They have at least five short, varied movements, which are linked together without a break. The continuo part is often treated as a partner in the counterpoint, and so can be interesting.

Ten trio sonatas, Z802–811 (2 violins, continuo) 5–8m; up to D3–
This second set was published posthumously in 1697. Confusingly, the publisher entitled them 'Ten Sonata's in Four Parts': but actually the instrumentation is identical to that of the previous set. They resemble those of that set, but are more varied; they are thought to have been composed over a wider period of his life. Most have five or six movements. No. 6 in G minor, Z807, however, is a single long *Adagio* movement (but is full of variety). No. 9 in F, Z810, is known as 'The Golden Sonata', and has long been the most popular of all Purcell's trio sonatas. It is in five movements.

## Duet or Trio Sonata

<u>Sonata in G minor, Z780</u> (violin, continuo; or violin, bass viol, continuo)   7m; D3–
This was first published in 1899, based on a manuscript having two parts, as a
sonata for violin and keyboard. However, it is now thought that it is probably a trio
sonata for violin, obbligato bass viol and continuo, the bass viol part having been
lost; it has been published with this part in a hypothetical reconstruction of 1959
by Thurston Dart.

# RACHMANINOFF
### 1873–1943; Russia

Serge Rachmaninoff was one of the greatest, and the last, of the Russian romantic composers. He was also one of the outstanding pianists of his time. As a late
romantic continuing to compose through the first half of the twentieth century,
critics for many years had little good to say about him. However, his music had
a popularity with the public that ensured that much of it continued to be performed, and by the end of the twentieth century his greatness as a composer had
become recognized by all. He developed a very distinctive personal style, and had a
notable gift for melodies of great length and expressive quality. He left Russia in the
Revolution of 1917, living subsequently in America and touring as a pianist though
also continuing to compose. His chamber output is small and has just one major
work, the cello sonata, and two early piano trios. A few early pieces or fragments
are not discussed here.

## Piano Trios

*Trio élégiaque* no. 1 in G minor (1892)                                             15m; D3
Not published until 1947, this is in a single, slow movement, most of it sad. Though
immature, it is beautiful music, enjoyable to play for all, and not very difficult.

*Trio élégiaque* no. 2 in D minor, op. 9 (1893, rev. 1906, 1913)
                                                                    45m; D3+ (piano harder)
Dedicated 'to the memory of a great artist' – Tchaikovsky, who had just died. Its
form, in three movements with the second a set of variations, replicates that of
Tchaikovsky's great piano trio. Rachmaninoff's trio is too early to be really characteristic of him, but aspects of his mature style can be recognized. As one would
expect, it cannot match the power and scope of its prototype; and it is very long.
Nevertheless, for those who like Russian music, this is an enjoyable work. Violin
and cello have plenty of opportunities to enjoy, though the lion's share goes to the
piano, the writing for which is demanding.

## Duet Sonata

Op. 19 in G minor (1901) (cello, piano)                    36m; D4 (piano harder)

This beautiful sonata is Rachmaninoff's only mature chamber work, written following the second piano concerto. The cello spends much of its time singing, often high. By contrast, the piano part is full of notes and very demanding.

# RAVEL
## 1875–1937; France

Maurice Ravel is one of the most respected of French composers. He was a younger contemporary of his compatriot Debussy, and studied as a pupil of Fauré at the Paris Conservatoire. He reached maturity early, composing in an impressionist style comparable to that of Debussy. However, his style continued to develop, and included the use of bitonality and influences such as oriental music and jazz. His output includes several chamber works, of which the two earlier are probably the most popular. He did not use opus numbers.

## String Duo

Sonata for violin and cello (1920–2)                              21m; D5

Unfortunately for amateurs, this is a virtuoso tour de force and out of reach. Musically it is sometimes harsh, but it also has interest and beauty.

## String Quartet

String quartet in F (1902–3)                                      29m; D4+

This quartet is popular with audiences and often appears in professional concerts. It is fresh and lovely; its distinctive textures and atmosphere are those of Ravel's early impressionist style, showing the influence of Debussy's quartet of ten years earlier. Technically, however, this is much more difficult than the Debussy quartet. The first movement is playable, but the second with its brilliant pizzicato writing is more demanding. In the very slow third movement, the main problem is coordination through the many tempo changes, when (in the absence of cues) it is difficult to know what the other parts are doing. The difficulty of the last movement is its fast 5/8 tempo. Successful sight-reading is unlikely even by experienced amateurs: it needs advance practice and perhaps study with the score.

## Piano Trio

Piano trio in A minor (1914)                                      28m; D5

This is a fine, complex and beautiful work. However, it is very difficult, and sophisticated instrumental effects are exploited in all parts. Only the most experienced and capable amateurs could consider attempting it.

## Ensemble Work including Wind Instruments

<u>Introduction and Allegro (1905)</u> (harp, flute, clarinet, string quartet)

11m; D3 (harp harder)

First in this ensemble is the harp: this is effectively a miniature concerto, even including a substantial cadenza. The flute and clarinet have plenty to play, but the string parts are not without interest. An opportunity to play such delectable music in an ensemble with a harp is not to be missed.

## Duet Sonata

<u>Sonata in G (1923–7)</u> (violin, piano) 18m; D4+

Sometimes called Sonata no. 2 (no. 1 being an early work of 1897). Those interested in jazz may particularly enjoy the second movement *Blues*, which calls for some jazz techniques. Probably most difficult is the last movement *Perpetuum mobile*.

# REICHA
## 1770–1836; Bohemia, Austria, France

Anton (or Antoine) Reicha was born in Prague. He spent the years 1794–9 in Hamburg and 1802–8 in Vienna; he knew Haydn, and became a friend of Beethoven. He then spent the rest of his life in Paris, becoming professor of composition at the Conservatoire, where his many notable pupils included Liszt, Berlioz and Franck. He was important as a musical theorist, was interested in fugue and wrote a treatise on composition. His own principal instrument was the flute. He composed a good deal, including orchestral music, operas and much chamber music. He declared in his memoirs that he considered his twenty-four wind quintets to be his finest published compositions. Posterity has endorsed this: whereas most of his music is forgotten, the wind quintets continue to be played. Published between 1817 and 1820, they are the earliest important works for the combination.

## Wind Quintets

Reicha's quintets are for what became the standard grouping of flute, oboe, clarinet, horn and bassoon; they all offer a second flute as an alternative to the oboe. The natural horn was expected. They are substantial and ambitious works, all in four movements. First movements almost all begin with a slow introduction. The slow movement is normally second. Third is a minuet, of which the nature and structure vary a good deal; many are of scherzo character (sometimes but not always marked as such). They may have one or two trios, or the whole movement may be in sonata form. Reicha's treatment of the ensemble gives the most prominent role usually to the flute followed by the oboe, but the writing is unfailingly democratic and all players have enjoyable solos. The writing is often brilliant and technically demanding, especially in the later quintets. As compared with the almost contemporary wind quintets of Danzi, Reicha's are on a larger scale and more difficult to play.

### Op. 88 no. 1 in E minor                                              20m; D4–
The second movement is a set of variations. This first quintet is the shortest of the twenty-four, and relatively modest in scope. Clarinet in C is required.

### Op. 88 no. 2 in E♭                                                    27m; D4–
This is probably the best-known and most popular of Reicha's wind quintets. The first movement *Allegro moderato* opens on the bassoon, exemplifying the democracy that prevails throughout. Contrary to Reicha's usual practice, the minuet comes second. The clarinet is in B♭.

### Op. 88 no. 3 in G                                                     24m; D4
The clarinet is in C.

### Op. 88 no. 4 in D minor                                              29m; D4–
Clarinet in C is required, but a change to B♭ is necessary for the second movement, which is a set of variations.

### Op. 88 no. 5 in B♭                                                    31m; D4
The clarinet is in B♭. The introduction to the first movement includes entertaining written-out cadenzas for horn and clarinet. Subsequent movements bring some brilliant, demanding passages for all.

### Op. 88 no. 6 in F                                                     30m; D4
The clarinet is in C. The minuet, of *ländler* character, has two trios, which unusually follow one another without an intervening return to the minuet.

### Op. 91 no. 1 in C                                                     28m; D4
Clarinet in C is required. Unusually, this quintet does not start with a slow introduction.

### Op. 91 no. 2 in A minor                                              30m; D4
The slow movement is a set of variations. The clarinet is in C.

### Op. 91 no. 3 in D                                                     23m; D4
A relatively lightweight work. Clarinets in both A and B♭ are needed.

### Op. 91 no. 4 in G minor                                              33m; D4+
This quintet has some brilliant and technically difficult writing. The clarinet is in C.

<u>Op. 91 no. 5 in A</u>                                    30m; D4
The clarinet is in A.

<u>Op. 91 no. 6 in C minor</u>                              32m; D4
Clarinets in B♭ and C are required, for two movements each. This is among the most distinctively original and delightful of these quintets.

<u>Op. 99 no. 1 in C</u>                                    29m; D4+
The clarinet is in C. The minuet is marked *Scherzo*, but the whole work has a good deal of scherzo character. It also calls for some brilliant and technically demanding playing.

<u>Op. 99 no. 2 in F minor</u>                             30m; D4
Clarinet in B♭ is required except for the slow movement, which is for clarinet in C.

<u>Op. 99 no. 3 in A</u>                                    34m; D4
This quintet (which is sometimes erroneously listed as being in F) unusually has slow introductions to both the first movement and the finale. It requires clarinet in A.

<u>Op. 99 no. 4 in D</u>                                    32m; D4
The clarinet is in A. This delightful quintet is rather martial in character. It has a particularly demanding minuet-scherzo.

<u>Op. 99 no. 5 in B minor</u>                             32m; D4
Clarinets in both A and C are required.

<u>Op. 99 no. 6 in G</u>                                    30m; D4
The clarinet is in C. The *Andante* second movement is entitled *Air-Fantaisie*.

<u>Op. 100 no. 1 in F</u>                                   31m; D4
Clarinet in C is required.

<u>Op. 100 no. 2 in D minor</u>                             32m; D4
A fine and powerful work. The clarinet is in C. All players (especially, perhaps, the flute) are put through their paces.

<u>Op. 100 no. 3 in E♭</u>                                  30m; D4+
The clarinet is in B♭. This quintet is memorable for its fine, sombre and powerful *Lento* second movement. The speed called for in the finale is demanding.

<u>Op. 100 no. 4 in E minor</u>                             34m; D4
Clarinet in A is required. The second movement *Andante con variazioni* gives opportunities to every instrument.

<u>Op. 100 no. 5 in A minor</u>                             32m; D4+
Clarinets in both C and A are required. This quintet, too, has a theme and variations.

<u>Op. 100 no. 6 in B♭</u>                                                    37m; D4

The clarinet is in B♭. This final quintet of the series is a fine and entertaining work.

———————

There also exists one further quintet (sometimes described as no. 25 in F minor) made up of four odd movements.

## Other Chamber Works

Another work by Reicha that is sometimes played is his clarinet quintet in B♭, op. 89. A further quintet, op. 107 in F for oboe and strings, has an alternative version for clarinet. There are also quintets with strings for flute, horn and bassoon, six quartets for flute and strings and an octet for four winds and four strings. Among other works, Reicha composed about twenty string quartets and ten string quintets (three with two cellos and the remainder with two violas). Of works with piano, most are with strings (piano trios and violin sonatas), but a few include wind instruments.

# RICHTER
### 1709–1789; Moravia, Germany

Franz Xaver Richter was born in Moravia (part of what is now the Czech Republic) but spent most of his life in Germany. For some time he lived in Mannheim, and he is considered a composer of the Mannheim school. He is not a major figure. However, his string quartets deserve attention, partly because they are charming but also because they are the best representatives of the period of two or three decades from 1750 when the baroque period was coming to an end but the classical style was not yet established. Richter was among the composers who began at this time to write works for two violins, viola and cello without continuo, before the creation of the string quartet as we know it.

## String Quartets

Richter's quartets, published as a set of six, may have been composed as early as 1757 – about the time when Haydn began his opp. 1 and 2. They are attractive and indeed are arguably better than those five-movement divertimento quartets by the young Haydn. All but one are in three movements; they are very contrapuntal and have much of late baroque character. They are enjoyable to play, especially because they give real freedom and equality to all four players; their enterprising cello parts may particularly be appreciated. They make a useful change from the usual repertoire.

These quartets are usually known as op. 5. However, this designation was not used in the first publication of 1768 in London but appeared in the second publication of about 1772 in Paris. The two publications differ both in order and in that the C major quartet in the first publication disappeared in the second, being replaced by one in G minor. Consequently there are seven quartets and their numbering is confused, modern editions being inconsistent. Reference by key is safest. The numbering given below is that of c.1772 (which strictly is the only valid numbering that refers to op. 5); the numbers from 1768 (where applicable) are shown in brackets. Publishers from whom some or all of the quartets are available today include Amadeus (all seven), Ourtext, Edition Silvertrust and Breitkopf & Härtel.

### Op. 5 no. 1 (no. 5) in G

16m; D3

Good but not easy; both outer movements are vigorous.

### Op. 5 no. 2 (no. 2) in B♭

16m; D3

The speed of the demisemiquavers in the *Allegretto* first movement is difficult.

### Op. 5 no. 3 (no. 3) in A

15m; D3–

Very attractive. The last movement is a minuet and trio.

### Op. 5 no. 4 (no. 6) in D

14m; D3–

### Op. 5 no. 5 in G minor

15m; D3

This quartet is the only one to have four movements. (As the substitution in the c.1772 publication, was it composed later than the others, and perhaps influenced by Haydn?) Most of it is excellent. The second movement includes long, energetic solos for both viola and cello. However, the finale, a minuet and trio, may be thought an anticlimax.

### Op. 5 no. 6 (no. 4) in E♭

15m; D3

An excellent and enjoyable quartet, one of the best of the set.

### (No. 1) in C

14m; D3

Also very good. The last movement is headed *Rincontro*, which means meeting again.

## Other Chamber Works

Richter's other chamber works are mostly for typical baroque combinations, usually in sets of six. They include trio sonatas, sonatas for flute or violin with continuo, and duets for two flutes or violins.

# SAINT-SAËNS
## 1835–1921; France

Camille Saint-Saëns played a major part in the later nineteenth-century renaissance of French music. He was not really an innovator: he wrote mostly in classical forms, and his language is generally conservative. However, his music is often delightful and has an enjoyable elegance. The best of it, such as some of the concertos and other orchestral works, continues to be performed. He composed a considerable body of chamber music. It does not today have a major position in the repertoire – except for the unique trumpet septet, which is deservedly popular and is frequently heard. However, most of the other chamber works are still played occasionally, especially the seven duet sonatas, which form a valuable series. Saint-Saëns's writing for the piano is often admirably light and transparent.

Although Saint-Saëns's music is thought of as always charming and understandable, from about the time of his sixtieth birthday in the mid-1890s his style changed. Although still finely constructed and full of interest, his music became less immediately attractive. (This change might be compared with that in Fauré in a similar period.) This later music is generally less popular – for example, the second cello concerto (op. 119, of 1902) is almost unknown, whereas the first (op. 33, of 1872) is one of his most frequently played works. Nevertheless, some of the later chamber works are of interest.

Saint-Saëns also composed many small pieces, mostly for one instrument with piano. Moreover, there is his most popular composition, *The Carnival of the Animals* – which is in no conventional sense a chamber work. It is for eleven instruments (two pianos, two violins, viola, cello, double bass, flute, clarinet, glass harmonica – usually in practice glockenspiel or similar – and xylophone); players may well enjoy an opportunity to take part in it.

## String Quartets

Saint-Saëns's two string quartets are not highly regarded and are rarely played. The first is probably the finer, but the second is the more playable.

<u>Op. 112 in E minor (1899)</u>                                          31m; D4+

Musically big and quite attractive, but difficult. There is good interest for all, but the first violin part is often prominent – the dedicatee was the violinist and quartet leader Eugène Ysaÿe.

<u>Op. 153 in G (1918)</u>                                                 27m; D4–

In three movements: pleasant and relatively straightforward, but musically unexciting.

## Piano Trios

<u>Op. 18 in F (1863)</u>                                                  29m; D3

A four-movement work: youthful, fresh and delightful throughout. It is particularly attractive and original for its light, open textures. Technically it is fairly straightforward.

Op. 92 in E minor (1892)                                                    35m; D4

This is a large-scale and ambitious trio, in five movements. The outer movements are the largest and the most serious. 5/8 and 5/4 timings are used for the second movement. The centre of the work is the beautiful *Andante con moto*. This is an enjoyable trio to play; the writing for strings is idiomatic and good, though some of the piano writing is demanding.

## Piano Quartet

Op. 41 in B♭ (1875)                                                        32m; D4

On a large scale, this quartet is full of original and fresh writing, which makes it attractive to play. It is elegant and engaging, with much variety; it does not seek profundity. The strings are given plenty of enjoyable material, and they are not drowned by the piano. Its form is cyclic, the last movement bringing back material from the previous movements.

## Piano Quintet (piano, string quartet)

Op. 14 in A minor (c.1855)                                                 30m; D4

Early as this is, it is characteristic of the composer and contains much interesting music. The piano part is demanding, though not unduly thick or heavy. Piano quintet ensembles seeking something else to play might try this.

## Ensemble Work including a Wind Instrument

Septet in E♭, op. 65 (1880) (trumpet, piano, 2 violins, viola, cello, double bass)

18m; D3

When asked to compose this work, Saint-Saëns initially wrote reluctantly. However, the unlikely and challenging inclusion of a trumpet in a chamber ensemble caught his imagination, and the completed septet seems a miracle, a perfect and unrepeatable work of genius. It is in four short movements and shows inspiration from the baroque suite: one movement is a minuet, another a gavotte. Its material is unfailingly delightful, and Saint-Saëns's treatment of the ensemble is masterly. The strings (except the double bass) have many enjoyable opportunities. The trumpet is often set against the other players, but sometimes, playing low in its register, it merges into the ensemble. The piano part is not heavy. Every player will surely enjoy playing this work. The trumpet is in E♭.

## Duet Sonatas and another Duet

Op. 75 in D minor (1885) (violin, piano)                                   23m; D4+

This is a really excellent work, one of the composer's best. But for most amateurs some sections will be too difficult.

<u>Op. 102 in E♭ (1896)</u> (violin, piano)                                             23m; D4
Compared to its predecessor this is cooler and more classical, but nevertheless attractive and interesting.

<u>Suite in D minor, op. 16 (1862)</u> (cello, piano)                           23m; D4+
Showy and full of bravura: too difficult for most to play, and hardly worth the effort for those who can.

<u>Op. 32 in C minor (1872)</u> (cello, piano)                                      21m; D3
Perhaps Saint-Saëns's most popular sonata; its mood is sometimes quite serious, but it is unfailingly fresh and attractive.

<u>Op. 123 in F (1905)</u> (cello, piano)                                            33m; D4+
Typically for late Saint-Saëns, immediately memorable melodies are lacking. Nevertheless, this is a compellingly fine sonata; but it assumes great technical mastery.

---

Saint-Saëns's last three sonatas, all written in the year in which he died at the age of eighty-six, are for wind instruments, for the players of which they are a valuable possession. They are relatively modest and small-scale, but although late they are attractive and enjoyable for players. The composer had planned to continue with further sonatas.

<u>Op. 166 in D (1921)</u> (oboe, piano)                                            12m; D4
Lightweight musically, but attractive and interesting throughout its three movements.

<u>Op. 167 in E♭ (1921)</u> (clarinet, piano)                                      16m; D4
A mellow, gentle and beautiful four-movement work. The clarinet is in B♭.

<u>Op. 168 in G (1921)</u> (bassoon, piano)                                        13m; D4
In three movements: attractive music that well shows the bassoon's capabilities.

# SCHOENBERG
## 1874–1951; Austria, America

Arnold Schoenberg (originally Schönberg) was born in Vienna. He was largely self-taught in composition, though he probably learned much through his friendship with the composer Alexander Zemlinsky, three years his senior. His first maturity may be dated at about 1899, when he composed in a late romantic style. His string sextet of that year, *Verklärte Nacht*, is one of his most popular works. As his development continued, his chromaticism became more free and the tonal basis increasingly tenuous, especially in his second string quartet, completed in 1908. In 1909, with the three pieces for piano, op. 11, he was the first composer to become atonal. This was a free atonalism, but he later developed and employed in his compositions from about 1923 the 'method of composing with twelve notes', also known as the twelve-tone method, dodecaphony or serialism. He used this method for the rest of his life, but regarded it as a natural development from his earlier tonal music, which he did not disavow. From 1925 he held a teaching position in Berlin, but in 1933 with the coming to power of the Nazis his Jewish ethnicity caused him to be dismissed; he moved to America in 1934.

Schoenberg led what became known as the Second Viennese School, in which his most important pupils were Berg and Webern; more widely, he has been perhaps the most influential of all twentieth-century composers. Nevertheless, his music remains controversial. For both technical and musical reasons, most of his chamber works are rarely played for pleasure. All are technically difficult, the later works more so.

## String Trio

String trio, op. 45 (1946)                                        19m; D5
A twelve-tone work, in a single movement though there are five sections. It is extreme in its contrasts and is full of extended technical devices. Some of it is extremely difficult.

## String Quartets

String quartet in D (1897)                                        26m; D4
Schoenberg's earliest surviving substantial work, published posthumously. It is remarkably conventional, but playable and attractively melodious.

String quartet no. 1 in D minor, op. 7 (1904–5)                   46m; D4+
In a single enormous movement, though within this there are four sections, the central two having the character of scherzo and slow movement. The whole is immensely varied and complicated. Harmonically Schoenberg has developed, but this remains tonal and is not discordant. Some consider it a masterpiece; but for others it is a turgid and indigestible monster. Whichever, technically it is very difficult (though its demands are not really virtuoso), made worse by its length.

String quartet no. 2 in F♯ minor, op. 10 (1907–8) (string quartet, voice)   31m; D4+
After the previous quartet, this returns to the convention of four movements and a normal duration. However, very unconventionally (and for prospective players, inconveniently!), it also requires a soprano voice: the third and fourth movements are settings of poems by Stefan George. Moreover, Schoenberg's stretching of tonality here reaches almost the end of the road: the last movement is without key

signature and is close to atonality. Its first performance in Vienna in 1908 provoked a near-riot. Nevertheless, some may find this musically more comprehensible than its predecessor.

String quartet no. 3, op. 30 (1927)                                            32m; D5
Written to a commission from Elizabeth Sprague Coolidge, this is a twelve-tone work. It has four movements, approximating to the classical layout; the last movement is headed *Rondo*. Few technical effects are used, but it is very difficult.

String quartet no. 4, op. 37 (1936)                                            34m; D5
This, too, was a Coolidge commission. It uses the twelve-tone method, and is again in four movements. The technical demands on the players are perhaps even greater than in its predecessor.

## String Sextet

*Verklärte Nacht (Transfigured Night)* (1899)                                  29m; D4+
This well-known single-movement work is a rare example of programmatic chamber music. It is based on a poem by Richard Dehmel, which the music closely follows. The story is one of intense feeling: two lovers walk through a wood at night, and the woman confesses that she is to bear the child of another. The man accepts this: the child will be transfigured by their love to be as if it were his. The music vividly conveys the intensity. Its style, deriving principally from Brahms and Wagner, is pure late romanticism, scarcely troubled by harmonic extension beyond this. Technically it is difficult, but it is approachable by capable amateurs who are prepared to work hard. It is also often heard in Schoenberg's later arrangement for string orchestra.

## Ensemble Works including Wind Instruments
Performances of these works often use a conductor.

Serenade, op. 24 (1920–3) (clarinet, bass clarinet, mandolin, guitar, violin, viola, cello, voice)                                                             32m; D5
Made problematical as a chamber work by the fourth of its seven movements, short but forming the centrepiece, which requires a baritone voice. This movement is twelve-tone, the rest is free atonal. Most of the music is light in intent – but technically very difficult.

Wind quintet, op. 26 (1923–4) (flute, oboe, clarinet, horn, bassoon)           38m; D5
This is Schoenberg's first major fully twelve-tone work. In compensation for the revolutionary new technique, it has a very classical four-movement structure; the first movement even has an exposition repeat. The clarinet is in A.

Suite, op. 29 (1924–6) (E♭ clarinet/flute; clarinet; bass clarinet/bassoon, piano, violin, viola, cello)                                                      30m; D5
The middle clarinet requires instruments in both A and B♭. There are four movements. This is again a twelve-tone work.

## Duet with Piano

*Phantasy*, op. 47 (1949)                                                      10m; D5
Twelve-tone; virtuoso violin.

# SCHUBERT
### 1797–1828; Austria

Of all early deaths among composers, that of Franz Schubert at thirty-one seems the most tragic, the one by which the world has surely lost the greatest potential quantity of wonderful music. But Schubert was prolific, and his achievement in the years he had was prodigious. He is known above all as a composer of songs, and in this medium he is supreme. However, all the major forms were also important to him: he composed operas, choral music, orchestral music, a great deal for the piano, and a substantial corpus of chamber music. Although he stood at the beginning of the romantic period, he was rooted in classicism. His place is with Haydn, Mozart and Beethoven: the four great composers of the classical era.

From when he began composition at about the age of thirteen, chamber music, mostly string quartets, figured large in his output. The models of his earlier music were mainly the classicism of Haydn and Mozart. He developed quickly, and by his late teens was composing masterpieces, with his own distinctive voice, although their scope was still that of his classical models. Because his life was so short, the chamber works of his early years are numerically more than half the total of his output. The first chamber work in which he may be considered to have reached his full maturity is the 'Trout' Quintet, of 1819. By this time his style was entirely his own. He continued to develop remarkably to the very end of his life, taking him musically into new worlds. What is by common consent his greatest chamber work, the C major string quintet, was composed only two or three months before his death. His entire life was spent in Vienna, where for almost the whole period Beethoven was the dominant composer; yet his largely self-taught development was remarkably independent of Beethoven. He offers us an alternative view of outstanding greatness in music. He is perhaps the greatest melodic genius the world has known. His development towards the coming romantic era followed a path quite different from that of Beethoven. He was a master of musical architecture. An aspect often noticeable is his interest in key relationships and in surprising modulations.

Schubert is sometimes criticized for his music being too long – what Schumann (referring to the 'Great C Major' symphony) called its 'heavenly length'. Indeed, most of the chamber-music masterpieces of his final years – the last two string quartets, the string quintet, the two piano trios, the octet – are very lengthy. It may be argued that their content justifies their length. Nevertheless, players may choose somewhat to moderate the duration by omitting repeats, particularly the first movement exposition repeats, which Schubert still marked.

Schubert gained little recognition in his lifetime, and few of his works were published until after his death, often many years after. At publication, many were given an opus number, usually unrelated to the date of composition. Which works were early or late was often not obvious. However, in 1951 O.E. Deutsch published his great thematic catalogue of Schubert's works in chronological order, and since then it has become general practice to refer to works by Deutsch (D.) numbers. But scholarship moves on: a few of these, too, are now recognized as inaccurate. Opus numbers are also shown here where applicable because they are the only numbers appearing in older published editions.

As most of Schubert's works remained unpublished when he completed them, he had no reason to continue to work on compositions in progress if something seemed to be going wrong, or if he became attracted to working on something else. In consequence some compositions were left unfinished. Of his chamber music, a mature string quartet and a string trio were both abandoned with one fine movement complete and a second unfinished. The completions of many of Schubert's unfinished works that have in recent years been provided by Brian Newbould may be of interest to some.

## String Trios

### D. 471 in B♭ (1816) 8m; D2
Only a single movement: Schubert abandoned the work after writing 39 bars of an intended second movement. But it is a delightful and useful piece – charming and well written for all, yet undemanding musically and technically.

### D. 581 in B♭ (1817) 21m; D3+
Unusually for Schubert, this is for some people a disappointing work. It can seem at least in parts to lack the composer's magic touch, and it tends to be undemocratic, with most of the musical interest given to the violin. Moreover, it is quite difficult, with some awkward florid ornamental writing (especially for the violin). These criticisms apply principally to the first two of its four movements. The third movement minuet, especially, is a different matter: both charming and democratic, with the viola having the melody throughout the trio.

## String Quartets
Schubert has left us a long series of string quartets – fifteen if two incomplete works

are included. He wrote them through much of his life, beginning almost in his first efforts at composition. All the earlier quartets were written for the family quartet, in which he played the viola; his brothers Ferdinand and Ignaz played the violins, and his father the cello. Every year from 1811 to 1816 saw the composition of one or more quartets. Then came a break. When he resumed composing for the medium, initially in 1820 but with a will in 1824, it was for a wider public, and these final works are major masterpieces of the repertoire.

In addition to the works discussed here, Schubert in his early years composed a number of minuets and German dances for string quartet, which some may wish to investigate.

Still in use are many old editions of Schubert's quartets lacking Deutsch numbers; and the early quartets in particular are not always easy to identify. Incipits of the first violin part are provided here to assist.

Schubert's string quartets may be divided chronologically into three groups. Those composed between 1811 and autumn 1813 number seven, one of which exists only in part; two or more further quartets are lost. These are very early works, among Schubert's earliest extended compositions, written before he first attempted a piano sonata or a symphony. In them, he was learning his craft, and was not yet a master of it. These quartets are not widely known and they do not usually appear in professional recitals. Nevertheless, for playing for pleasure, they are valuable and should not be ignored. Almost from the beginning they are characteristic of Schubert, showing his distinctive charm, melodic genius and captivating invention. Material is well distributed among the players. It is interesting to watch Schubert's progress through them. They are also less difficult to play than his mature masterpieces. Nevertheless, they are not actually technically easy: most of them are more difficult than the early quartets of Mozart, so as a group they are not among the best quartets for beginners to start with. For moderately capable amateurs, however, they are playable and most are delightful. Probably the best of the seven are D. 32, D. 36 and D. 46.

Obtaining sheet music for these very early string quartets is less easy than with the later quartets. The edition of Schubert's string quartets in two volumes by Peters and other publishers includes of these only the misleadingly numbered D. 94. The modern Bärenreiter edition includes every quartet, and Volume II contains D. 18, D. 32, D. 36 and the fragmentary D. 68. But to obtain D. 46 and D. 74 would require two further volumes of this edition. However, these quartets are also available separately elsewhere.

<u>D. 18 in mixed keys (c.1811)</u>                                          18m; D2

This first quartet is the only one that indeed seems weak and is in places obviously naïve and simple. Nevertheless, it contains a good deal that can be enjoyed; and it is easy to play. (That it ends in a different key from that in which it begins probably indicates adventurousness rather than incompetence!)

<u>D. 94 in D (c.1811–12)</u>                                             21m; D2+

Being included in the popular Peters two-volume edition, this quartet is quite often played. It is now recognized as being earlier in date than its Deutsch number implies. It is a major advance on its predecessor and contains much attractive material.

<u>D. 32 in C (1812)</u>                                             18m; D2+

This is Schubert's first really convincing quartet: enjoyable and entertaining throughout. Perhaps best are the outer movements. Long known only in two movements (the first and third), the complete quartet was first published in the 1950s, so it is incomplete in older editions.

<u>D. 36 in B♭ (1812–13)</u>                                             26m; D3+

A large-scale quartet, and remarkably good. Especially vigorous is the first movement. The material is distinctive and attractive throughout, and there is excellent textural variety, giving plenty of interest to all the parts. However, some of it is technically quite difficult.

<u>D. 46 in C (1813)</u>                                             23m; D3

When first approached, this quartet may be thought less attractive than its immediate predecessors; but closer acquaintance should reveal it as full of characteristically Schubertian charm. It is also rather easier than D. 36.

<u>D. 68 in B♭ (1813)</u>                                             16m; D3+

Unfortunately the two middle movements are lost. What we have, however, is good and the interest is well distributed among the players, so it is worth playing.

<u>D. 74 in D (1813)</u>                                                                     22m; D3

Disappointing: it seems strange and (in contrast to its predecessors) lacking in Schubert's usual charm. This applies particularly to the vigorous and forceful outer movements, which are long, have much scrubbing and are without lyrical relief. Only the minuet really seems typical of the composer.

---

Although the next quartet followed shortly after the previous work, it may be regarded as the first of a second group. The four quartets composed between November 1813 and 1816 are still early, but they arguably represent Schubert's first maturity. This was the period in which he composed the earliest of his songs to be considered matchless masterpieces, such as *Gretchen am Spinnrade* (October 1814), and the early symphonies (the third dates from May to July 1815). These quartets are better known than their predecessors; they sometimes appear in professional concerts and they are included in the two-volume editions of the quartets. They are still of classical pattern and modest scope, but they are works of a master composer.

<u>D. 87 in E♭ (op. 125 no. 1) (1813)</u>                                                26m; D2

This quartet, the last of five completed during 1813, is remarkably different from its predecessors. Compared to them it may seem simple; certainly it is easier to play. But it has a new perfection, and its musical content is full of Schubert's personal character. All movements are good, but especially memorable is the *Prestissimo* scherzo.

This is one of the best quartets by any composer for inexperienced players to try.

<u>D. 112 in B♭ (op. 168) (1814)</u>                                                      31m; D3

This is a hauntingly beautiful quartet, full of Schubert's characteristic freshness of melody, and remarkably original. The opening is immediately arresting, beginning on unaccompanied first violin, which is soon joined by the viola. Also particularly original is the finale, moving in dotted semibreves but gradually being taken over by fluttering quavers; much of its material was later reworked to become the scherzo of the 'Great C Major' symphony. Though less easy than its predecessor, it is not technically difficult. The first movement may be thought excessively long if the exposition repeat is included.

### D. 173 in G minor (1815)                                                    23m; D3+

Quite a tough G minor work: excellent, single-minded and quite compact. However, compared to its immediate predecessors it shows less of Schubert's distinctive character and more influence probably of Mozart. The semiquavers of the last movement may need advance practice!

### D. 353 in E (op. 125 no. 2) (1816)                                          22m; D4

More technically demanding than any previous quartet, Schubert was probably in this work no longer thinking mainly of the family quartet. It is tight, terse and interesting in all parts. Nevertheless it is on the whole disappointing, perhaps because its material lacks charm and there is little relaxation. The trio of the minuet and the finale may be thought best. In the second movement, a slower tempo than the 2/4 *Andante* marking might suggest may be found preferable both musically and technically.

Players using at least some copies of the Peters edition are warned of a surprising error in the viola and cello parts: in the first movement, bars 5 to 8 after letter B are completely wrong. A solution is to paste in correct bars copied from a score or from online.

———

Eight years followed before Schubert next completed a string quartet. Midway through that time, however, he began a quartet in C minor, but finished no more than the first movement. That movement, nevertheless, is remarkably original and perfect, and has a major place in the repertoire. He then completed three quartets in 1824–6: they are very different from each other, but each is an outstanding monument of the string quartet repertoire.

### D. 703 in C minor ('Quartettsatz') (1820)                                   10m; D4

The name simply means 'quartet movement'. Considering the scarcity of short works for string quartet, this is a very useful addition to the repertoire. It is an exquisite work, and one that is of completely mature Schubert, profoundly unlike any other composer. Even its form is strikingly original, the coda being an exact recapitulation of the remarkable opening material. However, it is technically difficult, especially for the first violin.

Before he abandoned the *Andante* second movement, Schubert wrote almost three minutes of beautiful music: playing it is fascinating, though it ends in frustration. (One way of obtaining parts is to write them out from the score included, for example, in the Lea Pocket Score.)

D. 804 in A minor (op. 29) (1824)          36m; D4–

The principal theme of the second movement also appears in Schubert's incidental music to *Rosamunde*; this is sometimes used as a nickname for the quartet. Lyrical, wistful and highly original in its textures, this work is unlike anything else. The first three movements are broadly consistent in their character and mood, though the minuet is strikingly sad for music in that form. The finale, in the major, is cheerful yet still seems appropriate to the rest. This quartet is very popular with both audiences and players. Technically it is the easiest of Schubert's three great last quartets.

D. 810 in D minor ('Death and the Maiden') (1824)          43m; D4

This is one of the most popular of all string quartets, and it appears frequently in concert programmes. Its nickname comes from Schubert's song *Der Tod und das Mädchen* of 1817, which gave the theme for the variations that form the slow second movement. It is a remarkably powerful and unified work; every movement is in the minor (only the trio of the minuet moves to D major), and the final movement in tarantella rhythm continues in the minor key to the end. Certainly its mood is sombre, but surely to be doubted are writers who suggest that it is a programmatic work 'about' death. Rather, it is a minor-key masterpiece of exceptional power, musical invention and beauty, full of superb writing for string quartet.

This quartet is difficult but also rewarding and enjoyable to play. Every player has music of vital power and interest throughout. It is long: the first movement, with its exposition repeat, lasts over fifteen minutes. That repeat is often omitted in professional performances.

D. 887 in G (op. 161) (1826)                                            51m; D4

After the tremendous power of the D minor quartet, amazingly Schubert has here given us something even larger and more ambitious. The energy of much of the music, the originality of its textures and the quality of its musical content are exceptional. Mainly in the outer movements, the interplay of G major and G minor is a major part of its character. The last movement, a pounding rondo again in tarantella rhythm, is of remarkable resourcefulness and interest. For many, this is the greatest of Schubert's quartets, and its remarkable qualities are widely acknowledged. Nevertheless, some critics also find fault with it. Its technical difficulties are not much greater than those of the D minor quartet, but its length is gruelling. With the repeat, the first movement lasts over twenty minutes. Cellists have particular cause to love this quartet: their instrument is treated generously throughout, and especially in the slow movement.

## String Quintets

The two works in this grouping could hardly be further apart in both date and importance.

Overture in C minor, D. 8 (1811) (2 violins, 2 violas, cello)                9m; D2+
Schubert's earliest surviving completed chamber work. Despite being so early, it is surprisingly good and is worth trying at least as a novelty. (Schubert also arranged it for string quartet.)

D. 956 in C (op. 163) (1828) (2 violins, viola, 2 cellos)                54m; D4
Schubert's last chamber work: and it is universally agreed that it is his greatest. Many consider it the greatest chamber work by any composer. Others might say it is the most loved. Certainly it is astonishingly rich and powerful, yet meltingly lovely. Its general mood is of happiness and of luminous beauty, though it does contain some darker music. Most loved of all is the great *Adagio* second movement – a movement of beauty unsurpassed perhaps by anything else in music. The whole quintet is technically quite difficult; but so wonderful are the melodies and so liberal their distribution to everyone that it is exceptionally rewarding to play. Perhaps most difficult for players are the slow sections, especially the remarkable 4/4 *Andante sostenuto* that forms the trio of the scherzo. Throughout the work the presence of two cellos gives a special sonority to the sound and also permits the free use of the cello as a melody instrument, making it especially beloved of cellists. The first cello is often given melodies high in its register, but the second cello part is enterprising and is perhaps the more difficult. Particularly memorable is the complicated and prominent second cello part in the wonderful final section of the *Adagio*.

In the *Adagio*, no change of tempo is marked for the vigorous F minor central section, but it is usual to take this faster. A general characteristic of Schubert's handwriting was an ambiguity between an accent and a decrescendo hairpin; the final bar of the quintet is probably an example of this. Scores and parts show a decrescendo, but musically this seems questionable; many professional performances favour an accent only.

This quintet has a unique position in the repertoire: there are other works for this combination, but nothing of remotely comparable stature.

## Piano Trios

As well as two smaller pieces, Schubert left two great piano trios that were written close together near the end of his life, and are products of his ripest maturity. They differ in character from the late string chamber music: unlike the seriousness of the latter, these are entertainment music in its most elevated form. Schubert's writing for strings with piano is distinctively his own, and gives great and exhilarating freedom to the strings; some may feel that these trios achieve an ideal balance of the instruments. The string parts are challenging. In particular, those of the cello are difficult because they spend much of their time in a high register: but if they can be managed, this makes them especially enjoyable. The piano writing, too, is demanding; a characteristic is many fast octave unison passages. Despite their technical demands, these trios are central to the repertoire and are much played by more capable amateurs.

Sonata in B♭, D. 28 (1812)                                                   10m; D3–

A single movement, presumably intended as a first movement; it is sometimes called 'Sonatensatz'. Despite its very early date it has charm.

Adagio in E♭, D. 897 ('Notturno', op. 148) (1827)                            9m; D3

This may well be a rejected slow movement for D. 898. It is unmistakably by the mature Schubert, and there are some who consider it among Schubert's most beautiful compositions. Others, however, find it disappointing: musically it lacks contrast, and the string parts are rather ungrateful to play.

D. 898 in B♭ (op. 99) (1827)                                                 41m; D4

Lyrical, relaxed, happy and delightful throughout, with scarcely anything of intensity. It is highly regarded and is perhaps the more frequently performed of Schubert's trios. However, it is long, and some would argue that it spins out its material too much.

D. 929 in E♭ (op. 100) (1827)                                               48m; D4–

Of the two trios this is the more forceful and at times passionate. Moreover, the slow movement is opened on the cello by a hauntingly memorable and expansive tune (which may have originated in a Swedish folk-song). In addition to its treatment in that movement, this tune returns twice in the finale. This trio is even longer than its companion: but it is so full of variety and incident that for many people its length never seems excessive.

Which is the finer of the trios is difficult to say. For amateur players, however, the Eb trio has the advantage that, partly because of its generally more moderate tempi, it is somewhat the easier.

## Piano Quartet

<u>Adagio and Rondo Concertante in F, D. 487 (1816)</u>     14m; D2 (piano harder)
This unusual work is not pure chamber music: it is firstly a showpiece for the piano. However, it is very charming and the strings will enjoy their parts, which though not difficult have considerable musical interest.

## Piano Quintet (piano, violin, viola, cello, double bass)

<u>D. 667 in A ('The Trout', op. 114) (1819)</u>     40m; D3+
The 'Trout' quintet is easily Schubert's best-known chamber work, with an enduring popularity. It was written when the twenty-two-year-old composer was on holiday, in response to a commission from an amateur. The result is music that is delightful and unclouded throughout. It is in five movements, so resembling an eighteenth-century divertimento. The name comes from a song of 1817 that provided the theme for the fourth-movement variations. Its demands on the players are considerable, but it is well written for the instruments and is always grateful. The cello is treated particularly generously, but all parts have delightful opportunities; even the double bass, though inevitably less free, has some interest and is granted one memorable solo. The piano writing has similar technical characteristics to that in the trios.

## Ensemble Works including Wind Instruments

<u>Minuet and finale in F for wind octet, D. 72 (1813)</u> (2 oboes, 2 clarinets, 2 horns, 2 bassoons)     10m; D2
Although this is an early work, and moreover is incomplete (there also exists an unfinished *Allegro* first movement), it is modestly charming and is worth giving an outing. The clarinets are in C.

<u>Octet in F, D. 803 (op. 166) (1824)</u> (clarinet, horn, bassoon, 2 violins, viola, cello, double bass)     62m; D4
The octet is another of Schubert's best-known and most popular works. It is thought that it was commissioned by an amateur clarinettist, Count Ferdinand Troyer, and that he asked for something similar to Beethoven's septet. Certainly the result both in its six-movement plan and in its cheerful and melodious character resembles

the Beethoven. Some would say it is even better! The main difference is that it adds a second violin. Schubert's melodic genius makes it a delight throughout, and though exceptionally long it sustains the interest. It is not difficult musically or for ensemble, but the brilliance of the writing is sometimes technically demanding. Leadership is shared between the clarinet and the first violin. Good solo opportunities are given to all except the double bass, but the latter nevertheless has an interesting part. Clarinets are required in B♭ and C.

## Duet Sonatas and other Duets

Chronologically these fall into two groups. The four sonatas for violin and piano were written during Schubert's first maturity in his late teens, when he produced distinctive and competent classical compositions of moderate scope. The remaining works are by-products of his great late period.

Sonata in D, D. 384 (Sonatina, op. 137 no. 1) (1816) (violin, piano)            12m; D2
The title 'sonatina' was given to this set of three works by the publisher rather than the composer: but it seems appropriate. They are small-scale, charming and easy to play. Musical interest is well distributed between the parts. Most players of any level of attainment will enjoy them, but for amateurs of modest technical ability or those first playing duet sonatas, they are ideal. This first sonata has only three movements, and is perhaps the most innocently lovely of the three.

Sonata in A minor, D. 385 (Sonatina, op. 137 no. 2) (1816) (violin, piano)    20m; D2
In four movements: again highly attractive, and rather larger in scope than its predecessor.

Sonata in G minor, D. 408 (Sonatina, op. 137 no. 3) (1816) (violin, piano) 18m; D2+
Also in four movements, rather tougher and less easy-going.

Sonata in A, D. 574 (Duo, op. 162) (1817) (violin, piano)            22m; D3+
A much more ambitious work than those of the preceding set. Though good, it never quite fulfils the promise of its evocative opening bars. It also makes some tricky demands on both players.

Rondo in B minor, D. 895 ('Rondeau brillant', op. 70) (1826) (violin, piano) 14m; D5
Very beautiful music; but it requires a virtuoso technique.

Fantasy in C, D. 934 (op. 159) (1827) (violin, piano)            24m; D5
Although it plays continuously and the structure is complicated, four movements can be recognized in it. The material is hauntingly beautiful, but virtuoso playing is required from both performers. One might think of it as Schubert's equivalent to Beethoven's 'Kreutzer' sonata.

<u>Sonata in A minor, D. 821 ('Arpeggione') (1824)</u> (usually cello or viola, piano)

26m; D4(cello, piano easier)/D3(viola)

One of the most beautiful, though not most profound, of Schubert's works; and for players one of the most useful. The arpeggione, or guitar-cello, the newly invented instrument for which the sonata was commissioned, rapidly disappeared. So this sonata has no 'owner', and is available to be played by any reasonable instrument. The arpeggione had frets and six strings, giving it a very wide range. Most obvious to play the sonata is the cello, which can play it almost as written (but not five- or six-note pizzicato chords!). However, the tessitura is high, making it difficult. It is also beloved of viola players, for whom it is rather easier: but publications have to adjust some passages to avoid notes below the viola compass. Other instruments that sometimes play it include double bass, flute and clarinet.

As the sonata was intended to show off the arpeggione, the piano part is subsidiary and is easier than might be expected. It is nevertheless more than just an accompaniment.

<u>Introduction and Variations on *Trockne Blumen*, D. 802 (op. 160) (1824)</u> (flute, piano) 20m; D5

The theme ('Faded Flowers') comes from Schubert's song-cycle *Die schöne Müllerin*. Flautists will be grateful that Schubert wrote this work for their instrument: but they may regret that sections of it demand virtuoso technique from both players. The flute part can alternatively be played by a violin.

# SCHUMANN
## 1810–1856; Germany

Robert Schumann is one of the greatest composers of the early romantic period. In the years up to 1840, he composed almost exclusively for solo piano, producing a series of very original and highly regarded works. From 1840, the year of his marriage to Clara Wieck, he branched out into other and larger forms, devoting 1842 to chamber music. More chamber works followed in later years.

But Schumann's life was ultimately a tragedy. From perhaps as early as 1828, he suffered from a mental disorder that caused episodes of depression and sometimes other symptoms. Later these episodes became more frequent and more severe, and in early 1854 he attempted suicide by throwing himself into the Rhine. Following this he was confined to an asylum until his death, was not permitted to see Clara, and composed no more. Right up to that final crisis, however, he continued to compose prolifically. There is a problem here: his illness affected the quality of his music. It perhaps affected some works even in the 1840s, and it is generally agreed that his music deteriorated in his last few years of composition. (Clara, with advice from Brahms, believed that at least some of his final works were unworthy of him, and should be suppressed. Works such as the violin concerto only finally emerged in the twentieth century.) The 'year of chamber music' in 1842 produced several major masterpieces, of which the piano quintet is generally considered greatest. None of his later chamber music quite matches the standard of these works, but most of it is much too good to be ignored.

As well as full-scale chamber works, Schumann wrote several sets of pieces for one or two instruments with piano. Some are programmatic. Though relatively insubstantial, they are attractive and warrant consideration as chamber music. They are usually fairly straightforward technically and many are useful in providing repertoire for neglected instrumental combinations. Adding to this usefulness, Schumann usually offered versions for alternative instruments.

After the works of 1842, Schumann changed (inconveniently for those who do not understand German) to using German instead of Italian performance directions.

## String Quartets

Schumann began his 'year of chamber music' by composing a set of three string quartets, which he dedicated to Mendelssohn. It is sometimes said that, as a pianist, Schumann's treatment of the string quartet is clumsy and his writing for the instruments is unidiomatic. Whether this is so is doubtful, but what matters more is their musical content: and these quartets are delightful, full of Schumann's whimsy, gentle sentiment and distinctive melodic invention. Moreover, for the most part they are grateful and enjoyable to play. All three are good, but by common consent the third stands head and shoulders above its fellows in its scale, scope and beauty.

Op. 41 no. 1 in A minor (1842)        26m; D3+

Very attractive, and probably the best of Schumann's quartets to try first. Especially lovely are the contrapuntal slow introduction to the first movement, and the third movement *Adagio*. Plenty of grateful opportunities are given to all. Both the scherzo and the finale are marked *Presto*; but the necessary speeds are not so fast as to make the notes unmanageable.

Op. 41 no. 2 in F (1842)        24m; D4–

This quartet is charming, fresh and delightful throughout, and its use of the ensemble is excellent. Some may prefer it to its predecessor. However, it is more difficult, the scherzo and finale in particular being demanding. Nevertheless, it is playable by capable amateurs, and it is an exhilarating experience to do so!

Op. 41 no. 3 in A (1842)        29m; D4

This is in every way a splendid work, certainly the finest of the set. It is also technically the most difficult, and unprepared amateurs may have difficulties – but do not be put off! The first and perhaps worst problem occurs in the first movement when, at the entry of the second subject on the cello (letter B in the IMC and Peters editions), the off-the-beat accompaniment starts before the tune. The remarkably original second movement is a scherzo in the form of variations. Observe the metronome marking, because it does not work musically if played too slowly. The following *Adagio molto* has no particular technical problems. Second violinists have been known to complain about their long sections of exposed double-stopped accompaniment: but they play an essential part in the music of an exquisite movement, and are not very difficult.

## Piano Trios

Schumann wrote three large-scale, four-movement trios, plus a set of pieces. They give plenty of good opportunities to the strings. Technically the string parts are quite difficult, but not unmanageable. However, these trios do suffer from the richness or thickness of the piano writing: for the pianist, the large number of notes can be both a technical problem and a musical one. These trios do not generally rely on speed for effect, so it may be sensible to choose tempi on the slow side.

### *Phantasiestücke*, op. 88 (1842)      19m; D3
*Fantasy Pieces* – Romanze, Humoreske, Duett, Finale: this is the first of Schumann's sets of pieces for chamber groupings (the high opus number is misleading). It is lightweight music, probably intended for amateurs. Though modestly charming, it is disappointing. The string parts are mostly unenterprising, though some amends are made in the Duett, where the two strings play throughout with a flowing piano accompaniment.

### Op. 63 in D minor (1847)      31m; D4
This is a really fine, large-scale trio, sombre but beautiful. It is perhaps the finest and most often played of the three; but it is also the one in which the thickness of the piano part is most marked.

### Op. 80 in F (1847)      27m; D4
Although lighter in emotional character than its predecessor, this trio is musically as attractive, and has a good deal of Schumann's charming gentle sentiment.

### Op. 110 in G minor (1851)      28m; D4–
Most critics regard this trio as showing a decline from its predecessors, and its material does indeed seem less immediately memorable and evocative than that of the earlier trios. On the other hand, it is still good music, and also a little easier than the other two.

## Piano Quartet

<u>Op. 47 in E♭ (1842)</u>                                                                    28m; D4

Following writing the great piano quintet, Schumann went on to provide it with this worthy companion. For all four players, this is one of the most exhilarating and enjoyable of works. It has wonderful, inventive and vigorous contrapuntal writing (especially in the finale), but also melting, heart-warming melodies. Particularly memorable is the main theme of the *Andante cantabile* third movement, which belongs especially to the cello – though all players have their chance with it. For the viola's turn, the violin has semiquaver decoration – not to be played too loudly! Towards the end of this movement the cellist is given fifteen bars' rest in which to lower the C string to B♭ for the last section. It has to be returned to normal pitch before the finale.

## Piano Quintet (piano, string quartet)

<u>Op. 44 in E♭ (1842)</u>                                                                    30m; D4–

Schumann's piano quintet is one of the monuments of chamber music: a work that seems an unflawed masterpiece. It is powerful, brilliant, full of extrovert vigour, yet also touchingly and tenderly lyrical. It is rich in masterly counterpoint. This was the first significant work for the combination, and Schumann's writing for it seems ideal. Every player has many enjoyable opportunities. The viola episodes in the *In modo d'una Marcia* second movement, based on the open C string, have a specially haunting quality. The pianist has many notes to play; but Schumann seems to have found a good balance: the part does not have the thickness encountered in the piano trios.

## Ensemble Work including a Wind Instrument

<u>Märchenerzählungen, op. 132 (1853)</u> (clarinet, viola, piano)                    15m; D3
*Fairy Tales*: four pieces. Musically of small scope, but as repertoire for this combination they are worth playing. The piano part is technically more demanding than those of the viola or clarinet. The clarinet is in B♭. A violin can be used instead of the clarinet.

## Duet Sonatas and other Duets

<u>Sonata no. 1 in A minor, op. 105 (1851)</u> (violin, piano)                        17m; D3
In three movements, moderate in its ambition; it is quite good although texturally rather monotonous. As a fairly easy romantic sonata it is a useful rarity.

<u>Sonata no. 2 in D minor, op. 121 (1851)</u> (violin, piano)                        33m; D4+
This is a great contrast to its predecessor: long, in four movements, powerful musically and technically demanding. It is not to be undertaken lightly.

Sonata no. 3 in A minor (1853) (violin, piano)                                     21m; D4

In 1853, as previously mentioned, Schumann with Dietrich and Brahms wrote the composite 'FAE Sonata' as a present for Joachim, Schumann providing the slow (second) movement and finale. Shortly afterwards, however, he wrote two further movements of his own to replace those of his colleagues: but the resulting sonata was suppressed and only finally published in 1956. It remains little known. Some may enjoy exploring it: it is less earnest and more charming than its predecessors.

*Märchenbilder*, op. 113 (1851) (viola, piano)                                     16m; D4–

*Fairy Tale Pictures*: four pieces, all attractive. A violin part is provided as alternative to viola.

*Fünf Stücke im Volkston*, op. 102 (1849) (cello, piano)                            17m; D4–

*Five Pieces in Folk-Song Style*: varied and excellent. An alternative is provided for violin.

Adagio and Allegro in A♭, op. 70 (1849) (horn, piano)                               9m; D3

Very attractive. Schumann provided alternative parts for cello or violin.

*Fantasiestücke*, op. 73 (1849) (clarinet, piano)                                   11m; D3

Three pieces: lyrical and enjoyable. The clarinet is in A. Alternative instruments are violin or cello.

*Drei Romanzen*, op. 94 (1849) (oboe, piano)                                        12m; D3

Three calm, gentle and beautiful pieces. They can alternatively be played on clarinet (in A) or violin.

# SHOSTAKOVICH
## 1906–1975; Russia

Dmitry Shostakovich was born in St Petersburg and from 1919 studied at the conservatoire there (at that time called Petrograd). He came to prominence early with the success of his first symphony in 1926. Although critical opinions vary, he was one of the outstanding composers of the twentieth century, and arguably the greatest symphonist since Mahler. His entire creative life was lived in the Soviet Union, and he suffered political interference in his life and his music. In 1936 he was denounced following Stalin's unfavourable reaction on seeing his opera *Lady Macbeth of the Mtsensk District*. The next year, he largely succeeded in restoring his position by composing the fifth symphony, in a more conservative style. However, he had further troubles later and in 1948 was again condemned, along with other prominent Soviet composers. This time his return to favour was slower, and was only complete after the death of Stalin in 1953.

Shostakovich was influenced by contemporary developments, but he retained a harmonic basis; all his works have an explicit key. His music is also often emotional. His substantial body of chamber music is dominated by the fifteen string quartets – interestingly, the same as the number of his symphonies. However, he only began the series in 1938, after the first denunciation and the fifth symphony. He perhaps felt better able to express himself freely in chamber music than in more public genres. In his later years he suffered health problems, including two heart attacks, and the music of this period developed a different and inward-looking character. Shostakovich did not usually make virtuoso demands in his chamber music: for capable amateurs the works are challenging but mostly playable. They hold a place both in the concert hall and with amateurs playing for pleasure. In several string quartets (as in other works), Shostakovich employs his personal motif DSCH, for Dmitry S(c)hostakovich – in German musical notation D-Es-C-H, in English notation D-E♭-C-B.

## String Quartets

Every Shostakovich string quartet is a fully mature work. However, the first is both musically and technically relatively simple, and is probably the best for amateurs to start on. The fourth, too, is one of the most playable. Easily the best-known and most popular is the eighth, which although more difficult can be enjoyed by most experienced amateurs. In general the quartets later than the eighth are technically and musically more difficult, so perhaps best not approached until after most of the earlier quartets. Shostakovich's quartets in parts are only published singly, so obtaining the complete series is not cheap.

No. 1 in C, op. 49 (1938)                                                   14m; D4–

In four movements, and of a brevity and lightweight character that make it a remarkable contrast to the massive fifth symphony composed the year before. Technically it is fairly straightforward; but amateurs may find it difficult even to approach the indicated metronome speeds of the third and fourth movements.

No. 2 in A, op. 68 (1944)                                                   34m; D4+

In contrast to its predecessor, this is a large-scale, splendid and forceful quartet. It is again in four movements; their sequence is that of classical precedent, and they have titles – Overture; Recitative and Romance; Waltz; Theme with Variations. Technically, though practicable for capable amateurs, it is a tough challenge. Much of the *Adagio* second movement is a first-violin recitative above potentially arm-aching sustained chords in the lower parts.

No. 3 in F, op. 73 (1946)                                                   32m; D4

Another powerful and large-scale quartet. It also shares with its predecessor the fact that it was composed under the shadow of the Second World War (though the programmatic headings that Shostakovich gave to the movements for the first performance, and later withdrew, were probably offered to propitiate the authorities following their criticisms of his ninth symphony). There are five movements.

### No. 4 in D, op. 83 (1949)                                                25m; D4–
Said to be in Russia the most popular of Shostakovich's quartets. Composed in the aftermath of the 1948 condemnation, it differs from its predecessors in character, probably in the hope of a favourable response (though in the event Shostakovich withheld it for some years). There are four movements, the third and fourth being played without a break. It is lyrical and rarely forceful. The influence of the Jewish music of Eastern Europe is noticeable, especially in the haunting final movement.

### No. 5 in B♭, op. 92 (1952)                                               30m; D4
In three long movements, played without a break. The opening motif on the viola is derived from Shostakovich's DSCH motto, and much of the quartet is thought to have personal significance for him. It is quite a tough work, but it contains much enjoyable music. Some writing for two or three players in octaves is difficult for intonation.

### No. 6 in G, op. 101 (1956)                                               24m; D4–
This quartet returns to the conventional four movements (the last two linked). It is also relatively relaxed and cheerful, with some straightforward themes and fairly diatonic harmonies. The second movement is a kind of waltz, the third a passacaglia. In the final cadence of each movement, Shostakovich introduces his DSCH motif (in the second movement, a third lower) played vertically – the notes sounded simultaneously. Although the final movement has some fairly difficult passages, overall this is one of the most approachable of the quartets.

### No. 7 in F♯ minor, op. 108 (1960)                                        12m; D4
This quartet is dedicated to the memory of Shostakovich's first wife Nina, who died in 1954; since then, he had had a second marriage and a divorce. This is his shortest quartet, in three movements to be played without a break, and its meaning is puzzling. The first movement seems quite simple and attractive; it is followed by a subdued but not obviously tragic *Lento*. Most challenging is the forceful fugue that follows, with grinding minor seconds. Eventually, however, this movement returns to the atmosphere of the first.

### No. 8 in C minor, op. 110 (1960)                                         21m; D4
This is by far the best-known of the string quartets. (It is also often heard in a version for string orchestra, made by Rudolf Barshai.) It was written quickly when Shostakovich was in Dresden (infamously destroyed in February 1945), and the dedication reads 'To the victims of Fascism and war'. Nevertheless, its true

meaning (or perhaps a further meaning) is thought to be autobiographical. The DSCH motif is pervasive, and there are many quotations from Shostakovich's previous works. Whatever its significance, it is remarkably powerful and evocative. There are five movements, played without a break. The first is a *Largo*, opening with a contrapuntal treatment of the DSCH motif; three forceful and often emotional movements follow before the finale returns to the opening tempo and material.

### No. 9 in E♭, op. 117 (1964)
26m; D4+

There are five movements, played without a break. The *Allegro* finale, twice as long as any other movement, is a tour de force, and much of it is frenzied and very difficult. Moreover, musically the whole quartet is not easy. Probably only very capable amateurs who are Shostakovich devotees should attempt it!

### No. 10 in A♭, op. 118 (1964)
24m; D4+

Composed immediately after no. 9, but musically much more approachable. There are four movements, with just the last two linked. Perhaps most obviously beautiful is the *Adagio* third movement, which is a passacaglia. This and the first movement are technically quite straightforward, and the finale is playable though challenging. Unfortunately, however, the second movement *Allegretto furioso* is really difficult, and makes this quartet impracticable for many.

### No. 11 in F minor, op. 122 (1966)
17m; D4

This is the first of what are considered Shostakovich's late quartets. It was dedicated in memory of the second violinist of the Beethoven Quartet, who had just died. There are seven short movements, to be played without a break. It seems like a series of miniatures, each quite different but related to a theme presented at the beginning. Other than the one-minute fourth movement *Étude*, it is technically straightforward.

### No. 12 in D♭, op. 133 (1968)
27m; D4+

There are only two movements, though the long second movement is clearly a scherzo, slow movement and finale linked together. Shostakovich begins with, and uses through the work, a twelve-tone row. But this is not a serial quartet: the treatment is tonal, and though some of it is musically difficult the use of harmony generally accords with his usual practice. It contains, however, some technically difficult passages, and should be explored only by experienced Shostakovich players.

### No. 13 in B♭ minor, op. 138 (1970)
19m; D4+

Dedicated to the viola player of the Beethoven Quartet, this quartet emphasizes the viola. Indeed, it both begins and ends on unaccompanied solo viola. The latter sends the viola exceptionally high and is then joined by the violins for an extraordinary

215

final note, a crescendo from *pp* to *sffff*. The quartet is in a single movement, in ABA form, the outer parts being *Adagio* with a faster central section. As in the preceding quartet, twelve-tone rows are employed within a tonal basis. There are also 'knocks' to be made by the wood of the bow on the belly of the instrument. Musically, the mood seems bleak. Amateurs could tackle it, but they should appreciate what they are taking on.

No. 14 in F♯, op. 142 (1973)                                                     27m; D4+

Of Shostakovich's late quartets, this is perhaps the most straightforward in its intentions. It is in three movements. The dedicatee this time was the cellist of the Beethoven Quartet. All players, especially the cellist, are given solos, sometimes declamatory. There are difficult passages for all, and some of those for the cello are very high-lying.

No. 15 in E♭ minor, op. 144 (1974)                                              36m; D4

This final quartet is Shostakovich's longest. It has six movements, played without a break and all marked *Adagio* or *Adagio molto*. Shostakovich was ill; he may have seen this as his requiem. Most of the music is withdrawn and bleak. Technically the notes are sometimes hard but not severely so. However, this is a string quartet like no other: difficult for an audience as it is for players. Before considering undertaking it, players should be aware of its character.

## String Octet

Two Pieces, op. 11 (1924–5) (4 violins, 2 violas, 2 cellos)                      10m; D4+

The first piece, Prelude, is tonal, lyrical and enjoyable. However, in the second (Scherzo), Shostakovich was experimenting: it is frenetic and dissonant. It is also too difficult for most amateurs to get much pleasure from it.

## Piano Trios

No. 1 in C minor, op. 8 (1923)                                                  13m; D4–

This attractive work from Shostakovich's student years was published only after his death. It is in one long and complex movement. Much of it sounds late romantic, but there are also plenty of hints of the later Shostakovich.

No. 2 in E minor, op. 67 (1944)                              27m; D4+ (cello harder)

Shostakovich here provided the outstanding piano trio of the twentieth century: a magnificent, serious, large-scale work. The seriousness reflects not only its composition in wartime but its dedication to a close friend who had just died. Technically much of it is difficult. Moreover, it begins with a very long passage (initially an unaccompanied solo) for the cello playing high artificial harmonics – for some cellists, hardly possible.

## Piano Quintet (piano, string quartet)

Op. 57 in G minor (1940)                                                31m; D4

This is one of Shostakovich's most popular works. It is on a large scale, in five movements (the first and second and the fourth and fifth played without a break). It differs from much of Shostakovich's music in having no harsh or forceful writing, and in that much of it is cheerful, sometimes exuberantly so. The slow second and fourth movements are sad but beautiful and sometimes emotional. Technically it is not easy but there are no severe problems. Unlike many piano quintets, it never indulges in bombastic piano writing.

## Duet Sonatas

Sonata in D, op. 134 (1968) (violin, piano)                              31m; D5

A splendid and expansive work, in three movements; but it is not playable by amateurs.

Sonata in F, op. 147 (1975) (viola, piano)                              30m; D4+

This is Shostakovich's last work. Perhaps the most memorable of its three movements is the long *Adagio* finale, which has obvious allusions to Beethoven's 'Moonlight' piano sonata. Much of this sonata could be attempted by capable amateurs; but some passages might be problematical. Also often played is a transcription for cello that Shostakovich approved.

Sonata in D minor, op. 40 (1934) (cello, piano)                         28m; D4+

A beautiful and distinctive work in four movements.

# SIBELIUS
### 1865–1957; Finland

Jean Sibelius is the most important composer to have been produced by Finland. He is regarded as a national hero: his music played a significant role in developing Finnish national consciousness in the years before the country gained independence from the Russian Empire in 1918. His style is of great originality, and although international critical opinions of his importance have fluctuated, his position as a major figure is secure. Much of his music is orchestral: symphonies and symphonic poems. In his young days he played the violin in chamber music and composed a number of chamber works, some of which have been published. They include a string quartet in A minor of 1889, a piano quintet in G minor of 1889–90 and a string quartet in B♭ major, op. 4, of 1890. However, these pre-date his first maturity, which he is often considered to have reached about 1892 with the tone poem *En Saga*. After this, regrettably, he composed only one full-scale chamber work, a string quartet, but this is a major contribution. Also in his maturity, he produced a sonatina for violin and piano, many pieces or sets of pieces for the same combination, and some pieces for cello and piano. However, these are rarely played; only the sonatina is considered here.

## String Quartet

Op. 56 in D minor (*Voces Intimae*) (1909)                                        32m; D4

The subtitle means *intimate voices* or *friendly voices*. At least for those who respond to Sibelius's sound-world, this is a wonderful quartet, one of the greatest of the early twentieth century. It is entirely unlike any other, both in its very original textures and in its structure. There are five movements, all of great power. The notes are not really very difficult, though achieving good intonation in the many unison passages is challenging.

## Duet Sonatina

Sonatina in E, op. 80 (1915) (violin, piano)                                        12m; D4+

Little known; musically modest, but technically too difficult for most amateurs.

# SMETANA
### 1824–1884; Bohemia

Bedřich Smetana is often considered the father of Czech music – the music of Bohemia. (Bohemia, formerly within the Austro-Hungarian Empire, is now part of the Czech Republic, and can also be taken broadly to represent its whole area.) In his homeland he is above all revered for his operas and for his cycle of symphonic poems, *Ma Vlast* (*My Country*). Chamber music forms only a small part of his output, but it is important, and for Smetana it was the medium for expressing matters of personal significance. His two string quartets are explicitly programmatic – the first such chamber works by any major composer. In 1876 Smetana became totally deaf, which largely ended his public musical career. However, his urge to compose and his ability were undiminished, and he now had much more time to devote to composition. The outpouring of the following years includes the two quartets, of which the first is his greatest chamber work.

## String Quartets

No. 1 in E minor (*From My Life*, op. 116) (1876)                                        27m; D4

This quartet is a rarity in being programmatic – the whole work charts the course of Smetana's life. It deservedly has a firm place in the repertoire. It is distinctive and fresh throughout; the writing is far from being traditional for the medium but it is enterprising and highly successful. The opening is beloved of viola players, who are given a long, declamatory (and difficult) solo above the lightest accompaniment. The second movement is a polka, with solos for viola and second violin going respectively up their C and G strings. In the slow third movement, the cello comes to the fore. The vigorous finale is interrupted towards the end by a held high E harmonic on the first violin, representing the sound in Smetana's ears that heralded his deafness. Overall the quartet is difficult: for many ensembles it will not be practicable, but for capable players it can be very enjoyable.

No. 2 in D minor (1882–3)                                    19m; D4

Smetana's last work, composed when signs were beginning of the decline into insanity that was soon to overtake him. The structure is baffling, and all movements have continual changes of tempo and material. The roles intended for the various movements are not obvious. On the other hand, the quartet contains much engaging material and is well written for the medium. It will be valued by those drawn to Smetana's music, but for others it may not be worth the effort required.

## Piano Trio

Op. 15 in G minor (1855)                                    29m; D4

A very fine trio, though it dates from before Smetana had developed his later style with its strong national character. It was written in memory of his first child, a daughter who died at the age of four, and is tinged with melancholy throughout. It is in three movements, and has much powerful and declamatory music. There are also many big, beautiful melodies for both violin and cello. For those who love uninhibitedly romantic music this may be a highly prized work. It is well written for the instruments, so for those with sufficient technique it can be very enjoyable to play.

## Duet with Piano

Two pieces *From my Homeland* (1880) (violin, piano)              12m; D4–
Attractive and characteristic.


# STRAUSS
### 1864–1949; Germany


Richard Strauss was one of the greatest composers of the late romantic period, and his operas and orchestral tone poems have a major position in the repertoire. From the point of view of the lover of chamber music, however, he is frustrating. He showed interest in the medium; but ultimately his contribution is slight. Four chamber compositions are among his early published works; but only the last of these, the sonata for violin and piano written just a year before his first outstanding orchestral masterpiece, *Don Juan*, is representative of the mature composer. Through the long years of success that followed, he devoted himself to tone poems and then operas, and produced no significant chamber music. Towards the end of his life, he returned to instrumental music in the classical forms; but the only work he then wrote for a chamber ensemble is the prelude to his last opera. In this period he also composed *Metamorphosen* for twenty-three solo strings, but this is not chamber music. Again for groups of larger than chamber size are Strauss's compositions for wind ensemble, which players may be interested in: there are two early works for thirteen wind instruments and two late works for sixteen.

## String Quartet

Op. 2 in A major (1879–80)                                                      31m; D4
Poor. This very early work is classical in character, has little melodic interest and no sign of the later Strauss. Moreover it is difficult. It is not worth the effort of playing.

## String Sextet

Prelude to *Capriccio*, op. 85 (1940–1)                                      12m; D3+
The opera addresses the question as to whether poetry or music is the greater art; the sextet is presented as a new work by the composer Flamand. Often played as an independent chamber work, it is a beautiful, lyrical and elegant *Andante con moto*, characteristic of the mature Strauss. Technically it is mostly straightforward, but achieving good ensemble is difficult.

## Piano Quartet

Op. 13 in C minor (1884)                                                          38m; D4
The writing resembles Brahms; there are only hints of the Strauss to come. Nevertheless, it is a fine work, rich and self-confident, with enjoyable parts for all.

———•◦•———

In 1893, Strauss composed two pieces for piano quartet. They are attractive though lightweight in character; some may wish to try them. They have no opus number.

## Duet Sonatas

Op. 18 in E♭ (1887) (violin, piano)                                            29m; D4+
The last of the early chamber works, and the only one to hold a firm place in the professional repertoire. It is splendid but difficult, its three movements full of music characteristic of the composer.

<u>Op. 6 in F (1882–3)</u> (cello, piano)                                        27m; D4

Beautiful, romantic and well balanced so that the cello is never drowned by the piano; but little in its style is personal to Strauss.

# STRAVINSKY
## 1882–1971; Russia

Igor Stravinsky was born near St Petersburg; after the 1917 Revolution, he left Russia and lived in France and later in America. Despite living outside the country for much of his life, he is always considered a Russian composer. His first fame came with his ballets for Diaghilev, starting with *The Firebird* in 1910. The most notorious was *The Rite of Spring* in 1913, which gave him a reputation as a musical revolutionary. A characteristic of his music throughout his life was his interest in rhythm; but otherwise he twice radically changed his compositional style. In his first maturity his music was nationalist Russian, influenced by folksong. After the First World War he became a neo-classicist. In the 1950s he took up serial technique and gradually developed his own version. Never conventional, he is considered one of the most important and influential composers of the twentieth century. He composed a number of works for chamber combinations. His dynamic approach to rhythm, often involving frequent changes of time signature, can be problematical for some.

After a few early works, Stravinsky did not use opus numbers.

## Works for String Quartet

<u>Three pieces (1914)</u>                                                      7m; D4

Untitled, but in a 1928 orchestral version these became *Danse*, *Excentrique* and *Cantique*. They are tonal but very unconventional. Much is fairly straightforward to play, but some technical demands appear in the second piece (inspired by the English music-hall comedian Little Tich).

<u>Concertino (1920)</u>                                                       7m; D4+

This single-movement work is what its name suggests: a miniature concerto, largely for the first violin. The other parts, however, are not negligible. It has Stravinsky's characteristic rhythmic vitality, and is technically quite difficult.

## Ensemble Works including Wind Instruments

There are two major works involving wind, both for unusual combinations of instruments. They are often performed with a conductor.

<u>Octet (1922–3)</u> (flute, clarinet, 2 bassoons, 2 trumpets, tenor trombone, bass trombone)                                                                15m; D4

This is one of Stravinsky's first neo-classical compositions. It is in three movements (the last two being linked): Sinfonia; Tema con Variazioni; and Finale. The clarinettist requires instruments in both B♭ and A; the trumpets are in A and C.

Septet (1952–3) (clarinet, bassoon, horn, piano, violin, viola, cello)      12m; D4
This work comes from the time of Stravinsky's transition from neoclassicism to serialism; the latter is evident mainly in the second and third of its three movements. The clarinet is in A.

Also for small ensembles including wind instruments are two suites from *l'Histoire du soldat* (*The Soldier's Tale*). The original is a theatre work, composed in 1918, with a small number of actors and dancers accompanied by seven musicians. In 1919 Stravinsky made a suite of five numbers for clarinet, violin and piano. He later made another suite of nine numbers for the original combination of instruments – clarinet, bassoon, cornet, trombone, percussion, violin and double bass.

## Duets with Piano

Duo concertant (1931–2) (violin, piano)      16m; D5
As its title suggests, this five-movement work requires a virtuoso technique.

Suite italienne (1932–3) (violin, piano)      18m; D4+
This popular suite is not really chamber music: it is six pieces with piano accompaniment. It was arranged (with violinist Samuel Dushkin) from numbers of the ballet *Pulcinella* of 1919–20. The ballet had been 'recomposed' by Stravinsky from music thought to be by the early eighteenth-century composer Pergolesi (but now known to be at least partly by others). Several of the pieces are readily playable by amateurs, but the last is really difficult.

A version for cello and piano of the *Suite italienne* was arranged by Stravinsky with the cellist Gregor Piatigorsky. The pieces selected are not all the same as those of the violin version.
    Another suite for violin and piano arranged by Stravinsky with Dushkin is *Divertimento*, from *Le baiser de la fée* (*The Fairy's Kiss*).

# TCHAIKOVSKY
## 1840–1893; Russia

Pyotr Il'yich Tchaikovsky is, with the wider public, one of the most popular of all composers, no doubt because of his wonderful melodies and the emotional intensity often found in his music. This popularity rests mainly on his large works, especially the symphonies, symphonic poems, overtures, concertos, ballet music and operas. Critical opinion has in the past been doubtful, but his position today is secure. He was an outstanding master of orchestration. His style is distinctive: he did not join with the nationalist Russian composers, he was uninfluenced by both Wagner and Brahms, and his greatest love was for the music of Mozart. Nevertheless, his music undoubtedly has Russian character. He began seriously to compose only in about 1863, but developed quickly and was producing masterpieces by about 1870. He is not a major composer of chamber music, but it is pleasantly surprising that he composed a considerable amount – especially since he sometimes made deprecatory comments about the medium. His chamber works have a place in the repertoire and playing them can be very enjoyable, though mostly they do not have the popularity of his orchestral music. Tchaikovsky's style of writing for chamber ensembles does not follow classical norms and may sometimes be unidiomatic; but it is mostly not too difficult for amateurs to play.

## String Quartets

There are three string quartets. They all come from the earlier part of Tchaikovsky's output, but none is to be considered immature; the second quartet is approximately contemporary with the first piano concerto, one of his most frequently played works. Of the three quartets the first is the most popular with both audiences and players, and is technically the easiest. Nevertheless, both other quartets are also fine works and should be played.

### No. 1 in D, op. 11 (1871)                                     31m; D3+

Tchaikovsky gives plenty of interest to all parts in this quartet, and it is well within the capabilities of most amateurs. Some of it is obviously Russian in character, and it is generally happy: there is none of Tchaikovsky's intensity here. The first movement is memorable for the subtle and fascinating rhythm of its opening theme. Most famous is the *Andante cantabile* second movement, which is often heard out of context in arrangements. This opens with a Russian folk tune; the treatment is simple and beautiful, but it is mostly a melody for the first violin with accompaniment for the other parts.

### No. 2 in F, op. 22 (1874)                                      36m; D4

A fine quartet, and more serious than its predecessor; indeed, the long and beautiful slow movement has Tchaikovsky's tragic emotional force. Particularly memorable is the second movement scherzo, with its distinctive rhythm of two bars of 6/8 and one of 9/8. Most of the writing in the quartet is enjoyable, but there are a few unidiomatic, quasi-orchestral passages, which some may not like – and they are difficult. Overall this quartet is much more demanding than its predecessor, but it should be manageable by experienced amateurs.

<u>No. 3 in E♭ minor, op. 30 (1876)</u>                                    36m; D3+ (cello harder)

This quartet was written in memory of the violinist Ferdinand Laub, and this determines the sombre and emotional character particularly of the first and third movements. The first is very long, but it is beautifully written and full of interest so that its length does not pall. The third, *Andante funebre e doloroso, ma con moto*, is the powerful, tragic core of the work. A solo for the second violin predominantly on a monotone evokes the chanting of an Orthodox priest. The quartet is in an uncomfortable key, but it is not particularly difficult. It is generous in solos for the cello (though some of these are not easy).

## String Sextet

<u>Op. 70 in D minor (*Souvenir de Florence*) (1887–92)</u>                              35m; D4

An attractive work of maturest Tchaikovsky. Its character throughout is cheerful and never intense. Despite its good qualities, however, some lack enthusiasm for this sextet. This may have something to do with its themes, which are not of Tchaikovsky's most heart-warming type. Players occasionally complain about the ostinato figurations or pizzicato patterns sometimes given to accompanying parts. Ricochet bowing is called for in the third movement. Overall it is not easy, but given adequate technique and a sympathetic approach it is good to play – and it is one of perhaps only five major works for the combination. It is sometimes performed by a string orchestra.

## Piano Trio

<u>Op. 50 in A minor (1881–2)</u>                                    50m; D4 (piano harder)

Of Tchaikovsky's chamber works, this is the one that departs furthest from normal conventions. But it is also probably the finest – a unique masterpiece. It is dedicated 'To the memory of a great artist': Nikolai Rubinstein, who was a virtuoso pianist and died in March 1881. Although exceptionally long, this trio has just two gigantic movements, of which the second is a set of variations – though the long final variation and coda effectively form a third movement. The music is often intense and tragic, but it is all of ravishing beauty. Technically the string parts are sometimes difficult though never unreasonable; but the piano part is as difficult as a concerto. Even more than with most piano chamber music, any decision to play this work depends on the pianist!

## Duets with Piano

<u>*Souvenir d'un lieu cher*, op. 42 (1878)</u> (violin, piano)                      17m; D3–4

Three pieces (also published separately): *Méditation*, *Scherzo* and *Mélodie*. Technically easiest and most popular with amateurs is *Mélodie*. All three are sometimes performed professionally in Glazunov's arrangement with orchestra.

# VAUGHAN WILLIAMS
## 1872–1958; England

Ralph Vaughan Williams (though not hyphenated, Vaughan Williams is his surname) was the first of the composers who, in the early twentieth century following the rise of Elgar, consolidated the revival of English music. Unlike Elgar, however, he was interested in English folksong and in the English composers of the sixteenth and seventeenth centuries. These influences form much of the basis on which he developed his very distinctive style, incorporating a modal element in his harmonies. This style is often considered to be characteristically English, and influenced many other English composers. He was a late developer, and in addition to his years at the Royal College of Music he studied with Bruch in 1898 and with Ravel as late as 1908. His maturity may be dated to about 1909–10. A few of his works (notably the *Tallis Fantasia* and *The Lark Ascending*) have become remarkably popular at least in England, and most of his nine symphonies are sometimes performed. Much other music, however, is little known, including most of his few chamber works. Technically they are playable by amateurs, but are not easy. In his early years Vaughan Williams played the viola, and his generous treatment of that instrument is prominent in the three works for string ensembles. He did not use opus numbers.

Works of possible interest not discussed below include the *Six Studies in English Folk Song* for cello and piano (with alternatives for clarinet, violin or viola). Another is *Household Music* (three preludes on Welsh hymn tunes): technically easy music for string quartet, available also to any other reasonable instruments. A potentially enjoyable opportunity is with an able singer to play the song-cycle *On Wenlock Edge* for tenor, string quartet and piano.

## String Quartets

No. 1 in G minor (1908, rev. 1921)                    28m; D4

By Vaughan Williams's standards rather an early work: it was composed immediately after his period of study with Ravel and is considered to show some French influence. There are nevertheless many Vaughan Williams characteristics, such as the folk-song qualities of the last movement *Rondo Capriccioso*, with its rustic opening theme. Though perhaps not a work to make converts to the composer, it is worth playing. The melodic material is freely distributed to all players – but especially to the viola.

No. 2 in A minor (1942–4)                    21m; D4

This is a tougher and finer work than its predecessor, and perhaps technically a little harder. It carries the dedication 'For Jean on her birthday': this was Jean Stewart, viola in the Menges Quartet. Vaughan Williams here gives even freer rein than in his other two string chamber works to his predilection for that instrument. The viola opens every movement and is prominent throughout; moreover, in the third movement scherzo all players except the viola are muted. The last movement Epilogue is subtitled *Greetings from Joan to Jean* in reference to the origin of its material in a proposed film about Joan of Arc.

## String Quintet (2 violins, 2 violas, cello)

Phantasy quintet (1912)                                                                15m; D4–

The best-known, the most obviously attractive and surely the finest of Vaughan Williams's chamber works. Its atmosphere is often rapt and lyrical in a way comparable to some of the composer's most popular works. It was written to a commission by William Cobbett, and so is in phantasy form. There are four movements, each continuing *attacca* to the next. The form means that it is short, which may be felt regrettable. The first viola is treated with special fondness: for example, it both opens and closes the first movement in unaccompanied solo. Nevertheless, all players are given good opportunities. Much of it is not difficult, but some will be challenged by the 7/4 *Prestissimo* second movement scherzo.

## Duet Sonata

Sonata in A minor (1954) (violin, piano)                                                27m; D5
Some of the writing for the violin makes virtuoso demands.


# VERDI
## 1813–1901; Italy

Giuseppe Verdi is generally considered the greatest Italian operatic composer, and one of the finest of any nationality. He composed very little other than opera, the only major work being the Requiem of 1874. Also, amusingly but fortunately for lovers of chamber music, in 1873 when in Naples and prevented from rehearsing his opera *Aida* by the illness of the soprano, he filled the time by writing a string quartet.

## String Quartet

String quartet in E minor (1873)                                                        23m; D4
After its composition, Verdi was dismissive about this quartet – perhaps as a way of deflecting critical comparisons with the classics. Though light in character, it is the work of a mature master and is surely the finest Italian quartet of the nineteenth century. With its Italian characteristics it is very different from almost everything else in the repertoire. Much of it is fast and brilliant, but the central section of the

third movement gives the cello what in an opera would surely be a tenor aria. It is a pity, perhaps, that the quartet is so difficult: but its charm and individuality make it worth the effort. With practice, it is playable by experienced amateurs.

# VIVALDI
## 1678–1741; Italy

Antonio Vivaldi was born in Venice and spent most of his life there. In 1703 he was ordained priest, but a year later he became inactive as such although he retained the status of priest for the rest of his life. For much of his career he had a position at the *Ospedale della Pietà*, an orphanage that specialized in the training of musical girls, for which he taught and composed. He was also much involved in opera, and he produced a good deal of religious choral music. In his last years his success in Venice waned and he moved to Vienna, but died in poverty shortly afterwards. Today he is one of the most popular composers of the baroque era, especially famous for his concertos.

Vivaldi's output was vast. There are over 500 concertos (more than 200 of them for violin) and over forty operas. By comparison with this, the quantity of chamber music is modest; but by other standards it is large. Only four sets of his chamber works were published in his lifetime, but many further compositions exist. Most of his chamber music is delightful, though it is sometimes suggested that, being largely composed under the influence of Corelli, it lacks the brilliant originality that he showed in some other fields.

There is some confusion over Vivaldi's output, at least in part because he often reused movements or material from previous works. Today, his works are usually identified by their numbers in the Ryom-Verzeichnis (RV), the catalogue by Peter Ryom, published in 1973–4, with subsequent updates.

## Trio Sonatas

Twelve trio sonatas, op. 1 (2 violins, continuo)                    5–10m; up to D3
These were first published in 1705; they are entitled *Sonate da camera*, and they include dance movements. Most are in four movements. No. 12 (in a single movement) is a set of variations on the well-known tune *La Follia* (also used by Corelli, among others). All are delightful music and enjoyable playing. They have RV numbers between 61 and 79, but not sequential.

Two trio sonatas from op. 5 (2 violins, continuo)                    7–9m; up to D3–
Published in 1716, this set contains two trio sonatas (along with four violin sonatas). Because the numbering in this opus continues from the op. 2 violin sonatas (*see* below), these two are numbered 17 (RV 76) and 18 (RV 72). Both are in

three movements. No. 18 is technically one of the easiest of Vivaldi's trio sonatas.

———•••••———

There also exist six further trio sonatas for two violins and continuo. RV 60 and 74 resemble those of opp. 1 and 5. RV 68, 70, 71 and 77 are different: their continuo parts are optional, so they can be played as duets for two violins. Their violin parts are technically more demanding than those of the normal trio sonatas.

Vivaldi also composed a number of trio sonatas for other combinations. With one exception, all are in three movements.

Trio sonata in C minor, RV 81 (2 oboes, continuo)                    7m; D2+

Trio sonata in C, RV 82 (violin, lute, continuo)                    10m; D3−

Trio sonata in G minor, RV 85 (violin, lute, continuo)                    9m; D2

Trio sonata in C minor, RV 83 (violin, cello, continuo)                    8m; D3
Considerable agility is asked of the cello. Note that this work could be played by a piano trio.

Trio sonata in D, RV 84 (flute, violin, continuo)                    7m; D3
This is technically quite demanding, especially for the flute.

Trio sonata in A minor, RV 86 (recorder, bassoon, continuo)                    11m; D3−
In four movements.

## Four-Part Sonatas

*Sonata a quattro* in E♭, RV 130 (2 violins, viola, continuo)                    4m; D2
Subtitled *al Santo Sepolcro*. It is charming but it has just two short movements.

Sonata in C, RV 779 (violin, oboe, organ, optional chalumeau)                    14m; D3−
Although usually listed as a four-part sonata with continuo, continuo is not expected: this is effectively a trio sonata for violin and oboe with the basso continuo played on the organ and (if present) chalumeau. The chalumeau is the predecessor of the clarinet: given the ability to read in C, its part could be played on a modern bass clarinet.

*Sonata a quattro* in C, RV 801 (flute/oboe, violin/oboe, cello/bassoon, continuo)
                    12m; D3−
An attractive work, which received a full RV number, implying probable authenticity, in 2001.

## Duet Sonatas

All Vivaldi's duet sonatas employ continuo.

## Violin

Twelve sonatas, op. 2            6–10m; up to D3

These sonatas were first published in 1709. Their RV numbers lie between 1 and 36, but are not sequential. Seven are in minor keys. They are of *sonata da camera* character, many of their movements being dances. All are in either three or four movements, which are frequently in two repeated halves. The continuo line is sometimes quite free and enjoyable.

Four sonatas from op. 5            7–10m; up to D3

This set of six works published in 1716 contains four violin sonatas; their numbers continue from op. 2 as 13–16.

Around twenty-seven further sonatas for violin and continuo exist, excluding some of doubtful authenticity or closely related to other sonatas. Two groups are sometimes referred to by name. The five 'Dresden sonatas' are known from copies taken to that city by Johann Georg Pisendel, who had come to know Vivaldi during some years he spent in Venice. The 'Manchester sonatas' are a group of twelve once owned by Cardinal Ottoboni in Rome; after his death in 1740, they came to England and eventually in 1965 were acquired by the Henry Watson Music Library in Manchester, where their significance was realized. Four were previously unknown, and two others known only in sections reused in a violin concerto.

## Cello

Six sonatas            10–15m; up to D3

This set was published in Paris in about 1739, without opus number (though they are sometimes referred to as op. 14). Their RV numbers are 40, 41, 43 and 45–47. All are in four movements.

There also exist at least two further cello sonatas, RV 39 and RV 42.

## Wind instruments

There are also a few sonatas for wind instruments and continuo: the following are the best-known and most probably authentic. Many further sonatas exist but are of more doubtful authenticity. (The set of six sonatas known as *Il Pastor Fido*, op. 13 (RV 54–59), for musette or alternative instruments, is now thought to be spurious.)

Sonata in C, RV 48 (flute, continuo)            9m; D3–

The best-known flute sonata attributed to Vivaldi; but even this one is of questionable authenticity.

Sonata in F, RV 52 (recorder, continuo)                                           8m; D3–

Sonata in C minor, RV 53 (oboe, continuo)                                        12m; D3

# WEBER
### 1786–1826; Germany

Carl Maria von Weber is a significant composer, important especially for his influence on nineteenth-century German opera, including Wagner. His most famous works are the three great operas of his last years, *Der Freischütz*, *Euryanthe* and *Oberon*. He also wrote instrumental music through most of his life, some of which is still played. He is important to clarinettists for his considerable number of works for their instrument. Of his small output of chamber music, only the clarinet quintet is well known. Nevertheless, the other works, too, have a distinctive charm and are useful additions to the repertoire.

## Piano Quartet

Piano quartet in B♭ (1806–9)                                                        28m; D3
Entitled *Grand Quatuor*, this work has no established opus number but is sometimes referred to as op. 8 or op. 18. The music is light in character and often quirky; some, indeed, is comical and is hard to play without a smile. But it is all well written and only moderate in its difficulties. Given that profundity is not expected, it makes enjoyable playing for all and is a useful addition to the piano quartet repertoire.

## Ensemble Works including a Wind Instrument

Trio in G minor, op. 63 (1818–19) (flute, cello, piano)                          24m; D3
Emotionally lightweight, but attractive and well written throughout. The slow movement is entitled *Schäfers Klage* (*Shepherd's Lament*), in reference to a Goethe poem (set by Schubert among others). As a rare chamber work including flute, this trio is well known to flautists. Its flute part is gratifying; the cello, too, is treated generously. The difficulties in all parts are only moderate, so this is a good trio for amateurs to play. The flute part can alternatively be played on a violin (though not all passages lie comfortably).

Quintet in B♭, op. 34 (1811–15) (clarinet, string quartet)   27m; D3 (clarinet harder)
This is Weber's finest chamber work, and the only one with an important position in the repertoire – after Mozart and Brahms, this is the third major clarinet quintet. However, the clarinet part, written for the virtuoso Heinrich Baermann, is brilliant and demanding. So in a sense this work breaks the usual rules of chamber

music and is a showpiece for clarinet: but the string players are not just accompanists. There are plenty of passages in which they come to the fore; and when they are accompaniments they are not boring. Given a clarinettist who can handle the part, experienced amateur string players will enjoy playing this work. Musically it is excellent throughout; there is nothing flippant or quirky here. The clarinet is in B♭.

## Duet Sonatas and another Duet

<u>Six progressive sonatas, op. 10 (1818–19)</u> (piano, violin)                    4–8m; D2
These little-known sonatas are 'dedicated to amateurs'. They are all short, in two or three movements, attractive but musically very lightweight. The violin part is often an accompaniment. Such technical progression as there is through them is gentle. Though indeed playable by most amateurs, they would perhaps not bear a lot of repetition.

<u>*Grand duo concertant* in E♭, op. 48 (1815–16)</u> (clarinet, piano)                    22m; D4
A full-scale work in three movements. It is a true duo, with the musical importance shared between the parts, and is good music as well as being a brilliant showpiece. The difficulties, too, are shared by both players. The clarinet is in B♭. Violin is offered as an alternative to the clarinet.

# WEBERN
### 1883–1945; Austria

Anton Webern began as a late romantic, but in 1904 he became a pupil of Arnold Schoenberg and gradually developed an atonal style. The first works that he published date from 1908, the year in which he completed his studies with Schoenberg. However, he remained passionately devoted to his former teacher, and when the latter in the 1920s introduced the twelve-tone technique, Webern adopted its principles in a strict form. His music was not widely known in his lifetime, but particularly in the 1960s and 1970s among the musical avant-garde Webern became a revered figure. He remains respected today, though probably only a limited proportion of the musical public understands or enjoys his music.

Webern composed a good deal of chamber music. Except for his earliest compositions, however, his works are far from conventional norms. Those from his atonal period but before he took up the twelve-tone technique are of extreme brevity – this being, his admirers say, because they are so concentrated. His later compositions are rather more extended, but still by usual standards very short. Also unconventional are their instrumental textures, with individual contributions often of only one or two notes at a time, and employing extremes of register and dynamics in close juxtaposition. Special instrumental effects such as sul ponticello, pizzicato, harmonics, col legno and long portamento are frequently used.

In addition to the music published with opus numbers during his lifetime, other works both early and mature were published after his death. Other than in the early compositions, the technical difficulties of his works usually make them impossible for most amateurs.

## String Trio

Movement (1925)                                                         2m; D5

String trio, op. 20 (1926–7)                                            9m; D5
In two movements; a complex and difficult work.

## Works for String Quartet

Slow movement (1905)                                                    9m; D4
This is tonal, in a romantic style, and is attractive. It is quite often played.

String quartet (1905)                                                  15m; D4
In a single extended movement. Though romantic, it shows early signs of Webern's movement towards atonality.

Rondo (1906)                                                           7m; D4

Five movements, op. 5 (1909)                                          11m; D5
Some of these movements are slow and technically fairly straightforward. This work may offer an approach, both musically and technically, for those wishing to enter Webern's sound world. It is sometimes heard in a later version for string orchestra.

Six bagatelles, op. 9 (1913)                                          4m; D5
At least two of these pieces last for less than half a minute.

String quartet, op. 28 (1936–8)                                      9m; D4+
This is perhaps one of Webern's easier mature works both musically and technically.

## Piano Quintet (piano, string quartet)

Piano quintet (1907)                                                 12m; D4
In one extended movement; although still in some ways romantic in character, it shows Webern's developing departure from tonality.

## Work including Wind Instruments

Quartet, op. 22 (1928–30) (violin, clarinet, tenor saxophone, piano)    6m; D5
In two movements. The clarinet is in A.

## Duet Sonata and other Duets

Four pieces, op. 7 (1910) (violin, piano)                4½m; D5

Three little pieces, op. 11 (1914) (cello, piano)        2½m; D4+

Cello sonata (1914)                                      2¼m; D5

# Appendix I

# Further Composers

In addition to the composers whose chamber works have been discussed, numerous others have composed and published chamber music. The following is a small selection from among them. Many of these further composers, whether included here or not, may well have produced chamber music that is enjoyable to play. One reason for exploring the byways of chamber music is simply the fun of trying what is different. Some of the music will be found dull and its neglect justified; but on the other hand, surprisingly fine works will be encountered. Sometimes one may even feel one has discovered a composer who is worth investigating more widely. A second motivation is to find more music for a group that has played all the available works by major composers (at least, those within its technical range) – particularly for combinations that have a small repertoire.

**Albinoni, Tomaso (1671–1751; Italy)**
Famous in his lifetime principally for his operas, Albinoni also composed much instrumental music, and it is for this that he is now mainly known. His chamber music includes a substantial number of trio sonatas, all with two violins, and sonatas for violin and continuo.

**Arensky, Anton (1861–1906; Russia)**
Arensky wrote in a style much influenced by Tchaikovsky. A little of his music is still played. There are five full-scale chamber works: two string quartets, two piano trios and a piano quintet. The first piano trio, op. 32 in D minor, was once highly popular. The second string quartet, op. 35 in A minor, is curiously scored for violin, viola and two cellos; but Arensky provided an alternative for conventional string quartet. Of its three movements, the long second, *Variations on a Theme of Tchaikovsky*, is well known in Arensky's arrangement for string orchestra.

**Beach, Amy (1867–1944; America)**
Usually known in her day as Mrs H.H.A. Beach, her compositions received considerable recognition during her lifetime in both America and Europe. Though largely forgotten

after her death, some interest has revived more recently. Her chamber works include a string quartet, a piano trio, a piano quintet, a substantial Theme and Variations for flute and string quartet, and a duet sonata for violin.

### Berwald, Franz (1796–1868; Sweden)

Berwald is recognized as a fine and distinctive composer. He had an attractive melodic gift, and his approach to form was frequently original. Some of his works (notably the four symphonies) continue to be performed. Most of his substantial body of chamber music dates from a productive period in his fifties, when he was at his best. Two string quartets, in particular, are played. There are also two piano quintets and four piano trios. From an earlier period are another string quartet, a quartet for piano, clarinet, horn and bassoon and a septet for clarinet, horn, bassoon, violin, viola, cello and double bass.

### Bloch, Ernest (1880–1959; Switzerland, America)

Bloch was highly regarded in his lifetime but has since become neglected, though he still has a following. He developed a powerful and personal style, which has a distinctive Jewish character. In his later works he incorporated aspects of contemporary techniques, including atonality. His chamber compositions include five string quartets, two piano quintets, two sonatas for violin and piano and a suite for viola and piano; there are also smaller pieces for string quartet and other combinations.

### Bridge, Frank (1879–1941; England)

Perhaps best known for having taught Britten (who later championed his music), Bridge remains a marginal figure. However, he composed many chamber works and some are occasionally played – mainly those from between his first maturity around 1905 and the end of the First World War. Later works, in which his style became more 'advanced', are less known. His output includes four string quartets, a string sextet, a piano quintet, two piano trios, and duet sonatas for violin and for cello. There are also a phantasie (his spelling) string quartet, phantasie piano trio, phantasie piano quartet, and a trio rhapsody for two violins and viola. Of his many shorter pieces for various chamber combinations, the *Three Idylls* for string quartet are quite well known.

### Chausson, Ernest (1855–1899; France)

A late developer who died early, Chausson perhaps never fulfilled his potential. His only mature chamber work is a piano quartet. A string quartet, incomplete at his death, was finished by d'Indy. There is an early piano trio. Probably best known, though not a normal chamber work, is his concerto for violin, piano and string quartet.

### Cherubini, Luigi (1760–1842; Italy, France)

Though born in Italy, Cherubini lived in France from the age of twenty-eight, eventually becoming director of the Paris Conservatoire. He is highly regarded but his music is rarely played. His principal output was of operas and religious choral music, but he also composed six string quartets (the second being largely an arrangement of a symphony). These are worth trying – the first is probably the best to start with, and is not difficult (D3). They are excellent in craftsmanship, but some would criticize their material as austere. The last four are late works, composed between 1834 and 1837, and technically rather harder than their predecessors. A string quintet with two cellos is disappointing.

### Clarke, Rebecca (1886–1979; England, America)

Born in Harrow of an American father and a German mother, Rebecca Clarke lived in America from 1939. Her two full-scale chamber works, a piano trio and a viola sonata, are quite often performed.

### Crusell, Bernhard (1775–1838; Finland, Sweden)

Crusell was a fine clarinet player. His output as a composer was small but includes three attractive quartets for clarinet, violin, viola and cello.

### Delius, Frederick (1862–1934; England, France)

Born in Bradford and generally considered an English composer, though his parents were German and from 1897 he lived in France. His style is late romantic, lyrical, influenced by Wagner and Grieg. It is distinctive and recognizable; he has passionate advocates but his music is not to everyone's taste. There are a string quartet (sometimes known as *Late Swallows*, the title of its third movement), three duet sonatas for violin and one for cello.

### Dittersdorf, Carl Ditters von (1739–1799; Austria)

Dittersdorf is perhaps best remembered for having joined Haydn, Mozart and Vanhal in string quartets – apparently playing second violin to Haydn's first. He is a representative example of the many lesser composers of the classical era. There is much chamber music: six string quartets, varying numbers of string trios and duos for different combinations, string quintets either with two cellos or cello and double bass, and works for wind ensembles.

### Donizetti, Gaetano (1797–1848; Italy)

Principally an opera composer: he holds a major position in today's operatic repertoire. He composed chamber music mainly in his early years from about 1817 to 1821. Eighteen string quartets are published. A few other works include a piano trio, a quintet for guitar and strings, sonatas with piano for violin, flute and oboe, and a sonata for flute and harp.

### Farrenc, Louise (1804–1875; France)

Until a recent revival of interest, Louise Farrenc's music was almost unknown. She was for thirty years professor of piano at the Paris Conservatoire, and she composed much attractive chamber music, most of which was published in her lifetime. It includes four piano trios (one having either clarinet or violin, another flute or violin), two piano quintets (with violin, viola, cello and double bass), a nonet for violin, viola, cello, double bass and wind quintet, a sextet for piano and wind quintet, and three duet sonatas (two for violin and one for cello).

### Gade, Niels (1817–1890; Denmark)

Denmark's most important nineteenth-century composer, Gade initially composed in a nationalist style, but after he spent some years in Leipzig the influence of Mendelssohn became predominant. Nevertheless, his chamber works are of interest. They include a string quartet, a string quintet with two violas, a string sextet, a string octet, a piano trio and three sonatas for violin and piano. Further works (including three more string quartets) should appear in a complete edition of his works that is in progress.

### Glazunov, Aleksandr (1865–1936; Russia)

A late romantic who lived into the era of the moderns, Glazunov fell only a little short of the greatest Russian composers. Some of his music, such as the violin concerto, is still performed. There are seven string quartets (of which no. 3 in G, op. 26, is entitled *Quatuor Slave*). Other works for string quartet include *Five Novelettes* and a *Suite in C*. There is a string quintet with two cellos. Glazunov's last chamber work, of 1932, is a full-scale quartet for saxophones (soprano, alto, tenor and baritone).

### Glinka, Mikhail (1804–1857; Russia)

Glinka is regarded as the founder of Russian music. However, his few chamber works were written early in his career, before he developed the distinctively Russian style displayed in his operas. Though unimportant, they are enjoyable to play. There are two string quartets, a sextet for piano, string quartet and double bass, and a trio for clarinet, bassoon and piano. Also sometimes played is an unfinished sonata for viola and piano.

### Hindemith, Paul (1895–1963; Germany)

One of the most important of twentieth-century composers: still respected, but now not much played. He developed his own musical system, retaining some tonal basis. He was remarkably prolific. His chamber music avoids virtuosic writing and is playable. There are seven string quartets and two string trios. Ensemble works involving wind instruments include a clarinet quintet, a quartet for clarinet, violin, cello and piano, an octet for wind and string instruments, a sonata for four horns and a septet including a trumpet. *Kleine Kammermusik*, op. 24 no. 2, is a wind quintet. Duet sonatas with piano are many: violin, viola and cello each have two or more; others are for flute, bassoon, oboe, clarinet, horn, alto horn/saxophone, trumpet, cor anglais, trombone, double bass and tuba.

### Howells, Herbert (1892–1983; England)

Howells's church music, which formed most of his output after the 1940s, holds an important place in the repertoire today. He also composed in other forms, including orchestral, choral and chamber music, though most of these works are less known. The chamber compositions include three for string quartet (*Lady Audrey's Suite*, a phantasy string quartet, and the string quartet *In Gloucestershire*), a piano quartet, a rhapsodic quintet for clarinet and string quartet, and duet sonatas for violin (three), oboe and clarinet.

### Kodály, Zoltán (1882–1967; Hungary)

Bartók, Dohnányi and Kodály were the three great Hungarian composers of the earlier twentieth century. Kodály's musical language remained firmly tonal, but he developed a very original style profoundly influenced by Hungarian folk music. He is highly regarded, but his chamber works (all composed before 1921) are marginal to the repertoire. They are mostly technically difficult. There are two string quartets, a serenade for two violins and viola, a duo for violin and cello and a sonata for cello and piano.

## Korngold, Erich (1897–1957; Austria, America)

Korngold began as a remarkable child-prodigy composer. In 1938 he moved to America. He remained throughout his life a late romantic; though today probably best known for his film music, he never forsook absolute music. His considerable number of chamber works includes three string quartets, a string sextet, a piano trio, a piano quintet and a sonata for violin and piano.

## Locatelli, Pietro (1695–1764; Italy)

Locatelli settled in Amsterdam in 1729. He composed ten trio sonatas, twelve sonatas for flute and continuo and eighteen for violin and continuo. As a violinist he made major advances in technique; his violin sonatas are technically demanding.

## Mahler, Gustav (1860–1911; Austria)

Famous mainly for his symphonies, the mature Mahler showed no interest in chamber music. However, his earliest surviving work, a piano quartet movement in A minor dating from 1876 (when he was a student at the Vienna Conservatory), is sometimes performed. Nothing of his later style can be recognized in it.

## Mendelssohn, Fanny (1805–1847; Germany)

Fanny (married name Hensel) was the elder sister of Felix Mendelssohn; throughout their lives the two remained very close, often discussing their latest compositions. Her principal published chamber works are a string quartet, a piano trio and a piano quartet. (The piano quartet is of 1823, so by usual standards early – and contemporary with Felix's piano quartets.) There may be further works still unpublished.

## Messiaen, Olivier (1908–1992; France)

This highly regarded, remarkably individual composer produced only one major chamber work, and that in the extraordinary circumstances of a prisoner-of-war camp in 1940–1. It is the *Quatuor pour le fin du temps*, for violin, clarinet, cello and piano. There is also a Theme and Variations for violin and piano.

## Nielsen, Carl (1865–1931; Denmark)

Considered his country's greatest composer, Nielsen was little known in his lifetime but has gained in international esteem since, especially for his six symphonies. He wrote a considerable amount of chamber music. There are four string quartets, of which those in G minor and F minor may be considered early works. Also early is a string quintet with two violas. Two duet sonatas are both for violin. His best-known chamber work is the genial wind quintet, op. 43, of 1922.

## Onslow, George (1784–1853; France)

Onslow was a Frenchman with an English father. Inherited wealth freed him from financial pressures and allowed him to compose what he wished: mostly chamber music. There are thirty-six string quartets. Of thirty-four string quintets, some have two violas, some two cellos, and some cello and double bass. He composed piano trios, piano quintets (with violin, viola, cello and double bass) and duet sonatas for violin and for cello. There is one wind quintet. Also including wind instruments are a nonet for winds and strings (with an alternative version as a sextet for piano, winds and double bass), and a septet for wind quintet, double bass and piano.

### Parry, (Sir) Hubert (1848–1918; England)

During his lifetime Parry was a major figure in the so-called English musical renaissance. His two short choral works *I was Glad* and *Blest Pair of Sirens* are still frequently performed. His chamber works include three string quartets, a string quintet with two violas, three piano trios, a piano quartet, a nonet for wind instruments (flute, oboe, cor anglais, two clarinets, two horns and two bassoons), several duet sonatas for violin and one for cello.

### Puccini, Giacomo (1858–1924; Italy)

This much-loved operatic composer composed no full-scale chamber works. However, his six-minute elegy for string quartet entitled *Crisantemi* (*Chrysanthemums*), of 1890, is a masterpiece – perhaps unique among works for the medium in its heart-on-sleeve emotion. (It is also sometimes performed by a string orchestra.) Three minuets for string quartet are early works.

### Raff, Joachim (1822–1882; Switzerland, Germany)

A facile and prolific composer whose music was widely performed in his day but has since been largely forgotten. Nevertheless, at least on a first impression, it can seem very attractive. His chamber works include eight string quartets, a string sextet, a string octet, four piano trios, two piano quartets, a piano quintet, five duet sonatas for violin and one for cello. (Some works are programmatic, for example the six-movement string quartet no. 7, op. 192 no. 2, entitled *Die schöne Müllerin*.)

### Reger, Max (1873–1916; Germany)

Reger wrote in classical forms, following in the tradition of Brahms but with awareness of new developments. He has been considered important, but his music is little played now; although technically excellent, it perhaps lacks obvious attractiveness. Despite his early death his output of chamber music is large. It includes five string quartets, two string trios, a string sextet, two serenades for flute, violin and viola, two piano trios (one with viola instead of cello), two piano quartets and two piano quintets. There are many duet sonatas for violin and for cello, and three for clarinet (one with viola alternative). Probably his most often-played chamber work is the last: the clarinet quintet in A, op. 146.

### Respighi, Ottorino (1879–1936; Italy)

Of Respighi's considerable number of chamber works, only three may be considered mature. These are two string quartets and a sonata for violin and piano; the second of these quartets, *Quartetto Dorico*, is sometimes played.

### Rimsky-Korsakov, Nikolay (1844–1908; Russia)

A composer notable for his brilliant orchestration; some of his orchestral works and operatic extracts remain highly popular in the concert hall. His chamber compositions, however, are rarely played. The principal works are two string quartets, a string sextet and a quintet for piano, flute, clarinet, horn and bassoon. Most date from relatively early in his output, but the string quartet in G is of 1897.

## Rossini, Gioachino (1792–1868; Italy)

In 1804, aged twelve and long before he came to fame as an operatic composer, Rossini composed six *sonate a quattro*, or string sonatas, for two violins, cello and double bass. When first published in 1825–6 they were in an arrangement for normal string quartet. They are popular (especially when performed by a string orchestra): highly tuneful whilst making no pretence to sophistication or true chamber-music character. Double bass players may especially enjoy the original version for the melodic opportunities given to their instrument.

## Russian collaborative chamber music

These works, all for string quartet, are connected with M.P. Belyayev, a wealthy chamber-music enthusiast who gathered round him a circle of Russian composers, and in 1885 founded the publishing house bearing his name. The most significant of the composers, at least in chamber music, was Borodin. The *B-la-f* quartet of 1886 has movements by Rimsky-Korsakov, Lyadov, Borodin and Glazunov, using a motto theme B♭-A-F based on Belyayev's name. It is easy to play (D2+) and favours the viola (Belyayev's instrument). *Les Vendredis* is a set of sixteen pieces (commemorating the musical evenings held on Fridays at Belyayev's home). Their ten composers again include Borodin; many are readily playable. A further collaborative string quartet, *Jour de Fête*, has no contribution from Borodin, who had died.

## Schumann, Clara (1819–1896; Germany)

Clara, née Wieck, married Robert Schumann in 1840. As well as being an outstanding pianist, she composed, mostly for piano. Of chamber works there are a piano trio, op. 17, and *Drei Romanzen* for violin and piano, op. 22.

## Spohr, Louis (1784–1859; Germany)

Spohr is perhaps unique in that, though now considered a minor composer, in his life-time he was regarded as highly important. He was also an outstanding violinist. His prolific output includes much chamber music. It is melodious and attractive, but lacks more substantial qualities. The writing is often florid and technically demanding (especially in first violin parts). Still played is the nonet, op. 31, for flute, oboe, clarinet, horn, bassoon, violin, viola, cello and double bass. Further works including wind instruments are an octet and (with piano) a septet and quintet. Of thirty-six string quartets, opp. 11, 43, 61, 68, 83 and 93 are of the *quatuor brillant* variety, so best avoided. Seven string quintets are all for the two-viola combination. There is one string sextet. Four double quartets offer repertoire for the string octet grouping. For piano and strings there are five trios and two quintets. Spohr's first wife was a harpist: there are seven sonatas for violin and harp.

## Stanford, (Sir) Charles Villiers (1852–1924; Ireland, England)

Born in Dublin, Stanford lived in England from the age of eighteen. He became a major figure in late Victorian English music, but most of his compositions are forgotten today. His chamber works (not all of which have been published) show much influence of Brahms. There are eight string quartets, two string quintets with two violas, three piano trios, two piano quartets, a piano quintet, a serenade for nine instruments (flute, clarinet, bassoon, horn, string quartet and double bass) and duet sonatas for violin (four), cello (two) and clarinet (with alternative for viola).

### Taneyev, Sergey (1856–1915; Russia)

Chamber music is prominent in the output of this pupil of Tchaikovsky. It is notable for contrapuntal mastery, but it is quite difficult, lacks melodic distinction and shows no Russian character. Nevertheless, it has its devotees. Published in his lifetime were six string quartets, two string quintets (one with two cellos, one with two violas), two string trios (one for two violins and viola, one for violin, viola and tenor viola – the last a very rare instrument), a piano trio, a piano quartet and a piano quintet.

### Tartini, Giuseppe (1692–1770; Italy)

Tartini was a violinist and composer, and most of his output is of works for the violin. The many sonatas for violin and continuo include the famous *Devil's Trill* sonata (which is of virtuoso difficulty). There are also some trio sonatas for two violins and continuo.

### Telemann, Georg Philipp (1681–1767; Germany)

In his lifetime, Telemann was regarded as Germany's most important composer. He later fell from favour, particularly by comparison with Bach and Handel, but today he has a place. He composed in all the genres of his time, and was exceptionally prolific. His chamber music includes many sonatas for one instrument and continuo, many trio sonatas for varying combinations, and also sonatas in four parts and larger.

### Walton, (Sir) William (1902–1983; England)

Walton holds a high reputation, mainly for his orchestral works; but his chamber compositions are less known. A string quartet of 1919–22 was subsequently withdrawn (but has been published); the piano quartet of 1918–21 was revised over half a century later. A second string quartet and a sonata for violin and piano date from the 1940s.

### Wesley, Charles (1757–1834; England)

This minor composer (son of the well-known hymn-writer of the same name, and nephew of John Wesley, founder of Methodism) is known for his six string quartets, published in 1778. They are charming, mostly in three movements, and technically probably the easiest quartets available (D1) – suitable either for beginners or for more experienced players exhausted after a long day!

### Wolf, Hugo (1860–1903; Austria)

Wolf's fame is based almost entirely on his outstanding achievement as a composer of songs. He has, however, a real place in chamber music with the seven-minute Serenade in G ('Italian Serenade') for string quartet – original and brilliant but quite difficult (D4). Also for string quartet are an intermezzo and an early, long, highly ambitious and difficult string quartet in D minor.

# Appendix II

# Repertoire by Instrumental Combination

For each identified instrument or instrumental combination, the following lists show the composers of chamber works that appear in this book. For details of the work or works, refer to the entry for the composer in Chapter 4 or Appendix I.

♦ An entry means that the composer left at least one work for the identified combination (but very early or insignificant works do not appear).
♦ Entries in **bold** mean that at least one work may be considered important and is of difficulty less than D5 (so should be playable by capable amateurs).
♦ Entries in normal text refer to composers in Chapter 4. Entries *in italics* refer to composers in Appendix I (which may nevertheless occasionally be identified as important, so ***bold italic***).
♦ Entries in square brackets [] are arrangements, reconstructions, not the intended instrumentation, or not really chamber music. (These too may sometimes be identified as important, so [**bold**].) Of the vast number of published arrangements, only those few that were made or approved by the original composer are normally mentioned.

## STRING DUO
### Two Violins
[**Bartók**]; Boccherini; *Dittersdorf*; [Haydn]; [**Mozart**]; **Prokofiev**; Reicha; [Richter]; Vivaldi

### Violin, Viola
Haydn; **Mozart**

### Violin, Cello
*Kodály*; Ravel; Reicha

### Viola, Cello
**Beethoven**; Danzi

**Two Cellos**
Boccherini

## STRING TRIO

**Violin, Viola, Cello**
**Beethoven**; Boccherini; *Dittersdorf*; **Dohnányi**; Haydn; *Hindemith*; Hummel; **Mozart**; *Reger*; Schoenberg; **Schubert**; Webern

**Two Violins, Viola**
[**Beethoven**]; *Bridge*; *Dittersdorf*; **Dvořák**; *Kodály*; *Taneyev*

**Two Violins, Cello**
Boccherini; *Dittersdorf*; Haydn; **Mozart**

**Other Combinations**
Hummel; *Taneyev*

## STRING QUARTET

*Arensky*; **Arriaga**; **Barber**; **Bartók**; *Beach*; **Beethoven**; Berg; *Berwald*; *Bloch*; Boccherini; **Borodin**; **Brahms**; *Bridge*; **Britten**; Bruch; Bruckner; *Chausson*; *Cherubini*; Danzi; **Debussy**; *Delius*; *Dittersdorf*; **Dohnányi**; Donizetti; **Dvořák**; Elgar; Fauré; **Franck**; *Gade*; Glazunov; *Glinka*; **Grieg**; **Haydn**; *Hindemith*; *Howells*; **Hummel**; Janáček; *Kodály*; Korngold; **Mendelssohn**; *Mendelssohn, Fanny*; **Mozart**; *Nielsen*; Onslow; *Parry*; **Prokofiev**; *Puccini*; *Raff*; **Ravel**; *Reger*; Reicha; *Respighi*; **Richter**; *Rimsky-Korsakov*; *[Rossini]*; *Russian Collaborative*; Saint-Saëns; **Schoenberg**; Schubert; **Schumann**; **Shostakovich**; **Sibelius**; **Smetana**; *Spohr*; Stanford; Strauss; Stravinsky; *Taneyev*; **Tchaikovsky**; **Vaughan Williams**; **Verdi**; *Walton*; **Webern**; *Wesley*; **Wolf**

## STRING QUINTET

**Two Violins, Two Violas, Cello**
**Beethoven**; Boccherini; **Brahms**; Britten; **Bruch**; **Bruckner**; Danzi; **Dvořák**; *Gade*; Haydn; **Mendelssohn**; **Mozart**; *Nielsen*; Onslow; *Parry*; Reicha; Schubert; *Spohr*; *Stanford*; *Taneyev*; **Vaughan Williams**

**Two Violins, Viola, Two Cellos**
Boccherini; [**Brahms**]; *Cherubini*; *Dittersdorf*; *Glazunov*; *Onslow*; Reicha; **Schubert**; *Taneyev*

**Two Violins, Viola, Cello, Double Bass**
Boccherini; *Dittersdorf*; **Dvořák**; *Onslow*

## STRING SEXTET

Boccherini; **Brahms**; *Bridge*; Dohnányi; **Dvořák**; *Gade*; *Korngold*; *Raff*; *Reger*; *Rimsky-Korsakov*; **Schoenberg**; *Spohr*; **Strauss**; **Tchaikovsky**

## STRING OCTET

### Four Violins, Two Violas, Two Cellos
*Gade*; **Mendelssohn**; *Raff*; Shostakovich; *Spohr*

### Four Violins, Two Violas, Cello, Double Bass
Bruch

## PIANO TRIO

*Arensky*; *Beach*; **Beethoven**; *Berwald*; **Brahms**; *Bridge*; Bruch; *Chausson*; Chopin; *Clarke*; *Donizetti*; **Dvořák**; *Farrenc*; **Fauré**; Franck; *Gade*; **Haydn**; **Hummel**; *Korngold*; **Mendelssohn**; *Mendelssohn, Fanny*; **Mozart**; *Onslow*; *Parry*; **Rachmaninoff**; *Raff*; Ravel; *Reger*; Reicha; **Saint-Saëns**; **Schubert**; **Schumann**; *Schumann, Clara*; **Shostakovich**; *Smetana*; *Spohr*; *Stanford*; *Taneyev*; **Tchaikovsky**; [Vivaldi]; [**Weber**]

## PIANO QUARTET

[**Beethoven**]; **Brahms**; *Bridge*; **Chausson**; **Dvořák**; **Fauré**; *Howells*; *Mahler*; **Mendelssohn**; *Mendelssohn, Fanny*; **Mozart**; *Parry*; *Raff*; *Reger*; **Saint-Saëns**; **Schubert**; **Schumann**; *Stanford*; **Strauss**; *Taneyev*; *Walton*; **Weber**

## PIANO QUINTET

### Piano, String Quartet
*Arensky*; Bartók; *Beach*; *Berwald*; *Bloch*; Boccherini; Borodin; **Brahms**; *Bridge*; Bruch; **Dohnányi**; **Dvořák**; **Elgar**; **Fauré**; **Franck**; [Hummel]; *Korngold*; [Mozart]; *Raff*; *Reger*; **Saint-Saëns**; **Schumann**; Shostakovich; *Spohr*; *Stanford*; *Taneyev*; **Webern**

### Piano, Violin, Viola, Cello, Double Bass
*Farrenc*; **Hummel**; *Onslow*; **Schubert**

## TRIO SONATA (Two Melody Instruments, Continuo)

*Albinoni*; **Bach**; **Corelli**; **Handel**; *Locatelli*; **Purcell**; Richter; *Tartini*; *Telemann*; **Vivaldi**

## FOUR-PART SONATA (Three Melody Instruments, Continuo)

**Corelli**; *Telemann*; **Vivaldi**

## ENSEMBLE INCLUDING DOUBLE BASS

Beethoven; *Berwald*; Boccherini; [Brahms]; **Bruch**; *Dittersdorf*; **Dvořák**; *Farrenc*; *Glinka*; Haydn; *Hindemith*; **Hummel**; Mendelssohn; *Onslow*; Prokofiev; *Rossini*; **Saint-Saëns**; **Schubert**; *Spohr*; *Stanford*; Stravinsky

## ENSEMBLE INCLUDING HARP

**Debussy**; *Donizetti*; **Ravel**; *Spohr*

## ENSEMBLE INCLUDING HARMONIUM

Dvořák

## ENSEMBLE INCLUDING GUITAR

Boccherini; *Donizetti*; Schoenberg

## WIND QUINTET (Flute, Oboe, Clarinet, Horn, Bassoon)

Barber; Danzi; *Hindemith*; **Nielsen**; *Onslow*; **Reicha**; Schoenberg

## ENSEMBLE INCLUDING FLUTE

Bach; **Barber**; *Beach*; **Beethoven**; Boccherini; [Brahms]; **Danzi**; Debussy; *Donizetti*; Elgar; *Farrenc*; **Handel**; **Haydn**; *Hindemith*; **Hummel**; Janáček; *Locatelli*; **Mozart**; *Nielsen*; *Onslow*; *Parry*; **Poulenc**; **Ravel**; *Reger*; **Reicha**; Richter; *Rimsky-Korsakov*; Schoenberg; *Spohr*; Stanford; **Stravinsky**; *Telemann*; **Vivaldi**; **Weber**

## ENSEMBLE INCLUDING OBOE

Barber; **Beethoven**; Boccherini; [Brahms]; **Britten**; **Danzi**; *Dittersdorf*; Elgar; *Farrenc*; Handel; **Haydn**; *Hindemith*; **Hummel**; Janáček; **Mozart**; *Nielsen*; *Onslow*; *Parry*; **Poulenc**; Prokofiev; **Reicha**; Schoenberg; Schubert; *Spohr*; *Telemann*; **Vivaldi**

## ENSEMBLE INCLUDING CLARINET

Barber; Bartók; **Beethoven**; *Berwald*; **Brahms**; **Bruch**; *Crusell*; **Danzi**; *Dittersdorf*; Dohnányi; Elgar; *Farrenc*; *Glinka*; **Haydn**; *Hindemith*; *Howells*; **Hummel**; Janáček; **Mendelssohn**; *Messiaen*; **Mozart**; *Nielsen*; *Onslow*; *Parry*; **Poulenc**; Prokofiev; **Ravel**; *Reger*; **Reicha**; *Rimsky-Korsakov*; Schoenberg; **Schubert**; **Schumann**; *Spohr*; *Stanford*; **Stravinsky**; **Weber**; Webern

## ENSEMBLE INCLUDING BASSOON

Barber; **Beethoven**; *Berwald*; Boccherini; [Brahms]; Bruch; **Danzi**; *Dittersdorf*; Elgar; *Farrenc*; *Glinka*; **Haydn**; *Hindemith*; **Janáček**; **Mozart**; *Nielsen*; *Onslow*; *Parry*; **Poulenc**; **Reicha**; *Rimsky-Korsakov*; Schoenberg; **Schubert**; *Spohr*; *Stanford*; **Stravinsky**; **Vivaldi**

## ENSEMBLE INCLUDING COR ANGLAIS

Beethoven; *Dittersdorf*; *Parry*

## ENSEMBLE INCLUDING SAXOPHONE

*Glazunov*; Webern

## ENSEMBLE INCLUDING HORN

Barber; **Beethoven**; *Berwald*; Boccherini; **Brahms**; Bruch; **Danzi**; *Dittersdorf*; Dohnányi; *Farrenc*; **Haydn**; *Hindemith*; **Hummel**; Janáček; **Mozart**; *Nielsen*; Onslow; *Parry*; **Poulenc**; **Reicha**; *Rimsky-Korsakov*; Schoenberg; **Schubert**; *Spohr*; *Stanford*; **Stravinsky**; *Telemann*

## ENSEMBLE INCLUDING TRUMPET

Corelli; *Hindemith*; **Hummel**; **Mozart**; **Poulenc**; Saint-Saëns; Stravinsky

## ENSEMBLE INCLUDING TROMBONE

**Poulenc**; **Stravinsky**

## VIOLIN, PIANO/HARPSICHORD/CONTINUO

*Albinoni*; **Bach**; Bartók; *Beach*; **Beethoven**; *Bloch*; Boccherini; **Brahms**; *Bridge*; Britten; **Corelli**; **Debussy**; *Delius*; **Dohnányi**; *Donizetti*; **Dvořák**; **Elgar**; *Farrenc*; **Fauré**; **Franck**; *Gade*; **Grieg**; **Handel**; [Haydn]; *Hindemith*; *Howells*; **Hummel**; *Janáček*; *Korngold*; *Locatelli*; **Mendelssohn**; *Messiaen*; **Mozart**; *Nielsen*; *Parry*; **Poulenc**; **Prokofiev**; Purcell; *Raff*; **Ravel**; *Reger*; Reicha; *Respighi*; [Richter]; **Saint-Saëns**; Schoenberg; **Schubert**; **Schumann**; *Schumann, Clara*; Shostakovich; Sibelius; Smetana; *Stanford*; **Strauss**; **Stravinsky**; *Tartini*; **Tchaikovsky**; *Telemann*; Vaughan Williams; **Vivaldi**; *Walton*; Weber; Webern

## VIOLA, PIANO/HARPSICHORD

[**Bach**]; [**Beethoven**]; *Bloch*; [Boccherini]; [**Brahms**]; **Britten**; *Clarke*; *Glinka*; *Hindemith*; **Hummel**; Mendelssohn; *[Reger]*; [**Schubert**]; **Schumann**; **Shostakovich**; *[Stanford]*; [Vaughan Williams]

## CELLO, PIANO/HARPSICHORD/CONTINUO

[**Bach**]; Barber; **Beethoven**; Boccherini; **Brahms**; *Bridge*; Britten; **Chopin**; **Debussy**; *Delius*; **Dohnányi**; *Farrenc*; **Fauré**; [**Franck**]; **Grieg**; *Hindemith*; **Hummel**; *Janáček*; *Kodály*; **Mendelssohn**; *Parry*; **Poulenc**; **Prokofiev**; **Rachmaninoff**; *Raff*; *Reger*; **Saint-Saëns**; [**Schubert**]; **Schumann**; **Shostakovich**; *Stanford*; **Strauss**; [Stravinsky]; [Vaughan Williams]; **Vivaldi**; Webern

## VIOLA DA GAMBA, HARPSICHORD/CONTINUO

**Bach**; **Handel**; *Telemann*

## FLUTE, PIANO/HARPSICHORD/CONTINUO

**Bach**; Danzi; *Donizetti*; **Handel**; *Hindemith*; **Hummel**; *Locatelli*; Mozart; **Poulenc**; **Prokofiev**; Reicha; Richter; Schubert; *Telemann*; **Vivaldi**

## OBOE, PIANO/CONTINUO

**Britten**; *Donizetti*; **Handel**; *Hindemith*; *Howells*; **Poulenc**; **Saint-Saëns**; **Schumann**; *Telemann*; **Vivaldi**

## CLARINET, PIANO

Berg; **Brahms**; Danzi; *Hindemith*; *Howells*; **Mendelssohn**; **Poulenc**; *Reger*; **Saint-Saëns**; **Schumann**; *Stanford*; [Vaughan Williams]; **Weber**

## BASSOON, PIANO

*Hindemith*; **Saint-Saëns**

## HORN, PIANO

**Beethoven**; Danzi; *Hindemith*; **Schumann**

## RECORDER, CONTINUO

**Handel**; **Vivaldi**

# Glossary

**Ad lib** (properly *ad libitum*): (a) optional; (b) allowing tempo alteration, embellishment or improvisaton at the performer's discretion

**Atonal:** employing no system of key or tonal centre

**Augmentation:** a device in which the time values of the notes of a melody are lengthened

**Bagatelle:** 'trifle'. A short and unpretentious piece

**Bariolage:** an effect on string instruments obtained by repeatedly playing the same note alternately on two adjacent strings (one of which is often open)

**Cadence:** a melodic or harmonic progression associated with the ending of a phrase, section or composition. Types include perfect, imperfect, interrupted and plagal

**Cadenza:** an ornamental embellishment of a cadence usually near the end of a movement; traditionally improvised and often indicated in the music by a pause

**Canon:** (a) a strict contrapuntal device in which a melody in one voice is continuously imitated by one or more other voices; (b) an accepted repertoire of works

**Cantabile:** in a singing manner; smoothly

**Cembalo** (or *clavicembalo*): Italian for harpsichord

**Chaconne:** a form similar to *passacaglia*

**Chromaticism:** the use of notes not belonging to the diatonic scale of the prevailing key

**Clavier:** usually, any keyboard instrument

**Coda:** a section added at the end of a movement

**Col legno:** 'with the wood'. To strike the strings of a string instrument with the stick of the bow

**Concertante:** denoting music that has a solo or concerto-like element

**Continuo** (properly *basso continuo*, also called *thoroughbass*): in baroque music, the instruments (usually but not necessarily two) playing the bass line

**Contrapuntal:** characterized by counterpoint

**Contrary motion:** of two parts, their simultaneous melodic movement in opposite directions (up and down)

**Counterpoint:** the technique of combining two or more simultaneous melodic lines

**Development:** see *sonata form*

**Diatonic:** passages, intervals and chords made up solely of notes belonging to a major or minor scale

**Diminution:** the opposite of *augmentation*

**Divertimento:** 'diversion' or 'amusement'. In the late eighteenth century, a lightweight, entertaining work typically in five or six movements, usually for a small group of players and perhaps performed outdoors

**Exposition:** see *sonata form*

**Fugato:** a passage in fugal style in a non-fugal movement

**Fugue:** a composition in which usually three or more voices enter imitatively and which continues throughout based on the employment of imitative counterpoint, usually with certain particular features

**Gavotte:** a French dance popular as an instrumental movement in the baroque era, in common time (4/4) and usually beginning with a two-crotchet upbeat

**Glissando:** (a) the same as *portamento*; (b) a sliding movement between two notes on an instrument such as the piano where intermediate notes are briefly heard

**Grace notes:** ornamental notes, printed small, and of unmeasured duration that is not included in the nominal bar length. Types include appoggiaturas and acciaccaturas

**Ground** (or *ground bass*): a short melodic bass line continually repeated below changing upper parts

**Harmonics:** on a string instrument, the notes of flute-like timbre obtained by lightly touching a string at a nodal point. When the string is open, the harmonics are 'natural'; when the string is stopped, they are 'artificial'

**Imitation:** the repetition of a melody in one part by another, not necessarily without alteration of pitch or other characteristics

**Intermezzo:** a movement of lighter character coming between longer and weightier movements of an extended work

**Inversion:** of a melody, turned upside down so that where the original rises, the inversion descends. A common feature of contrapuntal writing

**Ländler:** rustic triple-time dance mainly of Austria and Germany

**Minuet:** a slow or moderate-speed dance in triple metre, often used as a movement of a multi-movement work. Usually in ternary form with a central contrasting minuet known as the trio. From Beethoven onwards largely supplanted by the scherzo

**Modes:** the scales used in medieval European music. There are eight, to which four more were added in the early sixteenth century

**Moto perpetuo:** an instrumental piece in which rapid notes of equal length are continuously maintained

**Musette:** (a) a type of French bagpipe, powered by bellows strapped under the arm; (b) a dance of pastoral character with a drone bass suggesting the sound of the instrument

**Nocturne:** in the nineteenth century, following its use for the piano by Field and Chopin, a slow, lyrical, meditative piece (compare *notturno*)

**Notturno** (German *Nachtmusik*): in the later eighteenth century, an instrumental composition in several movements, light in character, for performance at night (compare *nocturne*)

**Obbligato:** obligatory (but is sometimes incorrectly used to mean optional)

**Ostinato:** a continuously re-iterated phrase or rhythm

**Passacaglia:** a form consisting of a set of variations above a ground bass; similar to *chaconne*

**Polonaise** (Italian *Polacca*): a stately Polish dance in triple time, usually with certain characteristic features

**Portamento:** on a string instrument, trombone or clarinet, a smooth sliding movement between two notes

**Recapitulation:** see *sonata form*

**Ricochet** (or *jeté*): a technique on string instruments in which the bow is 'thrown' onto the string, normally on a down-bow in the upper half, causing it to bounce producing several rapid staccato notes

**Romance:** a term lacking exact definition but often used for a lyrical and tender piece

**Rondo:** a form in which a main section is repeated multiple times, between which are at least two different episodes (as ABAC...A). Frequently used for final movements

**Scherzo:** 'joke'. A lively movement in fast triple time, often humorous. From Beethoven's time onwards it usually replaced the minuet used in earlier periods, like which it has a contrasting middle section or trio

**Serenade:** in the late eighteenth century and subsequently, a piece of instrumental music typically in five or more movements and light in character

**Serialism:** the twelve-tone system (see *twelve-tone*). Has later sometimes been interpreted more widely, however, with serial techniques applied also to elements other than pitch

**Siciliano:** music in 6/8 or 12/8 metre, usually in a minor key and often of pastoral character with a swaying rhythm

**Sonata form:** a structure frequently used for the first movement of a multi-movement work and sometimes also for other movements. There are three sections: the exposition, in which the thematic material is presented, normally in two groups as first subject and second subject; the development, in which this material is freely exploited, elaborated and juxtaposed; and the recapitulation, in which the material of the exposition is again presented, with some changes. A coda may follow. Key relationships are normally of central importance. The exposition may be marked to be repeated, also (less often) the combined development and recapitulation

**Sonata rondo:** a combination of sonata and rondo forms, sometimes used for final movements

**Sul ponticello:** on a string instrument, to play with the bow very close to the bridge, producing a ghostly, insubstantial, glassy sound

**Tarantella:** originally a southern Italian dance; a fast and inexorable movement in 6/8 time

**Ternary form:** a musical structure consisting of three sections, the third being a repetition of the first: ABA

**Tessitura:** the general pitch level of a part in a composition as related to the compass of the instrument playing it

**Tremolo:** 'trembling'. The very rapid alternation of two notes or (especially on a string instrument) reiteration of one note; the durations are usually though not always unmeasured

**Trio:** (a) a piece for three instruments or parts; (b) the central section of a minuet or scherzo, so called because it was originally in only three parts for contrast

**Twelve-tone** (or *twelve-note*): system of atonal composition in which all twelve notes of the equal-tempered chromatic scale are put in a fixed order, known as a tone-row, which forms the basis of a work (see *serialism*)

**Viol:** the family of bowed string instruments that preceded the violin family, in use from the late fifteenth to the mid-eighteenth century. The instruments have a flat back, frets and usually six strings, and are played upright, resting on the knees or held between the legs

**Viola da gamba:** 'leg viol'. Bass viol (the equivalent in the viol family of the cello)

**Violone:** usually now taken as double bass viol, though usage has been ambiguous

# INDEX

Entries in **bold** are composers who appear in Chapter 4; those in ***bold italic*** are composers who appear in Appendix I. Page numbers in **bold** distinguish principal references from others.

accompanied keyboard sonatas 23, 27
*Adagio for Strings* (Barber) 46
**Albinoni, Tomaso** 235
Allegri, Gregorio 19
'American', str qt (Dvořák) **94**, 95, 96
'Apponyi Quartets' (Haydn) 127-9
'Archduke', pf trio (Beethoven) 62
***Arensky, Anton*** 235
'Arpeggione Sonata' (Schubert) 208
**Arriaga, Juan Crisóstomo de** 41-2
Art of Fugue (Bach) 38, 43

Bach, C.P.E. 45
**Bach, Johann Sebastian** 14, 27, 31, 38, **42-5**, 49, 73, 87, 156, 159, 166, 176, 242
Bach, W.F. 159
Bagatelles, str, harmonium (Dvořák) 97
Balakirev, Mily 72
**Barber, Samuel** 16, 24, 38, **45-6**
baroque chamber music 12, **13-14**, 17, 23, 25-7, 29-30, 32, 39, 190-1
**Bartók, Béla** 12, 16, 17, 19-20, 25, 27, 37, 46-9, 90, 238
Bartók pizzicato 47, 48
baryton 110
Baselt, Bernd 104
basso continuo: see continuo

Bax, Arnold 17
***Beach, Amy*** 235
**Beethoven, Ludvig van** 14, 15, 18-20, 23-5, 27, 31, 40, **49-68**, 72, 73, 75, 100, 109, 122, 131, 133, 140, 144, 145, 148, 151, 152, 154, 157, 171, 187, 197, 206, 207
  late string quartets 20, 37, 47, 56-60
**Berg, Alban** 16, **68-9**, 195
Berlioz, Hector 187
***Berwald, Franz*** 236
Billroth, Dr. Theodor 11
'Bird, The', str qt (Haydn) 39, 121
*Birthday, The*, divertimento, wind, str (Haydn) 142
*B-la-f Quartet*, str qt 241
***Bloch, Ernest*** 236
**Boccherini, Luigi** 18, 21, 39, **69-71**
  'Boccherini's Minuet' 70
**Borodin, Aleksandr** 71-2, 90, 241
**Brahms, Johannes** 11, 15, 20, 21, 23, 24, 25, 27, 37, 38, **73-81**, 83, 90-2, 93, 96-7, 143, 196, 209, 212, 220, 223, 230, 240, 241
***Bridge, Frank*** 17, 81, **236**
**Britten, (Lord) Benjamin** 17, **81-3**, 236
**Bruch, Max** 20, 21, **83-5**, 225
**Bruckner, Anton** 20, 29, **85-6**

*Capriccio*, prelude to, str sextet (Strauss) 220

chamber sonata: see sonata da camera

'Chasse, La', str qt (Haydn) 113

***Chausson, Ernest*** 236

***Cherubini, Luigi*** 236-7

**Chopin, Frédéric** 86

church sonata: *see* sonata da chiesa

clarinet quintet, the 17, 25

clarinet trio, the 25

***Clarke, Rebecca*** 237

classical chamber music 11, 12, **14-15**, 18, 19, 20, 21, 22, 23, 25, 27, 30, 32, 33, 38, 39

Cobbett, W.W. **16-17**, 82, 226

'Compliment, The', str qt (Beethoven) 53

continuo 12, 13-14, 19, 23, 25-7, 29-30, 32, 39, 248

*Contrasts*, cl, vn, pf (Bartók) 25, 49

Coolidge, Elizabeth Sprague **17**, 82, 196

copyright 34

**Corelli, Arcangelo** 25, 31, **86-8**, 184, 227

***Crusell, Bernhard*** 237

Cui, César 72


**Danzi, Franz** 24, **88-9**, 188

'Death and the Maiden', str qt (Schubert) 203

**Debussy, Claude** 16, 27, **89-90**, 180, 186

***Delius, Frederick*** 237

Deutsch, O.E. 32, **198**, 199, 200

Dietrich, Albert 74, 212

difficulty ratings 37-8

'Dissonance, The', str qt (Mozart) 165

***Dittersdorf, Carl Ditters von*** 109, **237**

**Dohnányi, Ernő** 16, 18, **90-2**, 238

***Donizetti, Gaetano*** 237

Dowland, John 83

'Dream, The', str qt (Haydn) 123

'Dresden sonatas', vn, cont (Vivaldi) 229

'Drum, The', str qt (Mozart) 165

duet sonata, the 9, 12, 13-14, 15, 17, 21, 22, 25, **26-7**, 39

'Dumky', pf trio (Dvořák) 97

durations 12, **36**

**Dvořák, Antonin** 15, 19, 20, 21, 23, 24, 32, 38, **92-8**


editing 32-3

**Elgar, (Sir) Edward** 15, 16, 24, **99-100**, 184, 225

'Emperor, The', str qt (Haydn) 130

Esterházy family 109, 110, 127, 131, 137, 138


'FAE Sonata' 74, 80, 212

'Fandango', guitar qnt (Boccherini) 71

'Fantasia', str qt (Haydn) 131

*Fantasia On One Note* (Purcell) 184

*Fantasiestücke*, cl, pf (Schumann) 212

***Farrenc, Louise*** 237

**Fauré, Gabriel** **100-1**, 186, 192

'Fifths, The', str qt (Haydn) 130

figured bass 13, 30

realization 26, 30, 32, 104

first violin 18, 20, 22, 37

'Five, The' 72

*Folia, La*, variations, vn, cont (Corelli) 88

*Follia, La*, variations, trio sonata (Vivaldi) 227

'For Jean on her birthday', str qt (Vaughan Williams) 225

fortepiano 14, 23, 27

four-part sonata, the 19, 26

**Franck, César** 24, 90, **102**, 187

'Frog, The', str qt (Haydn) 123

*From my Homeland*, vn, pf (Smetana) 219

*From My Life*, str qt (Smetana) 218


***Gade, Niels*** 21, **27-8**

'Ghost, The', pf trio (Beethoven) 62

***Glazunov, Aleksandr*** 224, **238**, 241

***Glinka, Mikhail*** **238**

'Golden Sonata, The', trio sonata (Purcell) 184

*Grand duo concertant*, cl, pf (Weber) 231

**Grieg, Edvard** 90, **103-4**, 237

*Grosse Fuge*, str qt (Beethoven) 20, 57, **58-9**

'Gypsy Rondo', pf trio (Haydn) 40, 137, **139**

Handel, George Frideric  14, 25, 31, 40, 67, 87, **104-9**, 145, 159, 184, 242

'Harp, The', str qt (Beethoven)  55

harpsichord  13, 26, 27, 30, 42

Haydn, Joseph  12, 14-15, 18-20, 22-3, 25, 30, 32, 36, 37-8, 39-40, 49-50, 52-3, 61, 69, 73, **109-44**, 145, 157, 160-2, 164, 165, 167, 170, 174, 190-1, 197, 237

Haydn, Michael  167

'Haydn's Serenade', str qt movt  116

*Hindemith, Paul*  24, **238**

Hoboken, Anthony van  110, 111, 124, 134

'Hoffmeister, The', str qt (Mozart)  166

Hoffstetter, Roman  115

'How do you do?', str qt (Haydn)  121

*Howells, Herbert*  17, **238**

Hummel, Johann Nepomuk  15, 24, 25, 31, 40, **144-8**

'Hunt, The', str qt (Mozart)  39, 164, 165

*Ich bin der Schneider Kakadu*, variations, pf trio (Beethoven)  61

inexperienced players, suggested works for  39-40

*Intimate Letters*, str qt (Janáček)  149

Janáček, Leoš  25, **148-9**

Joachim, Joseph  74, 75, 76, 212

'Joke, The', str qt (Haydn)  121

'Kegelstatt', trio, cl, va, pf (Mozart)  173

'King of Prussia quartets' (Mozart)  166-7

Köchel, Ludwig von  **158**, 172, 177

*Kodály, Zoltán*  90, **238**

*Korngold, Erich*  239

'Kreutzer', sonata, vn, pf (Beethoven)  **66**, 148, 207

*Kreutzer Sonata*, str qt (Janáček)  148

*Lachrymae*, va, pf (Britten)  83

Landon, H.C. Robbins  134, 136

'Lark, The', str qt (Haydn)  127

Liszt, Franz  73, 102, 187

*Locatelli, Pietro*  239

*l'Uccelliera*, str qnt (Boccherini)  70

Lyadov, Anatoly  241

*Lyric Suite*, str qt (Berg)  69

*Mahler, Gustav*  212, **239**

*Malinconia, La*, section of str qt (Beethoven)  54

'Manchester sonatas', vn, cont (Vivaldi)  229

Mannheim School  88, 190

'Mannheim Sonatas', vn, pf (Mozart)  177

*Märchenbilder*, va, pf (Schumann)  212

*Märchenerzählungen*, cl, va, pf (Schumann)  211

*Mendelssohn, Fanny*  152, **239**

Mendelssohn, Felix  15, 19, 20, 21, 23, 31, 39, 77, 84, **149-156**, 209, 237, 239

*Messiaen, Olivier*  239

'Milanese Quartets' (Mozart)  161-2

'Military Septet' (Hummel)  146, 147

Miniatures, 2 vn, va (Dvořák)  93, 98

*Mládí*, wind sextet (Janáček)  149

Mozart, Wolfgang Amadeus  14, 18, 19, 20-1, 22, 23, 25, 27, 32, 37, 38, 39-40, 41, 49, 50, 51, 52, 53, 60, 61, 64, 65, 67, 68, 73, 88, 109, 112, 113, 120, 121, 122, 141, 144, 145, 147, 149, **157-80**, 197, 199, 202, 223, 230, 237

Mühlfeld, Richard  74, 80

*Musical Offering, The* (Bach)  43

*Musica Notturna delle Strade di Madrid, La*, str qnt (Boccherini)  70

Musorgsky, Modest  72

Nielsen, Carl  24, **239**

Onslow, George  239

opus numbers  30-1, 32

*Parry, (Sir) Hubert*  240

*Phantasiestücke*, pf trio (Schumann)  210

phantasy form  16-17, 82, 226, 238

piano quartet, the  23-4

piano quintet, the  15, 18, **24**

piano trio, the  22-3
piano with strings: *see* strings with piano
*Pohádka*, vc, pf (Janáček)  149
**Poulenc, Francis**  24, 27, **180-2**
**Prokofiev, Sergey**  16, 17, 27, **182-3**
Prussia, King Frederick the Great of  43
Prussia, King Frederick William II of  122, 166
publishers  31, 32-5, 37, 106-7, 112, 144, 145, 191, 199
*Puccini, Giacomo*  240
**Purcell, Henry**  14, 15, 25, 38, 82, 99, **184-5**

*Quartetto Serioso*, str qt (Beethoven)  55
'Quartettsatz', str qt movt (Schubert)  202

**Rachmaninoff, Serge**  16, **185-6**
*Raff, Joachim*  21, **240**
'Railwayman, The', str qt (Haydn)  127
'Rasumovsky Quartets' (Beethoven)  54-5
**Ravel, Maurice**  23, **186-7**, 225
'Razor, The', str qt (Haydn)  126
*Reger, Max*  240
**Reicha, Anton**  24, 88, **187-90**
repeats  36, 198
*Respighi, Ottorino*  240
**Richter, Franz Xaver**  19, **190-1**
'Rider, The', str qt (Haydn)  129
*Rimsky-Korsakov, Nikolay*  72, **240**, 241
*Ritirata di Madrid, La*, guitar qnt (Boccherini)  71
romantic chamber music  11, 14, **15**, 16, 18, 19, 20, 21, 22, 23, 24, 26, 30, 32
'Rondeau brillant', vn, pf (Schubert)  207
'Rosamunde', str qt (Schubert)  203
*Rossini, Gioachino*  241
*Russian collaborative chamber music*  72, **241**
'Russian Quartets' (Haydn)  120-1
Russian Revolution  182, 185, 221

**Saint-Saëns, Camille**  180, **191-4**
'Salzburg symphonies' (Mozart)  161
Scarlatti, Alessandro  19

Schmieder, W.  42
**Schoenberg, Arnold**  16, 17, 21, 24, 68, 84, **194-7**, 231
**Schubert, Franz**  14, 15, 18, 19, 21, 24, 25, 27, 32-3, 36, 38, 39, 40, 49, 55, 78, 79, 144, 154, 157, 171, **197-208**, 230
*Schumann, Clara*  78, 208, **241**
**Schumann, Robert**  15, 23, 24, 26, 29, 74, 78, 197, **208-12**, 241
*Seccatura, La*, clar qt movt (Hummel)  147
Second Viennese School  68, 195
*Serenissima, La*, str qt movt (Britten)  82
serialism  195, 215, 221, 222, 250
*Seven Last Words, The*, str qt, (Haydn)  123-4
sheet music  32-5
**Shostakovich, Dmitry**  16, 19, 21, 23, 24, 27, 182, **212-17**
**Sibelius, Jean**  16, **217-18**
*Six, Les*  180
**Smetana, Bedřich**  **218-19**
*sonata da camera*  14, 87, 227, 229
*sonata da chiesa*  14, 87, 105, 182
'Sonatensatz', vn, pf (Brahms)  80
*Souvenir de Florence*, str sextet (Tchaikovsky)  224
*Souvenir d'un lieu cher*, vn, pf (Tchaikovsky)  224
**Spohr, Louis**  20, 21, **241**
'Spring', sonata, vn, pf (Beethoven)  66
'Spring', str qt (Mozart)  164
Stadler, Maximilian  170
***Stanford, (Sir) Charles Villiers***  241
Stockhausen, Karlheinz  17
'Storm, The', str qnt (Beethoven)  60
**Strauss, Richard**  16, 38, **219-21**
**Stravinsky, Igor**  25, 84, 180, **221-2**
string duo, the  18
string quartet, the  14, 16, 18, 19-20
    quatuor brillant  20, 241
string quintet, the  18, **20-1**
string octet, the  21
strings alone, ensembles of  18-21
string sextet, the  15, 18, **21**

strings with piano, ensembles of 21-4
string trio, the 18
*Summer Music*, wind qnt (Barber) 46
'Sun Quartets' (Haydn) 118-20
'Sunrise, The', str qt (Haydn) 130
Svendsen, Johan 21

*Taneyev, Sergey* 242
*Tartini, Giuseppe* 242
Tchaikovsky, Pyotr Il'yich 21, 185, **222-4**, 235, 242
*Telemann, Georg Philipp* 242
*Temporal Variations*, ob, pf (Britten) 83
*Terremoto, Il*, movt, str qt (Haydn) 124
'Tost Quartets' (Haydn) 124-7
trio sonata, the 13, 14, **25-6**, 39
'Trout', quintet, str, pf (Schubert)
twentieth-century chamber music 11, 12, **15-17**, 18, 19, 23, 24, 25, 27, 29, 31

urtext 33, 34

Vanhal, Johann 109, 237

Vaughan Williams, Ralph 16, 17, 20, 38, 81, **225-6**
Verdi, Giuseppe **226-7**
*Verklärte Nacht*, str sextet (Schoenberg) 194, 196
viols, consorts of 12, 16, 38, 184
Vivaldi, Antonio 25, **227-30**
*Voces Intimae*, str qt (Sibelius) 218

Wagner, Richard 73, 85, 92, 99, 102, 196, 223, 230, 237
*Walton, (Sir) William* 242
Weber, Carl Maria von 15, 25, 27, 88, 89, **230-1**
Webern, Anton 16, 17, 68, 195, **231-3**
*Wesley, Charles* 37, 39, **242**
wind instruments, ensembles of or including 12, 17, **24-5**, 26, 28, 38, 39
wind quintet, the 24
*With two obbligato eyeglasses*, duet, va, vc (Beethoven) 51
*Wolf, Hugo* 242
WoO numbers 31